Power, Politics, and Tariffs: The Hidden Strategies Behind Global Trade Wars

Alan Bennett

Copyright and Moral Rights Notice

© 24 February 2025 Alan Bennett. All rights reserved. This book, titled "Power, Politics, and Tariffs: The Hidden Strategies Behind Global Trade Wars", including all text, content, and intellectual property, is protected under international copyright laws and moral rights provisions. The author asserts moral rights to be identified as the creator of this work and retains full rights over reproduction, distribution, adaptation, and derivative works.

This book may not be copied, reproduced, stored in a retrieval system, or transmitted in any form, by any means (electronic, mechanical, photocopying, recording, or otherwise), without prior written permission from the author.

This work is protected internationally under the Berne Convention for the Protection of Literary and Artistic Works and the Universal Copyright Convention (UCC). Any unauthorized use, distribution, or reproduction of this content without the author's express consent will be subject to legal action.

For permissions or inquiries, please contact the author at alanbennett108@gmail.com.

Published by Prominence Publishing, Inc.

ISBN: 978-1-990830-85-3

Acknowledgments

I would like to express my deepest gratitude to my wife, Zorica, whose unwavering support and encouragement have been invaluable throughout the writing of this book.

I would also like to thank Zerah Bennett and Philippa Jones for their invaluable assistance in editing.

About the Author

Alan Bennett – International Trade Law Expert & Author

Alan Bennett is a distinguished former lawyer specializing in international trade law. Throughout his legal career, he provided strategic counsel to multinational corporations navigating complex regulatory disputes, including cases that culminated in determinations by the World Trade Organization (WTO).

In addition to his legal practice, Alan was an Adjunct Professor in the Postgraduate Faculty of Law at the University of Sydney, where he lectured in courses for 25 years on: WTO Dispute Resolution and International Import-Export Law and Regulation. His academic contributions have shaped the understanding of international trade law for generations of students and practitioners.

Alan also served as a contractual consultant for the International Monetary Fund's (IMF) Legal Division in Washington, D.C., where he was engaged in drafting import laws for nations requiring legal and regulatory frameworks to support their trade policies.

Now an esteemed author, Alan continues to influence the field through his publications on international trade law, providing in-depth analysis and insights into the evolving global trade landscape.

Preface

In an era where global trade is no longer defined by cooperation but by strategic competition and economic confrontation, understanding the complexities of trade wars is more essential than ever. The rules-based international trading system, built over decades to ensure fairness and predictability, now faces its greatest challenges. Countries are increasingly leveraging tariffs, economic sanctions, and trade barriers not merely as regulatory tools but as weapons of economic influence and geopolitical maneuvering.

This book, *Power, Politics, and Tariffs: The Hidden Strategies Behind Global Trade Wars*, examines the evolution of international trade conflicts, the legal frameworks governing them, and the strategies employed by nations to navigate and manipulate global commerce. It explores the fundamental principles of tariff policies, trade agreements, and dispute resolution while critically assessing the weaknesses of existing institutions, particularly the World Trade Organization (WTO). The chapters analyze landmark trade disputes, the rise of economic nationalism, and the implications of digital trade, carbon tariffs, and supply chain disruptions.

A central theme of this book is the inadequacy of current trade regulations to address modern challenges. The legal frameworks that once upheld the stability of global trade are increasingly exploited, circumvented, or rendered obsolete in the face of rapid technological change, state-controlled economies, and shifting geopolitical alliances. The book proposes substantive reforms, including a Misuse of Country Market Power Framework, to replace outdated anti-dumping measures, and explores alternative models for regulating international trade more effectively.

This work is not merely an academic exploration—it is a practical analysis that challenges conventional thinking and provides innovative policy recommendations. As governments rethink their trade strategies and international institutions struggle to maintain authority, the need for a new trade order—one that balances economic fairness with strategic pragmatism—has never been more urgent.

As the global economy stands at a crossroads, *Power, Politics, and Tariffs: The Hidden Strategies Behind Global Trade Wars* offers a critical examination of where we are and where we might be headed. Whether you are a trade policy expert, a business leader, or a concerned global citizen, this book provides the insights needed to navigate the shifting tides of international commerce.

Alan Bennett
March 2025

Table of Contents

Book 1: The Role, Effects and Formulation of Tariffs

Part 1: Tariffs – What are they? Their role

Chapter 1: Introduction – The Changing Landscape of Global Trade.... 1

Chapter 2: What Are Tariffs? 5

Chapter 3: Global Trade in Transition – From Expansion to Strategic Competition 11

Chapter 4: Protectionism vs. Free Trade... 19

Chapter 5: The Digital Economy and Tariffs on Data Transfers: Emerging Trade Barriers in the Digital Economy 25

Chapter 6 33

Environmental Tariffs and Carbon Border Adjustments 33

Chapter 7: Tariffs as Economic Instruments: Strategic Divergence in U.S., EU, and Chinese Practice 39

Part 2: Tariffs - Effects

Chapter 8: Historical Lessons from the Smoot-Hawley Tariff Act and Other Protectionist Measures 45

Chapter 9: Case Studies in Tariff Weaponization 51

Chapter 10: Tariff Disputes in WTO History....................................... 61

Chapter 11: Impact of Tariffs on Emerging Markets............................. 65

Chapter 12: The Impact of Tariffs on Inflation: A Commercial Observation 73

Chapter 13: Tariffs and Supply Chain Disruptions............................... 81

Chapter 14: Currency Manipulation and Its Role in Trade Wars 87

Part 3: Tariffs – Formulation

Chapter 15: The Influence of Lobbying on Tariff Policy 95

Chapter 16: The Role of Economic Sanctions in Global Trade 103

Chapter 17: China's Belt and Road Initiative and Its Impact on Trade Wars.. 109

Chapter 18: Trade Wars and Potential Resolutions 113

Chapter 19: The Role of Developing Nations in Global Trade Wars ... 119

Chapter 20: Trade Wars and Economic Nationalism 127

Book 2: International Trade Rules & Trade Wars

Part 4: Introduction to International Trade Rules

Chapter 21: Why Trade Wars Need International Rules 137

Chapter 22: The Establishment of the World Trade Organization – Challenges in Trade Governance 143

Chapter 23: Trade Wars: The Fragility of Rules................................. 149

Chapter 24: Leveraging 2025 Technology in the Administration of WTO Agreements 155

Part 5: General Agreement on Tariffs and Trade 1994 – The Foundations of International Trade

Chapter 25: Non-Tariff Barriers to Trade... 163

Chapter 26: GATT – The Evolution of GATT and Its Analytical Framework.. 169

Chapter 27: Most-Favored Nation Principle – Foundation Principle of GATT 175

Chapter 28: Tariff "Bindings" – Article II of GATT 181

Chapter 29: "National Treatment" Principle – Article III of GATT .. 189

Chapter 30: Emergency Action Exemptions – Articles XX & XXI of GATT 197

Chapter 31: Free Trade Agreements – Article XXIV of GATT........... 205

Chapter 32: The Inadequacies of Free Trade Agreement Dispute Resolution Mechanisms.. 213

Part 6: WTO 1995 – Global Trade Governance and Regulations

Chapter 33: The WTO Dispute Settlement Understanding............... 221

Part 7: WTO Trade Protection Tools

Chapter 34: Agreement on Safeguards 231

Chapter 35: The Anti-Dumping Agreement and Article VI of GATT 237

Chapter 36: The Agreement on Subsidies and Countervailing Measures (SCM Agreement) 243

Chapter 37: The Agreement on Import Licensing............................ 247

Part 8: Investment, Intellectual Property & Trade Measures

Chapter 38: The Agreement on Trade-Related Aspects of Intellectual Property Rights (TRIPS)... 255

Chapter 39: Special Requirements Related to Border Measures Under the TRIPS Agreement 265

Chapter 40: The Agreement on Trade-Related Investment Measures (TRIMs) 275

Part 9: Sector-Specific WTO Agreements

Chapter 41: The Agreement on Agriculture (AoA) 281

Chapter 42: The Agreement on Sanitary and Phytosanitary Measures (SPS) 287

Chapter 43: The Agreement on Technical Barriers to Trade (TBT) 293

Part 10: Customs Valuation Rules Under WTO

Chapter 44: Customs Valuation under Article VII of GATT and the WTO Customs Valuation Agreement (CVA) 301

Chapter 45: The Harmonized Tariff System... 307

Chapter 46: The Agreements on Rules of Origin (ARO) 313

Chapter 47: The Agreement on Pre-shipment Inspection 319

Chapter 48: Publication and Administration of Trade Regulations under Article X of GATT and WTO Agreements 327

Part 11: Future of International Trade and WTO Reforms

Chapter 49: The WTO Trade Facilitation Agreement – A Framework for Easier Trade 337

Chapter 50: Reforming the Anti-Dumping Regime – Addressing the Misuse of Country Market Power 345

Part 12: Final Reflections – The Future

Chapter 51: Author's Commentary:Final Reflections on WTO Reform353

Book 1
The Role, Effects and Formulation of Tariffs

PART 1
Tariffs – What are they? Their role

Chapter 1

Introduction –
The Changing Landscape of Global Trade

In 2025, the United States unleashed a wave of aggressive trade policies that sent shockwaves through the global economy. With most of the 165 member nations of the World Trade Organization (WTO) feeling the squeeze, retaliatory tariffs erupted worldwide, triggering economic upheaval.

Once-stable trade agreements fractured, long-standing alliances strained under economic pressure, and global supply chains buckled under the weight of uncertainty. From Beijing to Berlin, São Paulo to Sydney, governments scrambled to shield their economies from the fallout. What began as policy shifts soon spiraled into an escalating cycle of protectionism and countermeasures—a battle that would come to define the new era of *trade wars*.

The United States Reciprocal Trade Bill and Its Implications

On January 24, 2025, Congressman Riley M. Moore introduced the United States Reciprocal Trade Bill, a legislative measure designed to empower President Trump to address trade imbalances caused by foreign tariffs and non-tariff barriers. If enacted, the bill would grant the President the authority to impose *reciprocal tariffs* on imported goods from nations that impose restrictive tariffs or other trade barriers against the U.S.

The significance of this policy lies in its broad interpretation of "harmful trade imbalances." Beyond standard tariffs, the bill also scrutinizes non-tariff barriers (NTBs)—a catch-all category for domestic taxes, administrative policies, licensing restrictions, and regulatory requirements that, in the administration's view, unfairly hinder U.S. exports.

At present, the bill is under review by the House Committee on Ways and Means and the Committee on Rules. However, the administration has chosen not to wait. On February 13, 2025, President Trump ordered the Office of the U.S. Trade Representative (USTR) and the Department of Commerce to conduct an extensive review of foreign tax regimes, particularly value-added taxes (VAT) and digital services taxes (DST), which are perceived as disproportionately harming U.S. exporters.

The administration argues that these measures are necessary to correct long-standing trade deficits and restore balance. However, this approach has ignited major legal and economic concerns, particularly regarding the United States' obligations under WTO agreements.

Legal Challenges and WTO Compliance

At the heart of the issue is whether the U.S. can unilaterally impose reciprocal tariffs without violating WTO rules.

The General Agreement on Tariffs and Trade ("GATT") is one of the agreements within the WTO. Under Article II of the GATT, WTO members agree not to impose tariffs beyond their pre-agreed "bound rates" unless formally renegotiated. Article XX and Article XXI of GATT outline specific exceptions, but retaliatory tariffs in response to non-tariff barriers or foreign tax policies fall outside these exemptions.

If enforced, reciprocal tariffs could violate WTO commitments, triggering international disputes, retaliatory tariffs, and a potential breakdown of trade relations. While the administration argues that VAT and DST regimes distort trade, most WTO members consider them standard fiscal policies, not discriminatory trade practices.

Critically, VAT systems often include rebates on exports, ensuring that foreign consumers (including U.S. buyers) are not disadvantaged. As such, the argument that VAT regimes constitute an unfair trade barrier lacks substantive legal basis under WTO law.

Unilateral U.S. tariffs would almost certainly provoke retaliatory measures, triggering broader economic instability. Rather than strengthening global trade leadership, such actions could weaken U.S. credibility in future negotiations, undermine multilateral agreements, and accelerate a shift toward protectionist trade policies worldwide.

While multilateral engagement remains a more stable and rules-based approach, the Trump administration appears to anticipate the shortcomings of WTO-led diplomacy. The multilateral system is slow, consensus-driven, and often produces weak, delayed outcomes—a reality that has contributed to growing skepticism about its effectiveness.

The History and Context of Trade Wars

Trade wars are nothing new. For centuries, nations have engaged in tariff battles, economic coercion, and retaliatory restrictions. From the Smoot-Hawley Tariff Act of 1930, which deepened the Great Depression, to the U.S.-China tariff war of the 2010s, history repeatedly demonstrates that escalating protectionism leads to economic volatility.

In the 21st century, trade wars have become a defining feature of international relations, driven by geopolitical realignments, economic nationalism, and the erosion of WTO authority.

The WTO, established to foster predictability and fairness in global trade, now faces an existential crisis. Its rules, designed for a 20th-century economy, struggle to accommodate modern geopolitical shifts, digital economies, and state-controlled economic models like China's.

The United States' aggressive trade policies have exposed the WTO's weaknesses, raising urgent questions about its continued relevance and ability to enforce trade discipline.

Recent Developments and Global Reactions

On February 18, 2025, China formally condemned the U.S. for imposing a 10% tariff on all Chinese imports, warning that these *"tariff shocks"* could trigger a global recession.

During a heated WTO meeting, China accused the U.S. of violating multilateral trade rules and escalating tensions. In retaliation, China implemented countermeasures and filed a dispute at the WTO.

Adding to the uncertainty, the confirmation of Howard Lutnick as U.S. Secretary of Commerce has reinforced the administration's hardline trade stance. A seasoned Wall Street executive, Lutnick dismisses concerns about inflationary risks and remains a strong advocate for leveraging tariffs as a bargaining tool.

Despite WTO warnings to avoid retaliatory actions, trade tensions continue to escalate, intensifying global concerns about economic instability and protectionist fragmentation.

The Shift Toward Regional Trade Agreements

With WTO inefficiencies mounting, many nations are pivoting toward regional trade agreements, bypassing multilateral frameworks.

Examples include:

- **The Comprehensive and Progressive Agreement for Trans-Pacific Partnership (CPTPP)**: giving Asia-Pacific economies greater autonomy in shaping trade policies.

- **The African Continental Free Trade Area (AfCFTA)**: promoting intra-African trade and reducing reliance on WTO-led negotiations.

These agreements increase trade efficiency but also weaken the WTO, fragmenting global trade governance and accelerating the decline of multilateralism.

Author's Commentary: Rethinking Global Trade in the 21st Century

As global trade fractures, the WTO risks obsolescence unless it adapts. Its survival depends on radical modernization, including:

1. **Redefining WTO Mandates**: Expanding its role beyond tariff regulation to address modern trade challenges like digital taxation, state subsidies, and geopolitical trade restrictions.

2. **Streamlining Dispute Resolution**: The WTO's legal processes are slow and ineffective. A fast-track arbitration system could prevent prolonged trade conflicts.

3. **Reforming Membership Rules**: Countries with state-controlled economies (e.g. China) often manipulate loopholes. Stronger enforcement mechanisms are needed to ensure fair competition.

The book will explore these themes in depth, assessing whether the WTO can be reformed or whether a new trade order—based on regional blocs and strategic alliances—will replace it.

At stake is the future of global trade governance. Will rules-based commerce survive, or are we entering an era of economic nationalism, fractured markets, and perpetual trade conflicts?

The answers will shape the next phase of globalization—for better or worse.

Chapter 2

What Are Tariffs?

Introduction

Trade protectionism encompasses a range of policies and measures that governments employ to shield domestic industries from foreign competition.

Among these measures, tariffs are one of the most widely used tools.

Understanding what tariffs are and how they function is essential to comprehending the broader discussion on trade wars and the escalation of tariffs, particularly in recent years under the Trump administration.

Defining Tariffs

In the context of international trade, the term "tariff" generally refers to the customs duty imposed on imported goods. This duty is calculated by applying a specified rate—known as the tariff rate—against the "customs value" of the imported product.

Tariffs are usually expressed as a percentage of the customs value (*ad valorem* tariffs), such as 5% or 10%. However, some tariffs are structured differently. For example, a country may impose a tariff based on a fixed amount per unit of measurement, such as:

- $X per liter of alcohol for alcoholic beverages,
- $Y per kilogram for tobacco products, or
- A combination of both methods, such as 5% of the customs value plus $10 per kilogram.

Regardless of the specific tariff structure, the fundamental effect remains the same: importers are required to pay a designated customs duty to the government of the importing country. This duty becomes a component of that country's revenue.

Once the duty is paid, and assuming there are no additional regulatory restrictions (such as import licensing or quarantine requirements), the goods are cleared through customs and enter what is referred to as "home consumption"—meaning they can be distributed, sold, or used within the country.

Variability of Tariff Rates

Tariff rates differ from country to country. For instance:

- India may impose a 5% tariff on imported plastic goods, whereas the European Union might levy only a 2% tariff on the same products.
- A motor vehicle exported from Japan to the European Union might attract a 20% tariff, while the same vehicle exported to Indonesia could enter duty-free.

Each country retains the sovereign right to determine the duty rates applied to different categories of imported goods. However, this ability is subject to limitations imposed by the international trade system, particularly through the WTO.

Bound Tariffs and WTO Regulations

While countries set their own tariff rates, they are often constrained by the concept of "bound" tariffs under the WTO framework.

A bound tariff represents the maximum rate a country has agreed to apply to a specific category of imported goods.

This commitment is established under Article II of the General Agreement on Tariffs and Trade (GATT), which binds all 165 WTO member countries to their declared tariff ceilings, barring a few exceptions.

Bound tariffs are intended to create trade predictability and stability, preventing countries from arbitrarily raising tariffs for political or economic gain. If a country wishes to increase a tariff beyond its bound rate, it must enter formal negotiations and offer compensation to affected trading partners.

WHAT ARE TARIFFS?

How Tariffs Work: An Example

To illustrate how tariffs function, consider the following example:

- The United States imposes a 15% tariff on imported steel from China.
- If the customs value of a shipment of steel from China is $300,000, the U.S. tariff of 15% is applied, resulting in an import duty of $45,000.
- This duty must be paid before the goods can be cleared for home consumption and enter the U.S. market.

If the U.S. government decides to increase the tariff on Chinese steel from 15% to 25%, the first question under WTO rules would be whether this new tariff exceeds the U.S.'s bound rate for steel.

If the bound rate registered with the WTO was 15%, then raising the tariff to 25% would violate international trade agreements.

Such an action could be subject to review by the WTO Dispute Settlement Body, and the U.S. might have to negotiate compensatory measures with affected trading partners.

Illustrative Cases

Thailand – Customs and Fiscal Measures on Cigarettes (DS371)

- **Context:** Thailand imposed high tariffs and customs valuations on imported cigarettes, leading to a WTO dispute filed by the Philippines.
- **Key Issue:** The WTO found that Thailand's customs valuation system unfairly inflated the duties imposed on imported cigarettes.
- **Outcome:** The WTO ruled that Thailand's measures were inconsistent with GATT obligations, highlighting the need for transparent and predictable tariff applications.
- **Relevance:** This case illustrates how tariffs, if improperly applied, can become hidden trade barriers and lead to disputes.

India's Tariff Commitments and WTO Disputes

- **Context:** India imposed tariffs on information and communication technology (ICT) products, exceeding its bound commitments under WTO rules.

- **Key Issue:** India classified new technologies under unbound categories, leading to disputes with major trading partners.
- **Outcome:** The WTO ruled that India's tariff measures violated its obligations, reaffirming that tariff commitments must be honored.
- **Relevance:** This case underscores the importance of adhering to WTO-bound tariff rates and the legal complexities surrounding evolving product classifications.

The Impact of Tariffs

Tariffs generally increase the cost of imported goods, and this additional cost has downstream effects:

1. **Absorption by Importers**: Importers may choose to absorb the increased duty, reducing their profit margins.
2. **Passing on the Cost**: More commonly, businesses pass on the higher costs to consumers by increasing retail prices.
3. **Supply Chain Disruptions**: Higher tariffs can lead to changes in global supply chains as businesses seek alternative sourcing options to avoid increased costs.

Tariffs and Trade Wars

As tariffs rise, so does the potential for retaliatory trade measures by affected countries. This can escalate into full-scale trade wars, where countries continually impose and increase tariffs in response to each other's policies.

A prime example of this occurred in the U.S.-China trade war (2018–2020), which led to hundreds of billions of dollars in tariffs being placed on a range of goods. The effects were significant:

- **Global Supply Chain Disruptions**: Companies were forced to shift production away from China to avoid higher costs.
- **Increased Consumer Prices**: Tariff-induced cost hikes affected industries ranging from electronics to agriculture.
- **Retaliatory Measures**: China imposed counter-tariffs on American goods, impacting farmers and manufacturers.

The Future of Tariffs in International Trade

Given the resurgence of tariff-based policies, particularly under the Trump administration, it is crucial to evaluate how such measures affect global trade stability. While tariffs can serve as economic tools to protect domestic industries, excessive reliance on them can undermine global trade cooperation and lead to prolonged economic instability.

The WTO and other international institutions continue to advocate for tariff reductions and negotiated settlements, emphasizing the benefits of open trade. However, as major economies—including the United States—turn to tariffs as strategic bargaining tools, the future of multilateral trade agreements remains uncertain. The author believes that the outlook for the WTO is "gloomy" and this view is explained in greater depth later.

Author's Commentary: The Strategic Role of Tariffs in Global Trade

Understanding the mechanics and implications of tariffs is fundamental to grasping the complexities of modern trade policy. Tariffs have long been a cornerstone of economic strategy, shaping national and international commerce by influencing trade flows, protecting domestic industries, and serving as leverage in geopolitical negotiations.

Historically, tariffs were one of the primary means by which governments generated revenue. Before the widespread adoption of income taxes in the 20th century, tariffs provided the financial backbone for many national economies. Even today, in developing nations with weak tax infrastructures, customs duties remain a crucial source of government income.

However, tariffs are far more than just a fiscal tool. They serve strategic economic and political purposes, often reflecting broader national interests. Governments impose tariffs to:

1. **Protect Domestic Industries**: By raising the cost of imported goods, tariffs shield local businesses from foreign competition, allowing them to grow and stabilize. This is particularly significant in emerging industries where domestic firms may struggle against established global competitors.

2. **Address Trade Imbalances**: Tariffs are used to counteract trade deficits by discouraging imports and encouraging domestic production. However, while this may offer short-term relief, it often provokes retaliatory tariffs, leading to long-term economic distortions.

3. **Enhance Bargaining Power**: Tariffs are frequently deployed as negotiating tools in international trade agreements. Governments use them to extract concessions, demand fairer terms, or retaliate against perceived trade injustices.

4. **National Security Considerations**: Some industries, such as defense, energy, and technology, are deemed vital to national security. Governments impose tariffs to reduce reliance on foreign suppliers, ensuring critical industries remain under domestic control.

Despite these objectives, tariffs often produce unintended consequences, including higher consumer prices, supply chain disruptions, and global trade tensions. Their impact depends on a variety of factors, such as the structure of the economy, the elasticity of demand for imports, and the response of trading partners.

Today, as the United States and other major economies increasingly use tariffs as economic and geopolitical weapons, the global trading system faces heightened instability. The resurgence of protectionist policies—exemplified by U.S.-China trade tensions, Brexit-related tariff disputes, and ongoing WTO legal battles—demonstrates how tariffs can disrupt long-established economic relationships and force governments to rethink their trade strategies.

Modern tariffs are no longer just about economics—they are geopolitical tools used to assert dominance, rebalance power structures, and reshape global trade rules.

However, tariff escalation is a double-edged sword. While they can serve as leverage, overuse of tariffs can erode trust in the international trading system, leading to fragmented trade blocs, retaliatory trade wars, and declining multilateral cooperation.

As the world grapples with uncertain economic conditions, policymakers face a delicate balancing act—one that requires reconciling domestic economic priorities with the need for global trade stability. The challenge lies not only in managing tariffs effectively but in ensuring that their use does not undermine the very trade frameworks designed to foster economic growth and international cooperation.

The next chapter will delve into the role of tariffs within the context of global trade in transition.

Chapter 3

Global Trade in Transition – From Expansion to Strategic Competition

Introduction

The trajectory of global trade has never been linear. From the early 20th century's expansionist period to the mid-century's protectionist turn, trade patterns have continuously evolved in response to economic, political, and technological shifts.

In the contemporary era, global trade is transitioning yet again, moving from integration and liberalization towards fragmentation and strategic realignments.

The trade policies of major economies, particularly those of the United States, the European Union, and China, have increasingly diverged, influencing global commerce in new and complex ways—including the 2025 initiatives by the Trump administration to empower the President to impose retaliatory tariffs on trading partners.

This chapter explores the evolution of global trade, highlighting key historical shifts, comparing the contemporary strategies of major trading powers, and examining the implications of recent trade developments, particularly the 2025 Trump administration initiatives and retaliatory actions taken by key global players.

Historical Evolution of Global Trade

Early 20th Century – The Foundations of Global Trade

The early 20th century witnessed rapid globalization, facilitated by technological advancements in transportation and communication. Nations like Britain, the

United States, and Germany dominated trade, leveraging industrialization and colonial networks to expand their commercial reach.

However, this period was disrupted by World War I, leading to a retreat from globalization and the adoption of protectionist policies.

Mid-Century Turmoil – War, Realignment, and Recovery

Between the interwar years and the aftermath of World War II, global trade dynamics shifted significantly:

- **Declining North-North Trade:** Industrialized nations reduced trade amongst themselves, forming regional trade blocs and focusing on domestic recovery.

- **Post-War Reconstruction:** The United States emerged as a dominant economic power, advocating for trade liberalization through institutions like the International Monetary Fund (IMF), the World Bank, and the General Agreement on Tariffs and Trade (GATT).

Post-War Era – Expansion and Integration

The latter half of the 20th century saw global trade flourish as developing economies integrated into international markets. North-South trade relations strengthened, with industrialized nations exporting manufactured goods and importing raw materials. Despite this growth, developing nations often remained at the lower end of the value chain.

Contemporary Era – Fragmentation and Strategic Shifts

The early 21st century introduced another wave of globalization, driven by digitalization and the rise of economies like China and India.

However, vulnerabilities in globalized trade became evident during the 2008 financial crisis and subsequent geopolitical tensions, notably the U.S.-China trade war. These challenges have led to the restructuring of supply chains and the emergence of "connector" economies such as Vietnam and Mexico.

Comparative Analysis of U.S., EU, and China Trade Strategies

Factor	United States	European Union	China
Policy Approach	Unilateral, protectionist, leveraging tariffs for economic and political aims.	Multilateral, adhering to World Trade Organization (WTO) principles, emphasizing regulatory consistency.	Strategic, state-directed, using tariffs to protect domestic industries and expand global influence.
Use of Tariffs	Implements tariffs to pressure trade partners and safeguard domestic employment.	Utilizes tariffs to enforce regulatory compliance and ensure fair competition.	Applies tariffs selectively to maintain industrial advantages and economic stability.
Trade Agreements	Prefers bilateral deals (e.g. USMCA) over multilateral arrangements.	Engages in regional pacts (e.g. EU Single Market, CETA).	Pursues a mix of bilateral and multi-lateral agreements to broaden global reach.
WTO Alignment	Often challenges or bypasses WTO rulings.	Strictly adheres to WTO regulations, seeking enforcement through legal channels.	Nominally aligns with WTO but faces criticism over subsidies and non-market practices.
Retaliation Tactics	Employs tariffs aggressively as a negotiation tool.	Implements countermeasures within a multilateral framework.	Utilizes tariffs, export controls, and regulatory restrictions in trade disputes.

Key Case Study: U.S. Steel Tariffs, EU Retaliation, and China's Response

Background: U.S. Steel Tariffs Under Trump (2018, Revisited in 2025)

In 2018, the Trump administration imposed 25% tariffs on steel and 10% tariffs on aluminum imports, citing national security concerns. This move provoked a backlash from allies and trade partners. By 2025, with President Trump's return to office, these tariffs were reinstated and expanded, affecting not only China but also European steel producers and Mexico.

EU's Countermeasures

The European Union responded with retaliatory tariffs targeting politically sensitive U.S. exports, including:

- Motorcycles,
- Bourbon whiskey,
- Blue jeans.

These measures aimed to exert economic and political pressure on key U.S. industries while adhering to WTO principles.

China's Response

China countered U.S. tariffs through a combination of strategies:

- **Direct Tariffs:** Imposed levies on U.S. agricultural products, high-tech goods, and automotive exports.
- **Export Controls:** Restricted the export of critical rare earth minerals essential for U.S. manufacturing.
- **Regulatory Actions:** Initiated antitrust investigations into American tech companies operating within China.

Trade Fragmentation and the Rise of New Economic Players

As trade wars escalate, certain nations have emerged as key "connectors," facilitating trade amid global tensions.

Case Study: Vietnam and Mexico as Trade Brokers

- **Vietnam:** Capitalized on U.S.-China tensions by attracting manufacturers seeking alternatives to China. The country has seen significant growth in its export share to the U.S. and has expanded global trade linkages.
- **Mexico:** Benefited from U.S. trade policy shifts, experiencing an expansion in nearshoring as companies relocate supply chains closer to North America.

The Role of Maritime Trade and Alternative Routes

Maritime trade remains the backbone of global commerce but rising geopolitical tensions have reshaped traditional shipping routes.

Key developments include:

- **Black Sea Conflict & Strait of Hormuz Threats:** Disruptions in these regions have led to increased costs and logistical complications.

- **Northern Sea Route Expansion:** Climate change has opened Arctic shipping lanes, presenting an alternative for Europe-Asia trade.

- **Belt and Road Initiative Rail Networks:** China has invested heavily in trans-Eurasian rail links to reduce dependence on maritime routes.

Author's Commentary: The Future of Global Trade in an Era of Strategic Competition

The evolution of global trade has always reflected a delicate balance between cooperation and competition. Historically, the post-World War II economic order was built on the assumption that free trade, governed by rules-based institutions, would promote stability, economic interdependence, and ultimately, global prosperity.

However, as geopolitical fragmentation accelerates, this vision is being tested. The international trading system is no longer defined by consensus-driven negotiations but by strategic competition, where major economies deploy tariffs, trade barriers, and economic coercion as instruments of power and influence.

The 2025 Trump administration's aggressive trade policies mark a significant departure from traditional U.S. trade diplomacy. This shift, combined with EU countermeasures, China's expanding economic statecraft, and the rise of regional trade blocs, underscores an urgent need for multilateral institutions to adapt.

Yet, the most pressing question remains: how can this reform take place? Who has the political will to drive it? And if reform does not materialize, what will be the consequences for the World Trade Organization (WTO) and the broader rules-based international trading system?

The Decline of the WTO and the Fragmentation of Trade Governance

The WTO, once hailed as the pillar of global economic cooperation, is now under immense strain. Its dispute resolution mechanism, designed to enforce compliance with trade agreements, has been paralyzed by political deadlock—most notably due to the U.S. blocking the appointment of appellate judges to its dispute settlement body. This institutional dysfunction has eroded confidence in the WTO's ability to mediate trade conflicts, leading to an unprecedented rise in unilateral trade actions.

The failure to adapt the WTO to the realities of 21st-century trade disputes has encouraged nations to pursue alternative strategies. Increasingly, we see a shift toward regional trade agreements (RTAs) and bilateral negotiations, bypassing the WTO's multilateral framework. Agreements such as the Comprehensive and Progressive Agreement for Trans-Pacific Partnership (CPTPP) and the African Continental Free Trade Area (AfCFTA) illustrate how nations are seeking more flexible, responsive trade arrangements that better align with their economic priorities.

While these regional agreements offer efficiency and strategic benefits, they also contribute to the fragmentation of global trade governance. Instead of a universal system where all nations adhere to common rules, we are witnessing the emergence of parallel economic spheres, where dominant players—the U.S., China, and the EU—set their own trade terms, often at the expense of weaker economies.

The Risks of a Fractured Trade Order

If the rules-based system continues to erode, it is not the major powers that will suffer the most, but rather the less powerful nations that depend on a stable, predictable trading environment.

1. **Developing Nations at a Disadvantage**: Smaller and developing economies rely on WTO protections to prevent economic coercion by larger nations. Without a functioning multilateral framework, these countries will struggle to compete, facing higher tariffs, reduced market access, and vulnerability to economic bullying.

2. **Trade Wars and Economic Instability**: Without a neutral body to regulate disputes, protectionism will escalate, leading to retaliatory tariffs, investment restrictions, and disruptions in global supply chains. This scenario could destabilize financial markets and exacerbate economic inequality.

3. **Technology and Trade Weaponization**: The digital economy and critical technology sectors (e.g. semiconductors, AI, and cybersecurity) have become central battlegrounds in trade disputes. If trade rules fail to adapt, we will see increased technological fragmentation, with nations creating rival tech ecosystems, restricting cross-border data flows, and decoupling key industries.

The Path Forward: Is There Hope for Reform?

The case for WTO reform is clear, but its execution remains highly uncertain. The U.S., EU, and China—the three most influential players—hold competing visions for trade governance, making consensus elusive. However, if no serious reforms are pursued, the consequences will be severe:

- The WTO risks becoming obsolete, relegated to a symbolic institution with no real authority.
- A multipolar trade system will emerge, dominated by regional blocs and ad-hoc economic alliances.
- Trade will become increasingly weaponized, used as a tool for diplomatic leverage and strategic coercion rather than economic growth.

To prevent this outcome, nations must recognize that economic interdependence is not a weakness but a necessity. Multilateral institutions, while imperfect, offer stability that no unilateral policy can replicate. Reforming the WTO will require pragmatic leadership, compromise, and a willingness to modernize trade regulations to reflect the realities of digital commerce, state capitalism, and national security concerns.

Conclusion: The Stakes for Global Trade

Trade is not just an economic function—it is a geopolitical force that shapes global power dynamics. As nations navigate this new era of strategic competition, they face a choice: strengthen multilateral cooperation or embrace an era of fragmented, conflict-driven trade policies.

If the world abandons the rules-based system, the biggest casualties will be the weaker economies that lack the leverage to negotiate favorable trade terms. Developing nations will be disproportionately affected, widening the economic gap between wealthy and poor nations.

This book will explore whether a new global trade order can emerge—one that preserves fairness and stability while adapting to the shifting realities of power, technology, and competition. The answer will define the future of globalization itself.

Chapter 4

Protectionism vs. Free Trade

Introduction

The interplay between protectionism and free trade has long been a defining feature of international commerce, shaping national policies and the structure of global markets. Each approach presents compelling arguments, shaped by diverse economic, political, and social considerations.

This chapter examines these contrasting perspectives, intending to present a balanced analysis of the benefits and challenges associated with each.

Understanding Protectionism and Free Trade

Protectionism involves the imposition of trade barriers such as tariffs, quotas, and subsidies to shield domestic industries from foreign competition.

Proponents argue that it safeguards national security, preserves local employment, and nurtures emerging industries. It has historically played a significant role in economic development, particularly in the industrialization phases of major economies such as the United States, Germany, and Japan.

Conversely, free trade promotes the unrestricted exchange of goods and services across borders, fostering efficiency, innovation, and economic growth through comparative advantage.

Classical economists, including Adam Smith and David Ricardo, championed free trade as the optimal system for global economic prosperity, arguing that nations benefit most when they specialize in producing goods where they hold a relative efficiency advantage.

The Law of Comparative Advantage: A Strong but Limited Principle

One of the most frequently cited arguments in favor of free trade is David Ricardo's law of comparative advantage, which asserts that nations should specialize in producing goods where they have a relative advantage, even if another country is more efficient in producing everything.

This principle has historically guided trade liberalization policies, supporting the idea that global efficiency is maximized when nations focus on what they do best.

Strengths of Comparative Advantage

1. **Efficiency Gains**: When countries specialize according to comparative advantage, global production increases, leading to lower costs and higher output.

2. **Consumer Benefits**: By allowing specialization, consumers benefit from lower prices and greater variety.

3. **Economic Growth**: Trade based on comparative advantage encourages market expansion and technological diffusion.

Criticism and Modern Challenges

However, while compelling in theory, the principle of comparative advantage has notable limitations in the modern economic and geopolitical context:

- **Static Assumptions**: Comparative advantage assumes that labor and resources remain relatively fixed. In reality, technological progress and policy interventions can shift a nation's advantages over time.

- **Supply Chain Vulnerabilities**: Heavy reliance on comparative advantage can lead to over-dependence on specific regions, making economies vulnerable to disruptions (e.g. COVID-19 shutdowns, semiconductor shortages).

- **Strategic Industries**: Some industries (e.g. defense, energy, semiconductors) are too vital to be left purely to comparative advantage, leading nations to implement protectionist policies to safeguard strategic capabilities.

- **Wage and Labor Disparities**: Comparative advantage does not account for labor exploitation or environmental costs, which can create unfair competitive advantages for low-wage, low-regulation economies.

The Debate on Economic Strategy

Roberto Mangabeira Unger, in *Free Trade Reimagined: The World Division of Labor and the Method of Economics*, critiques traditional free trade doctrines, asserting that they often overlook the dynamic capabilities of economies.

By "dynamic capabilities," Unger refers to an economy's ability to adapt, innovate, and diversify its production methods over time rather than being constrained by static comparative advantages. He argues that encouraging these capabilities can lead to more equitable and robust economic growth.

Unger advocates for a model that fosters national and regional diversity in production, challenging the rigid application of comparative advantage. His perspective highlights the potential weaknesses of an unrestricted free trade approach, particularly its tendency to concentrate economic activity in specific regions.

However, while Unger's argument is well-reasoned, an examination of global manufacturing patterns in 2025 suggests its limitations.

China's manufacturing dominance remains formidable, and even if other nations actively counterbalance this concentration, reversing China's pre-eminence would take many years—if it is even feasible. The long-term impact of reshoring or friend-shoring initiatives remains an open question.

Historical Context and Institutional Influence

The ascendancy of free trade as a dominant economic policy can be traced to the post-World War II era, marked by the establishment of institutions such as the General Agreement on Tariffs and Trade (GATT) and its successor, the World Trade Organization (WTO).

These institutions have played a pivotal role in reducing tariff barriers, facilitating dispute resolution, and fostering multilateral agreements aimed at economic integration.

The Uruguay Round of GATT negotiations led to substantial tariff reductions and culminated in the WTO's establishment in 1995. Similarly, the European Union initially provided its members with "free trade" internally while maintaining "common external tariffs."

The WTO's *Trade Facilitation Agreement* further streamlined customs procedures, reducing costs and delays for businesses worldwide. These frameworks were designed to prevent the protectionist measures that exacerbated the Great Depression and to encourage global economic interdependence.

However, as further discussed by Leonardo Baccini and Soo Yeon Kim in *Preventing Protectionism: International Institutions and Trade Policy*, these institutions have not been without criticism.

While they have successfully mitigated trade barriers, their strong emphasis on liberalization has often sidelined concerns about domestic economic stability. Moreover, developing nations frequently struggle to derive equal benefits from trade agreements, leading to critiques of systemic imbalances in global commerce.

Benefits and Critiques of Free Trade

Proponents of free trade, as illustrated in *Free Trade Versus Protectionism: A Source Book of Essays and Readings*, (compiled by Johannes Overbeek) emphasize its role in optimizing resource allocation, fostering innovation, and reducing consumer costs. This is exemplified by global value chains, which enable businesses to source inputs from the most cost-efficient locations.

Critics, however, argue that unrestricted free trade can result in significant economic disparities. The concentration of manufacturing in China—often attributed to decades of trade liberalization—illustrates the risks of over-reliance on a single nation for critical supply chains.

These concerns have led policymakers to advocate for "re-shoring" and "friend-shoring"—initiatives aimed at relocating critical industries to domestic markets or allied nations to enhance economic resilience and reduce strategic vulnerabilities.

Author's Commentary

The debate between protectionism and free trade is complex and multifaceted, with each approach offering distinct benefits and drawbacks. The optimal strategy depends on the economic priorities and geopolitical circumstances of individual nations.

While institutions like the WTO champion free trade, economic imbalances and strategic vulnerabilities necessitate a more measured approach. It would be unwise to adopt a rigid, dualistic stance by adhering exclusively to free trade or protectionism. Since both approaches entail significant risks, a balanced strategy appears most pragmatic.

For example, bilateral and regional Free Trade Agreements (FTAs) may offer a viable middle-ground solution, fostering trade while incorporating mechanisms to mitigate potential adverse effects. This approach reflects common sense in navigating the complexities of international commerce.

Finally, it is crucial to acknowledge that since the introduction of GATT in 1947, the nature of global trade has evolved significantly. The prevailing trade regulations, many of which originated in 1947, are now inadequate to address emerging economic realities. The theme of this book underscores the urgent need for reform to account for modern challenges, including:

- The impact of carbon tariffs on developing economies
- The digital economy and its implications for tariff structures
- The interplay between tariffs and inflation
- The role of emerging markets in trade negotiations
- The influence of currency manipulation on trade policies
- The role of state-owned enterprises in global commerce
- The intersection of international trade and climate policies
- The rise of economic nationalism
- The implications of trade wars for national security
- The relationship between trade and human rights policies
- The impact of artificial intelligence on global trade

The need for reform is clear, as most of the above issues currently have no or insufficient WTO regulation guiding stakeholders (including corporations involved in trade). It therefore seems clear that the global trading system must adapt to the economic and political realities of the 21st century.

Chapter 5

The Digital Economy and Tariffs on Data Transfers: Emerging Trade Barriers in the Digital Economy

Introduction

The digital economy has transformed global trade, enabling instantaneous cross-border data flows and the proliferation of digital services.

However, this rapid evolution has introduced new challenges, including the imposition of tariffs and restrictions on data transfers, which threaten to fragment the global digital marketplace.

This chapter explores these emerging trade barriers, with a focus on the European Union's Digital Services Tax (DST) and other regulatory frameworks affecting digital trade, while offering policy recommendations to navigate this complex landscape.

1. Defining Tariffs in the Context of the Digital Economy

Traditionally, a tariff is defined as a tax imposed by a government on imported goods, typically to protect domestic industries and generate revenue. According to the World Trade Organization (WTO), tariffs are "customs duties on merchandise imports."

This traditional definition raises questions about the applicability of tariffs to the digital economy, particularly concerning cross-border data transfers and digital services.

The core issue is whether digital products and services transmitted electronically qualify as "goods" and therefore fall within the scope of traditional tariff regulations.

A. WTO Moratorium on E-Commerce Tariffs

Since 1998, the WTO has maintained a moratorium on customs duties for electronic transmissions, effectively preventing member countries from imposing tariffs on cross-border data flows. This moratorium has been extended multiple times, most recently at the 13th Ministerial Conference in 2024, where it was renewed for an additional two years.

The moratorium reflects the recognition that imposing tariffs on electronic transmissions could hinder the growth of the digital economy and create complex enforcement challenges.

However, some member countries have expressed concerns that the moratorium limits their ability to generate revenue from the burgeoning digital trade sector, particularly as physical trade declines in relative importance.

B. The WTO's Lack of a Comprehensive Digital Trade Agreement

Despite the increasing importance of digital trade, the WTO does not currently have a dedicated agreement governing digital economy tariffs and taxation. Unlike traditional goods and services, which are covered under the General Agreement on Tariffs and Trade (GATT 1994) and the General Agreement on Trade in Services (GATS), digital products such as cloud computing, streaming services, and cross-border data transfers fall into a regulatory grey area.

This absence of a clear legal framework has led to diverging national approaches, where some countries impose unilateral digital services taxes (DSTs) or propose digital tariffs, while others advocate for a continuation of the WTO moratorium.

The lack of a uniform approach creates legal uncertainties, trade disputes, and growing calls for a modernized WTO framework that explicitly addresses digital commerce.

2. Emerging Trade Barriers in the Digital Economy

As digital commerce expands, governments are grappling with how to regulate and tax activities that transcend traditional borders. This has led to the emergence of trade barriers specifically targeting the digital economy.

A. Tariffs and Restrictions on Cross-Border Data Transfers

Cross-border data flows are essential for the functioning of the digital economy, supporting activities such as e-commerce, cloud computing, and international communications. However, several countries have implemented measures that restrict these flows:

- **Data Localization Requirements:** Some nations mandate that data about their citizens or operations be stored within their borders. For example, China's 2016 Cybersecurity Law imposes strict data localization and cross-border data transfer restrictions, potentially hindering international digital trade.

- **Cross-Border Data Transfer Restrictions:** Regulations that limit the transfer of data across borders can disrupt global operations of digital service providers, leading to increased costs and operational challenges.

These measures can create significant barriers for businesses that rely on seamless data flows, leading to increased operational costs and complexities.

B. Digital Services Taxes (DSTs)

In response to the challenges of taxing digital activities, several countries have introduced DSTs, which are taxes on selected gross revenue streams of large digital companies. These taxes primarily target major technology firms that operate across multiple jurisdictions.

As of 2024, 15 out of 37 OECD countries have implemented or proposed DSTs, including France, Italy, Spain, and the United Kingdom. These taxes are often seen as targeting U.S.-based multinational corporations, leading to trade tensions.

3. Case Study: The European Union's Digital Services Tax

The European Union's DST has been a focal point in discussions about taxation in the digital economy.

A. Overview of the EU's DST

The EU's DST is a tax on revenues generated from certain digital activities, including:

- Online advertising services
- Sale of user data

- Digital intermediary services that allow users to interact with each other

The tax applies to companies with significant global and EU revenues, effectively targeting large multinational tech firms.

B. Impact on U.S. Tech Firms

The **DST has significant implications** for major U.S. technology companies:

- **Financial Impact:** Companies like Google and Facebook face increased tax burdens on their European operations.
- **Trade Tensions:** The U.S. government views the DST as discriminatory against American firms, leading to heightened trade tensions between the U.S. and the EU. The result of this tension is evident in the January 2025 United States Bill: United States Reciprocal Trade Act, which proposes empowering the President to address harmful trade imbalances caused by foreign tariffs and non-tariff barriers placed on U.S. digital and manufactured goods.

4. Author's Policy Recommendations

To navigate the complexities of taxation and regulation in the digital economy, the following policy recommendations are proposed:

A. Standardizing Global Digital Trade Regulations

- **International Collaboration:** Countries should work together through international bodies like the OECD to develop standardized regulations that provide clarity and consistency for digital businesses operating globally.
- **Harmonization of Tax Policies:** Aligning tax policies can prevent double taxation and reduce the risk of trade disputes arising from unilateral measures like DSTs.

B. Avoiding Excessive Taxation That Discourages Innovation

1. **Balanced Taxation for the Digital Economy**
   - While governments seek to generate revenue from digital transactions, excessive taxation risks stifling innovation and

discouraging investment in emerging technologies such as artificial intelligence (AI), blockchain, and cloud computing.
- Striking the right balance is essential to ensure that companies continue investing in new digital solutions while also contributing fairly to the economies where they operate.

2. **Encouraging Taxation Models That Promote Growth**
    - Some alternative taxation models focus on value creation rather than blanket taxation, ensuring that companies are taxed where they genuinely add economic value rather than simply where they process transactions.
    - Governments could consider tax credits and incentives for tech firms investing in local innovation hubs, digital infrastructure, and workforce development.

3. **Avoiding Fragmentation in Digital Trade Rules**
    - A patchwork of digital taxes across different regions creates compliance burdens and regulatory uncertainty for companies operating internationally.
    - The OECD/G20 Inclusive Framework on Base Erosion and Profit Shifting (BEPS 2.0) has made efforts to harmonize global tax policies for digital businesses. However, delays in implementation have led some countries to unilaterally impose DSTs, increasing trade tensions.

4. **Preventing Trade Retaliation Through Overly Aggressive Taxation**
    - Countries implementing aggressive DSTs risk triggering retaliatory tariffs from affected trading partners, particularly the U.S., which has previously threatened tariffs against the EU in response to its DSTs.
    - Finding a diplomatic, rules-based solution through multilateral agreements is preferable to avoid escalating digital trade conflicts.

Author's Commentary

The digital economy represents one of the most significant transformations in global trade, redefining commerce, services, and market accessibility. Unlike traditional goods, digital products, cloud-based services, and cross-border data flows do not rely on physical movement across borders—yet they are increasingly subject to tariffs, taxation, and regulatory restrictions.

Governments worldwide are grappling with how to regulate and tax digital transactions, leading to the emergence of Digital Services Taxes (DSTs), data localization laws, and new trade barriers on digital commerce.

These developments highlight a growing tension: how to balance the need for fair taxation and regulatory oversight while ensuring that trade remains open, efficient, and globally integrated. The lack of a comprehensive WTO agreement on digital trade, data flows, and e-commerce taxation underscores the urgent need for new global frameworks that can provide clarity, consistency, and enforceable rules.

The Growing Role of Digital Services Taxes (DSTs) and Data Localization Laws

Many governments have introduced DSTs to ensure that multinational tech giants—such as Google, Amazon, Facebook, and Apple—pay taxes in the jurisdictions where they generate revenue rather than shifting profits to low-tax countries. While these measures are often framed as a tool to level the playing field, they also serve as de facto trade barriers, disproportionately affecting U.S.-based technology companies and exacerbating international trade tensions.

Similarly, data localization laws, which require companies to store and process data within national borders, have become a contentious issue. Countries such as China, India, Russia, and the European Union have implemented strict data localization requirements, citing reasons such as consumer protection, national security, and regulatory oversight. However, from a trade perspective, these laws fragment the global digital economy, increasing compliance costs, limiting market access, and stifling competition.

Tariffs on Data Transfers: A New Era of Digital Protectionism?

The introduction of tariffs on cross-border data flows represents a new dimension of trade protectionism. Unlike traditional tariffs on physical goods, these tariffs target the movement of digital content, intellectual property, and cloud-based services, raising fundamental questions about how trade policies should adapt to a world where data is the most valuable commodity.

Some key challenges include:

1. **Defining the Scope of Trade in Digital Services**: Unlike traditional goods, data does not have a physical presence, making it difficult to categorize, measure, and regulate within existing WTO frameworks.

2. **Regulatory Fragmentation**: Countries are adopting disparate digital trade policies, creating compliance challenges for businesses operating across multiple jurisdictions.

3. **Economic and Geopolitical Consequences**: Digital trade restrictions could entrench economic blocs, with the U.S., China, and the EU each pushing competing regulatory models, leading to technological and economic decoupling.

The Need for a Global Digital Trade Agreement

The WTO's failure to establish a comprehensive agreement on digital trade has led to policy fragmentation and uncertainty. While initiatives such as the Joint Statement Initiative (JSI) on E-Commerce seek to establish rules for digital trade, progress has been slow, largely due to political disagreements and competing national interests.

A modernized digital trade framework must address:

- The taxation of digital services to prevent unilateral DSTs that distort competition.
- Global data transfer standards to ensure that data flows remain open while respecting privacy and security concerns.
- Fair market access to prevent discriminatory barriers against foreign digital companies.

Without a coherent global strategy, the digital economy risks becoming a battleground for economic nationalism, digital protectionism, and regulatory fragmentation.

Conclusion: The Future of Digital Trade Governance

The digital economy is no longer a niche issue—it is the backbone of modern commerce. However, in the absence of clear, enforceable global trade rules for digital transactions, governments will continue to impose unilateral measures that disrupt cross-border trade.

The challenge is to develop a framework that balances innovation, taxation, and regulatory oversight while maintaining an open, competitive digital marketplace.

If international trade institutions fail to adapt, the world will see a divided digital economy, where data restrictions, DSTs, and trade conflicts further entrench economic and technological blocs. The need for global cooperation on digital trade has never been more urgent.

Chapter 6

Environmental Tariffs and Carbon Border Adjustments

Introduction

As global concerns over climate change intensify, trade policies are increasingly being used to enforce environmental standards. Among these policies, carbon border adjustments (tariffs imposed on imports from countries with weaker environmental regulations) have gained prominence.

The most well-known example is the *European Union's Carbon Border Adjustment Mechanism* (CBAM), which aims to level the playing field between domestic producers subject to strict environmental standards and foreign competitors from countries with lower regulatory requirements.

This chapter explores the role of carbon tariffs, the trade conflicts they may generate, and the implications for developing nations. Additionally, it considers how the World Trade Organization (WTO) governs environmental tariffs and how global trade law can adapt to address climate-related trade measures.

Finally, it examines how the Trump administration's 2025 tariff policy may impact environmental trade measures, including CBAMs.

1. The Role of Carbon Border Adjustments (CBAMs) in Trade

What Are Carbon Border Adjustments?

Carbon border adjustments are trade mechanisms designed to prevent carbon leakage, which occurs when industries relocate production to countries with weaker environmental regulations to avoid stringent domestic climate policies. By imposing tariffs on imports based on their carbon intensity, CBAMs aim to:

- Encourage carbon pricing parity across different economies.
- Reduce competitive disadvantages faced by domestic industries subject to strict environmental policies.
- Incentivize foreign producers to adopt cleaner technologies to access major markets.

The European Union's CBAM: A Case Study

The EU's Carbon Border Adjustment Mechanism (CBAM) is the most ambitious implementation of carbon tariffs to date.

Scheduled for full enforcement in 2026, it targets carbon-intensive imports such as cement, steel, aluminum, fertilizers, electricity, and hydrogen. Importers of these goods into the EU must pay a charge equivalent to the cost of emissions allowances under the EU's Emissions Trading System (ETS).

- **Impact on Global Trade**: CBAM is expected to increase compliance costs for foreign producers, particularly in countries with weak environmental policies such as China, India, and Russia.
- **Legal Challenges:** Some nations argue that CBAM constitutes a protectionist measure in violation of WTO rules.

The U.S. and other advanced economies are exploring similar models. In 2024, the U.S. proposed its own carbon tariff, targeting high-emission imports, signaling a shift toward climate-based trade policies.

2. Potential Trade Conflicts Arising from CBAMs

While carbon border adjustments are designed to combat climate change, they also raise serious geopolitical and economic concerns.

A. Countries with Lax Environmental Policies Face Economic Disadvantages

Developing nations—many of which rely on carbon-intensive industries—view CBAMs as a disguised form of protectionism. Countries like India, South Africa, and Brazil have criticized the EU's approach, arguing that it penalizes them for lacking the financial and technological capacity to transition toward greener industries.

B. Retaliatory Tariffs Could Undermine Climate Policies

CBAMs could provoke retaliatory tariffs from affected countries, particularly China and Russia, leading to a climate-related trade war. Affected nations may challenge CBAMs at the WTO's Dispute Settlement Body, arguing that they violate trade liberalization principles.

- **China's Response**: China has threatened to impose countermeasures if CBAM negatively impacts its exports.
- **Russia's Position**: Russia, a major exporter of steel and energy to the EU, claims CBAM is an economic weapon disguised as environmental policy.

C. Impact on Developing Nations

Developing nations argue that carbon tariffs disproportionately harm them, as they lack the resources to invest in green technologies. While the EU has proposed using CBAM revenues to finance climate adaptation funds for developing countries, critics argue that these funds are insufficient.

3. The Trump Administration's 2025 Tariff Policy and Its Implications for CBAMs

The 2025 U.S. trade policy under President Trump introduces a new layer of complexity for CBAMs and environmental tariffs. The administration's aggressive tariff strategy, particularly targeting major trading partners, could influence the global discourse on CBAMs in several ways:

A. Potential for Retaliatory Measures Affecting Environmental Goods

The imposition of tariffs by the U.S. has already led to retaliatory actions from affected countries. For instance, following the U.S. tariffs on Canadian and Mexican imports, both nations announced plans for reciprocal tariffs on American goods.

Such tit-for-tat measures could extend to environmental goods and services, complicating efforts to implement CBAMs and potentially leading to trade disputes that undermine environmental objectives.

B. Impact on Global Supply Chains for Renewable Energy

Tariffs on imports from countries like China, a major producer of renewable energy components, could disrupt supply chains for clean energy technologies.

This disruption may increase costs for renewable energy projects globally, potentially slowing the transition to greener energy sources.

C. Challenges to Multilateral Environmental Agreements

The U.S. administration's unilateral tariff actions may strain relationships within international bodies like the World Trade Organization (WTO) and United Nations Climate Framework.

If the U.S. imposes broad-based tariffs without aligning them with global environmental goals, it may create conflicts with countries advocating for CBAMs.

These developments suggest that while CBAMs aim to harmonize carbon pricing, they may instead become weapons in broader trade wars between the U.S., China, and the EU.

4. WTO Rules and the Legality of Carbon Tariffs

The legality of CBAMs under WTO rules is highly contested. Several General Agreement on Tariffs and Trade (GATT) provisions are relevant to the debate:

1. **GATT Article I**: The Most-Favored-Nation (MFN) Principle: Requires that all WTO members be treated equally. If CBAM disproportionately impacts certain countries, it may violate MFN rules.

2. **GATT Article III: National Treatment:** Prevents discrimination between imported and domestically produced goods. If CBAM only applies to imports and not to domestic products with similar emissions, it could be deemed unfair.

3. **GATT Article XX: General Exceptions:** Allows trade restrictions for environmental protection, provided they do not create arbitrary discrimination. As usual, it is possible to argue either way that this exemption applies and so it is by no means clear that the exemption does apply.

Several WTO dispute resolution cases have touched on environmental trade measures:

- *U.S. – Shrimp-Turtle Case (1998):* The WTO ruled that environmental measures can be justified under GATT Article XX, but they must be applied fairly and transparently.

- *Brazil – Re-treaded Tires (2007):* The WTO ruled that environmental objectives are legitimate but must be consistent and non-discriminatory.

If challenged, the EU may argue that CBAM aligns with GATT Article XX, justifying it as a legitimate environmental protection measure.

5. Author's Commentary

Environmental tariffs represent a bold but fraught attempt to align trade with climate action. CBAMs, in particular, reflect the emerging consensus among developed nations that environmental costs should be integrated into global commerce. Yet, despite their noble intent, these instruments risk exacerbating existing trade imbalances, penalizing developing economies, and provoking retaliation that undermines international cooperation.

As countries pursue climate goals, carbon border adjustments offer a means to discourage carbon leakage and reward sustainable production. However, unless accompanied by mechanisms for international equity—such as climate finance and technology transfers—they may deepen global inequalities.

The United States' 2025 return to aggressive unilateralism complicates matters. If American tariffs clash with CBAM implementation, particularly against allies and key exporters, a fracturing of climate-aligned trade coalitions could follow. A coordinated and inclusive approach, not competitive tariff escalation, is essential.

6. Conclusion: Pathways Forward for Trade and Climate Harmony

CBAMs and environmental tariffs are not simply technical tools; they are bellwethers of a larger transformation in global trade. Their success depends on balancing national interests with the shared imperative of climate stability.

A cooperative framework perhaps under a revamped WTO must emerge to guide this transition. Trade policies must uphold environmental integrity without succumbing to protectionism or geopolitical rivalry. For developing nations, genuine pathways to clean development, including financial support and market access, must be embedded in future trade arrangements.

If these principles are neglected, environmental tariffs may become instruments of division rather than progress. But if implemented with fairness, pragmatism, and multilateral resolve, they could mark a pivotal moment in the evolution of both trade law and climate policy.

CHAPTER 7

Tariffs as Economic Instruments: Strategic Divergence in U.S., EU, and Chinese Practice

Introduction

While Chapter 3 charted the broader evolution of global trade and the emerging paradigm of strategic competition, this chapter examines one of the most potent and contentious instruments of modern trade policy: the tariff.

Far from being mere fiscal tools for raising state revenue, tariffs today are wielded as instruments of geopolitical manoeuvring, economic coercion, and national identity assertion. Nowhere is this more evident than in the distinct strategies adopted by the United States, the European Union, and China.

This chapter provides an analysis of how each power deploys tariffs – not just as economic levers, but as expressions of ideology, institutional constraint, and strategic calculus. It moves beyond simplistic comparisons to explore underlying motivations, policy mechanisms, and predictive trajectories for the next decade.

1. The Strategic Logic Behind Tariffs

United States: Tariffs as Political Theatre and Economic Blunt Force

The U.S. has reconfigured its tariff use from a regulatory afterthought to a headline act of economic nationalism. Tariffs are often imposed not to encourage negotiations or regulatory compliance, but to send political messages, secure electoral bases, or punish adversaries.

Since 2018, and more intensively under the 2025 Trump administration, tariffs have been used:

- To shift public discourse toward national sovereignty and "America First."

- As a tactical device in electoral cycles, especially targeting swing-state industries (e.g. steel, agriculture).

- As a bypass of congressional scrutiny, using mechanisms like Section 232 (national security) and Section 301 (unfair trade practices).

European Union: Tariffs as Rules-Based Regulatory Enforcement

The EU's approach is restrained by internal consensus mechanisms and its commitment to multilateralism. Yet this does not render it passive. Tariffs in the EU context serve as:

- Reactive instruments against perceived unfairness (e.g. environmental or labor dumping).

- Tools to enforce regulatory equivalence, ensuring that trading partners meet EU standards.

- Part of a "smart retaliation" strategy-targeting symbolic exports to generate diplomatic pressure without full-scale escalation.

China: Tariffs as Tools of Industrial and Geostrategic Design

China's use of tariffs is embedded within a broader developmentalist and statist model. Unlike the U.S., which often reacts impulsively, China plans tariff regimes in line with Five-Year Plans, regional partnerships, and long-term technological self-sufficiency. Tariffs are used:

- To shield strategic sectors during phases of technological ramp-up (e.g. semiconductors, AI, EVs).

- As retaliation, often paired with non-tariff instruments like licensing delays, antitrust probes, or media pressure.

- With a view toward regional balancing, adjusting its tariff mix based on shifts in ASEAN, Africa, and South America.

2. Comparative Dynamics: Diverging Philosophies

Category	United States	European Union	China
Motivation	Political pressure; national security; leverage	Legal compliance; institutional trust; standardization	Developmentalism; industrial strategy; diplomatic leverage
Time Horizon	Short- to medium-term; often reactive	Long-term and consistent; rule-based	Long-term; embedded in strategic planning
Transparency	Often opaque, sudden, and politically driven	Highly documented and WTO-notified	Mixed; policy stated clearly, but state intentions sometimes opaque
Escalation Risk	High-tariffs used aggressively	Moderate-typically within WTO norms	High-retaliation blends tariffs with informal controls

3. Evolving Use-Cases and Emerging Trends

Instead of rehashing the steel tariff dispute, this section explores newer or underexamined examples where tariff strategy reflects deeper structural trends:

- **U.S. Tariff Threats Against Mexico (2024)**: Used to pressure immigration control, highlighting how tariffs are leveraged beyond trade issues.
- **EU Carbon Border Adjustment Mechanism (CBAM)**: A unique form of "green tariff" to enforce environmental standards across borders, likely to trigger WTO challenges.
- **China's Rare Earth Tariffs and Strategic Stockpiling**: Used not only to retaliate against U.S. tech sanctions but to shift global value chains toward China-centric production.

4. Future Trajectories: Beyond Tariffs?

Each economic power now confronts the limits of tariff reliance:

- **United States**: Risks diminishing returns as global partners develop tariff-avoidance strategies (e.g. rerouting through third countries).

- **European Union**: Faces growing pressure to combine its legalistic approach with firmer geopolitical stances, possibly moving closer to U.S.-style defensive trade policy.

- **China**: May pivot toward "tariff diplomacy", offering selective tariff reductions to reward alignment or punish dissent within the Global South.

Author's Commentary: Tariffs and the Return of Economic Sovereignty

Tariffs, once seen as crude relics of 19th-century mercantilism, have returned with renewed force—repurposed as instruments of sovereignty, symbolic resistance, and techno-industrial defense. In this era of geo-economic fragmentation, they serve less as tools to correct market failures and more as ideological totems.

Yet their overuse may sow the seeds of systemic instability. When tariffs become reflexive, they risk undermining supply chains, alienating allies, and triggering retaliation cycles that damage long-term growth. The U.S.'s tariff maximalism, China's policy opacity, and the EU's legal rigidity may each prove inadequate on their own.

If there is to be a future for cooperative trade, it will rest not in the elimination of tariffs, but in their disciplined re-imagination - as instruments of balance, not dominance. The current decade may well decide whether tariffs are remembered as a necessary defensive evolution or as the accelerants of a global trade conflagration.

Part 2
Tariffs - Effects

Chapter 8

Historical Lessons from the Smoot-Hawley Tariff Act and Other Protectionist Measures

Introduction

In the early months of 1930, as the United States reeled from the stock market crash of 1929, Congress debated a controversial bill that would change the course of global trade. Named after its key sponsors, Senator Reed Smoot and Representative Willis Hawley, the Smoot-Hawley Tariff Act was intended to protect struggling American industries by significantly raising tariffs on over 20,000 imported goods.

However, opposition mounted. Over a thousand economists pleaded with President Herbert Hoover to veto the bill, warning of economic retaliation and deeper depression. Their concerns, dismissed at the time, would soon prove prophetic as the legislation sent shockwaves through the global economy.

This chapter explores the Smoot-Hawley Tariff Act, its devastating impact, and its lessons for modern trade policy. Additionally, it examines other historical protectionist measures and compares them to modern trade disputes, drawing parallels between past and present economic consequences.

1. The Passage of the Smoot-Hawley Tariff Act

A. Economic and Political Justifications

The Great Depression had begun, and lawmakers were desperate to protect American businesses and jobs. They believed raising tariffs would shield domestic industries from foreign competition. The bill was driven by three primary justifications:

- **Protecting Domestic Jobs**: Supporters argued that higher tariffs would preserve employment by reducing competition from foreign imports.

- **Boosting Agricultural and Industrial Production**: Farmers and manufacturers lobbied for tariffs to secure local markets for their products.

- **Economic Nationalism**: Rising global economic instability fueled protectionist sentiment, with countries seeking to fortify their economies.

Despite these arguments, Hoover faced significant opposition. Leading economists warned of retaliatory measures from trading partners. Their warnings went unheeded, and the act was signed into law in June 1930.

2. The Immediate and Global Consequences of Smoot-Hawley

A. Retaliatory Tariffs and the Global Trade Collapse

The U.S.'s largest trading partners responded aggressively:

- Canada: Imposed tariffs on U.S. agricultural and manufactured goods, cutting trade by nearly 50%.

- Europe (France, Germany, UK): Enacted counter-tariffs, further shrinking trade volumes.

- Latin America (Argentina, Brazil, Mexico): Shifted trade toward European markets, weakening U.S. influence.

B. The Economic Fallout

- Global trade dropped by over 60%, compounding the Great Depression.

- U.S. exports fell by 66%, crushing domestic industries that had supported the bill.

- Farmers and manufacturers suffered severe demand declines, leading to bankruptcies and mass unemployment.

C. Political and Social Repercussions

- Rising nationalism and economic isolation fueled global instability.

- The lack of trade cooperation worsened relations between nations, contributing to geopolitical tensions leading up to World War II.

3. Other Historical Protectionist Measures

A. The Tariff of 1828 ("Tariff of Abominations")

This early U.S. tariff law imposed high duties on European imports, designed to protect Northern manufacturing but severely impacted the Southern states, who relied on European trade. The backlash contributed to sectional tensions, foreshadowing future conflicts in U.S. history.

B. Post-WWII Trade Liberalization

Learning from Smoot-Hawley's failures, the U.S. led efforts to liberalize trade:

- **GATT (1947)** established international trade norms, reducing tariffs globally.
- **The WTO (1995)** evolved to enforce trade rules, preventing unilateral protectionist measures.

C. The U.S.-Japan Trade Tensions (1980s)

- The U.S. imposed tariffs on Japanese car imports, attempting to protect the American auto industry.
- Japan responded by shifting production to U.S. factories, bypassing tariffs while maintaining market access.
- Unlike Smoot-Hawley, diplomatic negotiations prevented a full trade war.

4. Modern Parallels: Are We Repeating History?

A. The U.S.-China Trade War (2018-2020)

- The Trump administration imposed tariffs on Chinese goods, citing trade imbalances.
- China retaliated with tariffs on U.S. exports, particularly targeting soybeans and technology.
- The resulting trade war led to supply chain disruptions, economic uncertainty, and price increases.

B. Brexit and the Return of Trade Barriers

- The UK's exit from the European Union reinstated tariffs and trade restrictions, raising concerns about long-term economic impacts.

C. The 2025 United States Reciprocal Trade Act

- Proposed to counteract foreign tariffs and non-tariff barriers, reviving concerns over economic nationalism.
- Economists warn of potential trade retaliation and global uncertainty, echoing Smoot-Hawley's miscalculations.

5. Avoiding Another Smoot-Hawley Crisis

A. Strengthening Multilateral Trade Institutions

- Resolving disputes through WTO mechanisms rather than unilateral tariff hikes can prevent economic crises.

B. Prioritizing Trade Agreements Over Protectionism

- Agreements such as CPTPP and USMCA offer structured trade rules, reducing the risks of tariff escalation.

C. Avoiding Politicization of Trade Policy

- Trade policies should be driven by economic analysis, not short-term political gains.
- Tariffs should be used strategically, rather than as a default tool for political leverage.

Author's Commentary

As we transition from contemporary tariff strategies to historical perspectives, it is essential to reflect on the broader implications of protectionist measures. The Smoot-Hawley Tariff Act remains a defining moment in trade history, offering a cautionary tale about the unintended consequences of economic nationalism.

HISTORICAL LESSONS FROM THE SMOOT-HAWLEY TARIFF ACT

By examining the global trade collapse that followed its enactment, we gain crucial insights into the risks of protectionist policies and their cyclical nature in economic history.

History demonstrates that tariffs are more than mere economic instruments; they are deeply intertwined with political motivations, national security concerns, and diplomatic strategies. The Smoot-Hawley Tariff Act, much like modern tariff policies, was fueled by domestic pressures to protect local industries from foreign competition.

However, its ripple effects—marked by retaliatory tariffs, economic isolation, and a contraction in global trade—demonstrate the dangers of enacting protectionist policies without a broader strategic framework.

The lessons from Smoot-Hawley extend beyond the 1930s, as similar patterns have reemerged in modern trade conflicts, from the U.S.-China trade war to Brexit and beyond. The challenge for contemporary policymakers is to balance the immediate benefits of tariffs with the long-term stability of international trade. Strategic trade agreements, multilateral trade frameworks, and diplomatic negotiation remain crucial to preventing another Smoot-Hawley-style crisis.

Looking ahead, readers are encouraged to consider trade policies as integral components of global diplomacy and economic resilience. By learning from the past, we can make more informed decisions about the future, ensuring that trade policies foster stability rather than repeating the mistakes of history.

Chapter 9

Case Studies in Tariff Weaponization

Introduction

Tariffs have evolved beyond their traditional role as economic instruments used to protect domestic industries and generate revenue.

Increasingly, they are employed as strategic tools for achieving geopolitical objectives, exerting political pressure, and retaliating against perceived injustices. This phenomenon, referred to as the "weaponization" of trade, highlights how tariffs influence global economic relationships and policy decisions.

This chapter examines key case studies demonstrating the strategic use of tariffs in recent history. By analyzing these cases, we gain insight into the motivations behind such actions, their economic and political ramifications, and their broader implications for global trade.

The case studies include:

- The U.S.-China Trade War (2018–2020)
- U.S. Steel and Aluminum Tariffs (2018)
- The European Union's Carbon Border Adjustment Mechanism (CBAM)
- The 1973 OPEC Oil Embargo
- The Smoot-Hawley Tariff Act of 1930
- The 2025 U.S. Trade Initiatives

Each provides valuable insights into how tariffs extend beyond economic policy to influence international relations.

1. The U.S.-China Trade War (2018–2020)

Background and Key Events

The U.S.-China trade war exemplifies modern tariff weaponization. Initiated in 2018, it stemmed from U.S. concerns over China's trade practices, including allegations of intellectual property theft, forced technology transfers, and trade imbalances.

Key events:

- **March 2018:** The U.S. imposed steel and aluminum tariffs under national security provisions, with China as a primary target.
- **July 2018:** The U.S. levied 25% tariffs on $34 billion worth of Chinese goods, triggering immediate retaliatory tariffs from China.
- **September 2018:** Tariffs were expanded to $200 billion in Chinese imports, later increasing from 10% to 25%.
- **January 2020:** A "Phase One" trade deal paused escalation but left many tariffs intact.

Economic and Political Impact

- **Global Supply Chain Disruptions:** Companies shifted manufacturing away from China to mitigate costs.
- **Agricultural Struggles:** U.S. farmers suffered under retaliatory tariffs, prompting government relief measures.
- **Market Volatility:** Financial markets fluctuated with each policy change.
- **Strategic Decoupling:** The conflict accelerated discussions about reducing reliance on Chinese manufacturing, particularly in technology and telecommunications.

Lessons Learned

- **Complex Interdependence:** The trade war underscored the depth of global economic ties.

- **Limited Effectiveness of Tariffs:** While meant to address trade imbalances, tariffs often increased costs without achieving major policy concessions.
- **Geopolitical Consequences:** Tariffs escalated tensions, influencing global alliances and economic strategies.

2. U.S. Steel and Aluminum Tariffs (2018)

Background and Key Events

In March 2018, the U.S. imposed a 25% tariff on steel and a 10% tariff on aluminum imports, citing national security concerns under Section 232 of the Trade Expansion Act.

Key developments:

- **Broad Tariff Scope**: Initially applied to major trading partners, including allies like Canada and the EU.
- **Negotiated Exemptions**: Some countries secured exemptions or quotas.
- **Retaliatory Measures**: Affected nations imposed tariffs on U.S. exports, targeting products like bourbon and motorcycles.

Economic and Political Impact

- **Boost to Domestic Producers:** U.S. steel and aluminum industries gained short-term benefits.
- **Higher Costs for Manufacturers**: Downstream industries, including automotive and construction sectors, faced increased production costs.
- **Strained Diplomatic Relations**: The move sparked disputes within the WTO and among U.S. allies.

Lessons Learned

- **Balancing Protectionism**: Shielding domestic industries can come at the expense of higher costs elsewhere in the economy.

- **Diplomatic Repercussions**: Tariffs on allies can weaken strategic partnerships.
- **Legal Challenges**: Justifications under national security provisions can provoke legal disputes in trade institutions.

3. The European Union's Carbon Border Adjustment Mechanism (CBAM)

Background and Key Features

CBAM is the EU's attempt to address carbon leakage by imposing carbon costs on imports from countries with weaker climate policies.

- **Target Sectors**: Cement, steel, aluminum, fertilizers, and electricity.
- **Mechanism**: Importers must purchase carbon certificates to match EU pricing.
- **Implementation Timeline**: Gradual rollout, with full enforcement in the coming years.

Economic and Political Impact

- **Incentivizing Global Climate Policy**: Encourages non-EU countries to adopt stricter carbon regulations.
- **Trade Tensions**: Some nations view CBAM as a disguised protectionist measure.
- **Competitiveness Concerns**: Developing nations argue that CBAM disproportionately affects them.

4. The 1973 OPEC Oil Embargo

Background and Key Events

The 1973 OPEC oil embargo was a significant instance of economic weaponization. In response to U.S. support for Israel during the Yom Kippur War, Arab OPEC members imposed an oil embargo on the U.S. and other Western nations, causing global oil prices to quadruple.

Economic and Political Impact

- **Energy Crisis**: The embargo led to fuel shortages and economic recessions in affected nations.
- **Shift in Energy Policies**: Western countries invested heavily in alternative energy sources and strategic reserves.
- **Geopolitical Shifts**: The embargo altered diplomatic relationships and global energy dependence.

Lessons Learned

- **Economic Vulnerabilities**: Heavy reliance on foreign energy sources can be a strategic risk.
- **Trade as a Political Weapon**: The embargo illustrated how economic policies can be leveraged for geopolitical purposes.
- **Need for Energy Independence**: Many nations restructured their energy policies to reduce dependency on volatile regions.

5. The Smoot-Hawley Tariff Act of 1930

Background and Key Events

The Smoot-Hawley Tariff Act was introduced during the Great Depression to protect U.S. industries by imposing steep tariffs on imports. However, it triggered retaliatory tariffs from other countries, exacerbating the economic downturn.

Economic and Political Impact

- **Global Trade Decline**: International trade dropped significantly as countries imposed counter-tariffs.
- **Worsening of the Great Depression**: The act deepened economic hardships rather than alleviating them.
- **Policy Reversal**: The failure of Smoot-Hawley led to subsequent trade liberalization efforts.

Lessons Learned

- **Protectionism Can Backfire**: Overuse of tariffs can lead to economic isolation and global downturns.
- **Retaliation Is Likely**: Trade partners rarely accept tariffs without response, leading to trade wars.
- **Trade Cooperation Is Essential**: Smoot-Hawley demonstrated the need for multilateral trade agreements.

6. The 2025 U.S. Trade Initiatives

Background and Key Features

In 2025, the United States introduced trade initiatives aimed at bolstering domestic industries and recalibrating trade relations.

- **Tech and Semiconductor Tariffs**: New tariffs were imposed to reduce reliance on Chinese technology.
- **Re-Shoring Incentives**: Financial incentives encouraged companies to manufacture in the U.S.
- **Strengthened Export Controls**: Restrictions on AI technologies limited access for rival nations.
- **Imposition "across the board" retaliatory tariffs**: causing gross international unrest and indignation.

Economic and Political Impact

- **Increased Trade Tensions**: The measures led to further geopolitical disputes.
- **Boost to Domestic Manufacturing**: Industries benefited from government support.
- **Deteriorating Relations with Allies**: Some allies viewed the policies as economically isolating.

CASE STUDIES IN TARIFF WEAPONIZATION

Author's Commentary

The weaponization of tariffs is a defining feature of modern global trade conflicts, yet history suggests that governments consistently overestimate their effectiveness. From Smoot-Hawley's economic devastation to the protracted U.S.-China trade war, the assumption that tariffs will coerce adversaries into submission often proves misguided. Instead, tariff wars tend to escalate, entrench rival economic policies, and push nations toward alternative trade alignments.

The case studies in this chapter illustrate a fundamental paradox—tariffs are increasingly used as geopolitical tools, yet their ability to achieve clear, lasting strategic victories remains questionable. Despite their growing prevalence, modern tariffs rarely force meaningful concessions from adversaries. Instead, they trigger countermeasures, distort markets, and accelerate global economic fragmentation.

This raises a crucial question: Are tariffs becoming an outdated weapon in economic warfare?

The Persistence of Tariff Weaponization: Why Governments Keep Repeating the Cycle

Despite historical failures, nations continue to use tariffs as a primary instrument of economic statecraft. Several factors explain this persistence:

1. **Political Symbolism Over Economic Effectiveness**

   - Tariffs provide immediate, visible action in response to trade disputes, appealing to domestic political audiences.
   - Policymakers use tariffs to demonstrate strength, even when the long-term economic impact is negative.
   - The 2025 U.S. Trade Initiatives, for example, reinforce an America First agenda, regardless of whether they achieve tangible trade gains.

2. **Short-Term Gains, Long-Term Costs**

   - Tariffs can deliver initial benefits by shielding domestic industries or pressuring trade partners.
   - However, these advantages are often eroded by retaliation, rising costs for consumers, and shifting global supply chains.

- The U.S. steel and aluminum tariffs of 2018 temporarily boosted American producers but hurt downstream manufacturers, leading to higher consumer prices and trade tensions with allies.

3. **Strategic Rivalry and Economic Decoupling**

   - The U.S.-China trade war illustrates how tariffs are not just about trade—they are a means of economic containment.
   - China's response—expanding domestic subsidies, building alternative supply chains, and deepening ties with emerging markets—demonstrates how tariff weaponization can accelerate economic realignment rather than force submission.
   - The CBAM tariffs introduced by the EU highlight another dimension—climate policy is now intertwined with trade restrictions, reshaping global market access based on environmental compliance.

While tariffs remain a widely used tool, they increasingly fail to deliver decisive strategic victories. Instead, they foster prolonged economic standoffs that fuel protectionism, disrupt global markets, and encourage adversaries to develop countermeasures.

The Diminishing Effectiveness of Tariffs as an Economic Weapon

A key theme emerging from the case studies is that tariff weaponization is becoming less effective over time. This is due to three major global trade shifts:

1. **The Rise of Non-Tariff Economic Weapons**

   - Governments are increasingly relying on regulatory barriers, export controls, and investment restrictions to achieve economic dominance.
   - The U.S. AI and semiconductor export bans against China signal a move away from traditional tariffs toward targeted technology restrictions.
   - Supply chain control, rather than simple tariff escalation, may define the next phase of trade conflict.

2. **The Adaptability of Global Supply Chains**

- Unlike in the early 20th century, modern supply chains can quickly reconfigure in response to tariffs.
- The U.S.-China trade war led companies to shift manufacturing to Vietnam, Mexico, and India, minimizing tariff impact.
- The OPEC oil embargo of 1973 initially shocked global markets, but long-term consequences included the diversification of energy sources and investments in alternative fuel strategies.

3. **The Weakening of Multilateral Trade Institutions**

- The WTO's diminished role in regulating tariff disputes has emboldened nations to bypass formal trade mechanisms.
- Rather than seeking arbitration, major economies now impose unilateral tariffs, escalating conflicts rather than resolving them.
- This trend risks entrenching a fragmented trade order, where economic blocs replace global cooperation.

Taken together, these trends indicate that tariffs are losing their strategic edge. While they can still disrupt markets and signal economic aggression, their long-term effectiveness as coercive tools is increasingly questionable.

Conclusion: The Future of Trade Weaponization

The case studies in this chapter reveal a troubling cycle—governments repeatedly turn to tariffs as a weapon, experience retaliatory blowback, and ultimately fail to achieve their intended economic or political goals. The question is whether this pattern will continue or evolve into new forms of economic warfare.

Three possible futures exist:

1. **The Decline of Tariff Wars**: As supply chains adapt and non-tariff trade barriers become more dominant, tariffs may fade as a preferred method of economic coercion.
2. **The Expansion of Economic Weaponization**: Instead of disappearing, tariff strategies may evolve into broader regulatory trade wars, involving digital taxes, supply chain restrictions, and technology decoupling.
3. **A Shift Back Toward Structured Trade Agreements**: If the cost of trade fragmentation becomes too high, there may be renewed efforts

to rebuild multilateral trade frameworks—but this would require significant global cooperation.

This book will continue to explore whether tariff weaponization will remain a central feature of global trade or whether the next generation of trade conflicts will rely on entirely new economic tools. If history is any guide, nations will always seek to use trade as a form of power projection—the only question is how.

Chapter 10

Tariff Disputes in WTO History

Introduction

The World Trade Organization (WTO) serves as the primary international body governing trade disputes and tariff regulations. Over the years, it has adjudicated numerous tariff-related cases, shaping legal precedents that define fair trade practices.

These rulings establish critical guidelines on how nations can implement tariffs, prevent discriminatory trade barriers, and resolve disputes.

However, the WTO's ability to enforce decisions is increasingly challenged, especially when powerful economies disregard rulings. With protectionism on the rise, this chapter examines key WTO tariff dispute cases, explores the lessons learned, and evaluates the need for reforms to address the evolving global trade landscape.

1. Major WTO Tariff Dispute Cases

The WTO's dispute settlement mechanism has been instrumental in defining how tariffs align with global trade rules. Below are some of the most significant WTO tariff dispute cases that have influenced international trade policy.

A. United States – Import Prohibition of Certain Shrimp and Shrimp Products (1998)

Background

In 1998, India, Malaysia, Pakistan, and Thailand challenged a U.S. ban on shrimp imports harvested without turtle-excluder devices. The U.S. justified the ban under environmental conservation laws, citing the protection of endangered sea turtles under the Endangered Species Act.

WTO Ruling

The WTO's Dispute Settlement Body (DSB) ruled that while the U.S. had a legitimate environmental objective, its unilateral trade restrictions were discriminatory because:

- The ban did not provide equal treatment to all trading partners.
- The U.S. failed to engage in good-faith negotiations before imposing the restriction.
- The policy violated the non-discrimination principle under Article XI of GATT.

Implications

This ruling established a key legal precedent regarding trade restrictions based on environmental and sustainability concerns. It confirmed that countries can impose environmental trade measures, but they must be applied fairly and non-discriminatorily.

Author's Commentary: This case illustrates the delicate balance between environmental policy and trade law. While the protection of endangered species is undeniably important, the approach taken by the U.S. highlighted the pitfalls of unilateralism in international trade. A more consultative and multilateral process could have yielded the same environmental benefits without breaching WTO obligations.

B. Brazil – Re-treaded Tires (2007)

Background

In 2007, Brazil imposed an import ban on used and re-treaded tires to reduce environmental waste and public health risks. The European Union (EU) filed a WTO complaint, arguing that Brazil's policy was a disguised trade barrier, unfairly restricting European tire exports.

WTO Ruling

The WTO ruled in favor of Brazil, recognizing that:

- The ban was justified under Article XX(b) of GATT, which allows trade restrictions for the protection of human health and the environment.

- However, Brazil's inconsistent enforcement of the ban—allowing exemptions for Mercosur partners—violated WTO principles of non-discrimination.

Implications

This case reaffirmed that public health and environmental concerns can justify trade restrictions, but policies must be applied consistently to avoid violating WTO trade principles.

Author's Commentary: While Brazil's victory set an important precedent, it also exposed a common challenge in trade disputes—inconsistent enforcement. The decision suggests that environmental protections must not only be justified but also applied uniformly, without exceptions that might suggest protectionist intent.

This case serves as a warning that regulatory loopholes can undermine even the most well-intentioned policies.

C. *China – Rare Earth Exports (2014)*

Background

China is the world's largest producer of rare earth minerals, critical for electronics, renewable energy, and defense industries. In 2010, China restricted rare earth exports, citing the need for environmental protection and resource conservation.

However, the United States, Japan, and the EU challenged the restrictions, arguing that China was manipulating global supply chains for competitive advantage.

WTO Ruling

In 2014, the WTO ruled against China, finding that:

- The export restrictions were inconsistent with WTO rules, violating China's accession commitments.
- China could not use environmental concerns as a justification while favoring domestic industries with lower restrictions.

Implications

This ruling reinforced that WTO members cannot manipulate trade flows under the guise of resource conservation. It also underscored the importance of

WTO commitments, particularly for large economies with global supply chain influence.

Author's Commentary: China's actions in this case reflect a broader trend in global trade, where nations attempt to leverage natural resource dominance for strategic advantage.

The WTO's decision highlights the principle that trade restrictions must be based on legitimate and consistent policy applications rather than economic leverage. However, with increasing geopolitical tensions, it remains uncertain how effectively such rulings will be enforced in future disputes.

Author's Commentary

The legal precedents established by WTO tariff disputes have shaped global trade policies, reinforcing fair trade principles while highlighting enforcement challenges.

Cases like *Shrimp-Turtle, Re-treaded Tires, and Rare Earth* illustrate the complex balance between national policies and international trade obligations.

However, as powerful economies challenge the WTO's authority, concerns grow about its ability to enforce rulings. With rising protectionism and new trade tensions, WTO reforms are essential to maintaining a rules-based global trading system.

While the WTO remains the backbone of global trade governance, its authority is increasingly questioned.

The cases discussed demonstrate how WTO international trade decisions attempt to balance national sovereignty, economic policy, and global cooperation. Yet, without meaningful enforcement mechanisms, the credibility of WTO rulings will continue to erode.

Looking ahead, the real test will be whether nations uphold multilateral commitments or succumb to unilateral trade strategies, which history has shown to be economically disruptive.

Chapter 11

Impact of Tariffs on Emerging Markets

Introduction

Tariffs, as instruments of trade policy, have far-reaching implications, especially for emerging markets. These economies often find themselves disproportionately affected by tariff impositions due to their reliance on exports and limited capacity to absorb economic shocks.

Unlike developed economies, which often have diversified industries and extensive financial reserves, emerging markets frequently depend on a few key sectors, making them highly susceptible to trade barriers.

What Are Emerging Markets?

Emerging markets are economies that are in a transitional phase between developing and developed status. They typically exhibit rapid economic growth, increasing industrialization, and greater integration into the global economy. However, they also tend to have structural weaknesses such as income inequality, political instability, and vulnerability to external economic shocks.

The term "emerging markets" is widely used in financial and economic discourse but does not have an official definition within World Trade Organization (WTO) agreements or formal global trade policies. Instead, the WTO classifies its member countries into "developing countries" and "least-developed countries" (LDCs).

Developing countries, including many considered emerging markets, receive special rights and provisions within WTO agreements to assist their economic development and integration into global trade. While emerging markets share characteristics with developing economies, they are distinguished by their accelerated growth trajectories and increasing influence in global trade networks.

Illustrative examples of emerging markets include:

- **Brazil:** A key exporter of agricultural and industrial goods, with significant vulnerabilities to commodity price fluctuations and trade barriers.
- **India:** A fast-growing economy with a large services sector but facing trade challenges due to reliance on imported energy and raw materials.
- **China:** While approaching developed status, China remains an emerging market in certain respects due to ongoing economic reforms and regional disparities.
- **South Africa:** The most industrialized economy in Africa, yet highly dependent on commodity exports and vulnerable to external market fluctuations.
- **Indonesia:** A rapidly expanding economy benefiting from regional trade but still grappling with infrastructure and regulatory challenges.

This chapter explores the multifaceted impact of tariffs on developing economies, with a focused case study on U.S. tariffs imposed on Brazilian steel.

Additionally, it delves into broader economic consequences, the political dimensions of tariff policies, and strategies that emerging markets can employ to navigate and mitigate the challenges posed by such trade barriers.

1. Disproportionate Impact of Tariffs on Developing Economies

Economic Vulnerabilities

Developing economies are particularly susceptible to the adverse effects of tariffs due to several inherent vulnerabilities:

- **Export Dependence:** Many emerging markets rely heavily on a narrow range of export commodities. Tariffs targeting these goods can lead to significant revenue losses and economic instability.
- **Limited Diversification**: The lack of diversified industrial bases means that these economies have fewer alternatives to compensate for the loss of export markets affected by tariffs.

- **Capital Constraints**: Limited access to capital restricts the ability of businesses in developing countries to absorb increased costs resulting from tariffs or to invest in alternative markets and products.

- **Inflationary Pressures**: Tariffs can drive up the cost of imported raw materials and intermediate goods, leading to inflationary pressures that disproportionately affect lower-income populations.

- **Exchange Rate Volatility**: As tariffs disrupt trade balances, emerging market currencies can depreciate, increasing the cost of servicing foreign debt and making essential imports more expensive.

2. Case Study: U.S. Tariffs on Brazilian Steel

The imposition of U.S. tariffs on Brazilian steel exemplifies the challenges faced by emerging markets:

- **Background:** In March 2018, President Trump issued proclamations imposing tariffs of 25% on steel imports, citing national security concerns under Section 232 of the Trade Expansion Act of 1962. Brazil, as one of the top exporters of steel to the U.S., was significantly impacted. While some exemptions and quotas were later introduced, the overall effect remained damaging.

- **Economic Impact:** Brazilian steel exports to the U.S. faced substantial declines. Margins on Brazilian steel exports are lower than margins on steel sold domestically, particularly because they are lower-valued semi-finished products.

- **Broader Economic Consequences:** The tariffs led to job losses in Brazil's steel industry, affected the country's trade balance, and had ripple effects on ancillary industries such as mining and logistics.

- **Strategic Responses:** In response to the tariffs, major Brazilian companies like Gerdau and Braskem emphasized their substantial U.S. operations as a buffer against trade barriers. Gerdau, for instance, operates 11 steel production units in the U.S. and Canada, positioning itself to benefit from protected market policies.

This case study highlights how protectionist measures, though intended to safeguard domestic industries in the imposing country, can cause substantial harm to trading partners and disrupt global supply chains.

3. Political and Strategic Dimensions of Tariff Policies

Protectionism vs. Globalization

Tariffs are often implemented as a protectionist measure to support domestic industries. However, while protectionism can offer short-term gains for certain sectors, it can also lead to retaliatory measures, trade wars, and long-term economic stagnation. Emerging markets, which are highly dependent on international trade, often bear the brunt of these policies.

The Role of Trade Agreements and Dispute Resolution

The World Trade Organization (WTO) and regional trade agreements play a crucial role in mitigating the negative impacts of tariffs. However, enforcement mechanisms are often slow and politically charged, making it difficult for emerging economies to seek redress effectively.

4. Strategies for Emerging Economies to Navigate Tariff Challenges

To mitigate the adverse effects of tariffs, emerging economies can adopt several strategic approaches:

1. **Diversification of Export Markets**

   - Expanding trade partnerships beyond traditional markets can reduce dependence on any single economy and lessen the impact of targeted tariffs.
   - Strengthening economic ties with China, the European Union, and regional trade partners can create alternative revenue streams.

2. **Enhancing Domestic Value Addition**

   - Investing in the development of value-added industries can help countries move up the value chain, making their exports less susceptible to basic commodity tariffs and more competitive globally.
   - Developing manufacturing hubs can reduce reliance on exporting raw materials and increase self-sufficiency.

3. **Strengthening Regional Trade Agreements**

   - Participating in regional trade agreements can provide access to larger markets and create a buffer against external tariff impositions.

- Organizations like MERCOSUR, ASEAN, and the African Continental Free Trade Area (AfCFTA) offer platforms for collective bargaining and economic integration.

4. **Attracting Foreign Direct Investment (FDI)**

    - By creating a favorable investment climate, emerging markets can attract FDI, leading to technology transfer, infrastructure development, and enhanced production capabilities.
    - Encouraging joint ventures between local companies and multinational corporations can also help mitigate the impact of trade restrictions.

5. **Developing Robust Trade Facilitation Mechanisms**

    - Improving customs procedures, infrastructure, and regulatory frameworks can enhance trade efficiency and reduce costs, making exports more competitive despite the presence of tariffs.
    - Digital trade facilitation and streamlined logistics networks can lower trade costs and increase competitiveness.

Author's Commentary:

It is increasingly perplexing that certain economies—most notably China—continue to be classified as "emerging markets", despite their dominant role in global trade, technological advancement, and economic influence. The very notion that China, the world's second-largest economy, enjoys preferential trade treatment under any international trade framework raises fundamental questions about the legitimacy and fairness of the existing global trade system.

This classification grants unwarranted advantages to economies that no longer require developmental trade protections, while genuinely disadvantaged nations—many in Sub-Saharan Africa, South Asia, and parts of Latin America—struggle to access meaningful trade benefits, investment opportunities, and supply chain integration. The time has come for a thorough reassessment of which nations truly qualify for emerging market concessions and how trade policies can be restructured to ensure equitable economic development.

Recalibrating the Emerging Market Framework: A Necessary Reform

The process of identifying and prioritizing truly deserving economies requires a fundamental shift in global trade policy: Instead of relying on outdated GDP-based classifications, trade institutions must incorporate modern economic metrics, including:

1. **Industrial and Technological Development**: Nations with high-tech industries, advanced infrastructure, and global trade dominance should no longer benefit from "developing nation" exemptions.

2. **Access to Capital and Investment**: Economies with high foreign direct investment (FDI) flows, robust stock markets, and significant financial resources should not be treated on par with struggling low-income nations.

3. **Trade Surplus and Market Power**: Countries that consistently run trade surpluses and exert strategic control over key global supply chains should not be classified alongside fragile economies.

A modernized classification system must distinguish between economies that need trade concessions for development and those that have leveraged their status for geopolitical advantage.

The Path Forward: Regional Collaboration, Structural Reform, and Trade Realignment

Beyond reclassification, emerging economies that genuinely require trade support must be given clear pathways to sustainable economic growth. This requires:

1. **Regional Trade Cooperation**: Instead of relying on concessional agreements with advanced economies, emerging markets should strengthen regional alliances to promote intra-regional trade, industrial collaboration, and shared supply chain development.

2. **Investment in Innovation and Infrastructure**: Structural reform should focus on enhancing technological capacity, improving logistics and transportation networks, and fostering competitive industries, rather than over-relying on tariff preferences.

3. **A New Multilateral Framework for Developmental Trade Policies**: If the WTO survives its current crisis, it could play a critical role in restructuring trade policies to ensure that developing economies receive

meaningful support without allowing economic giants to exploit outdated classifications.

However, the WTO's future remains highly uncertain in an era where protectionism is resurgent, trade wars are escalating, and multilateral trade agreements are being increasingly bypassed in favor of bilateral and regional deals. The institution faces an existential crossroads: either modernize to remain relevant or risk becoming obsolete in a fragmented global trade order.

Conclusion: The Need for a Pragmatic Trade Model

The concept of emerging markets must evolve to reflect real economic conditions, not outdated political classifications. Trade policies should be restructured to provide meaningful advantages to struggling nations, rather than being manipulated by economic powerhouses seeking unfair trade advantages.

Ultimately, the question is not whether emerging markets should receive preferential treatment, but how to ensure that such treatment is reserved for those who truly need it. If the global trade system fails to address this issue, the very principle of fair trade will erode, leading to further protectionism, economic inequality, and the weakening of multilateral institutions.

Chapter 12

The Impact of Tariffs on Inflation: A Commercial Observation

Introduction: The Relationship Between Tariffs and Inflation

Inflation and tariffs are two of the most critical economic variables in global commerce, shaping consumer prices, trade relationships, and business strategies.

Inflation represents the rate at which the general price level of goods and services increases over time, eroding purchasing power and impacting economic stability.

Tariffs, on the other hand, are taxes imposed on imported goods, typically as a means of protecting domestic industries or as a tool of economic diplomacy. When tariffs increase, their direct and indirect effects ripple throughout the economy, influencing inflationary trends in complex ways.

This chapter provides a commercial observation of the impact of increased tariffs on inflation, defining key economic concepts, exploring mechanisms through which tariffs contribute to inflationary pressures, and illustrating these effects with some examples.

Understanding Inflation

Inflation is the rate at which the prices of goods and services rise over time. It is typically measured using indices such as the Consumer Price Index (CPI) and the Producer Price Index (PPI). Inflation can be categorized into different types:

1. **Demand-Pull Inflation:** Occurs when demand for goods and services exceeds supply, leading to price increases.

2. **Cost-Push Inflation:** Arises when production costs (such as wages, raw materials, and tariffs) increase, forcing businesses to raise prices to maintain profit margins.

3. **Built-In Inflation:** Results from the expectation of continued price increases, leading to wage-price spirals.

What Are Tariffs?

Tariffs are government-imposed taxes on imported goods, either as a percentage of the product's value (ad valorem tariffs) or as a fixed charge per unit (specific tariffs). Governments utilize tariffs for multiple purposes:

- **Revenue Generation:** Tariffs provide a source of government revenue.
- **Domestic Industry Protection:** By making imports more expensive, tariffs encourage consumers to buy domestically produced goods.
- **Trade Policy and Diplomacy:** Tariffs can be used as leverage in negotiations or as retaliatory measures in trade disputes.

However, the imposition of tariffs does not occur in isolation. Their effects extend beyond international trade and influence domestic economic conditions, particularly inflation.

How Do Tariffs Contribute to Inflation?

When tariffs are increased, they influence inflation through several channels:

1. **Higher Costs of Imported Goods**

    - Tariffs directly increase the cost of imported goods by adding an additional tax to their price. If domestic producers rely on imported raw materials or components, this raises production costs, which are then passed on to consumers.
    - **Example:** If the U.S. imposes a 25% tariff on steel imports, the cost of imported steel rises. This, in turn, increases production costs for industries relying on steel, such as automotive and construction sectors, leading to higher final product prices.

2. **Supply Chain Disruptions and Price Volatility**

   - Tariffs can lead to supply chain disruptions by forcing businesses to seek alternative suppliers, often at higher costs. This results in reduced efficiency and increased expenses, further fueling inflation.
   - *Case Study*: When the U.S. imposed tariffs on Chinese goods in 2018, American businesses faced shortages of essential components, leading to production delays and higher costs, which ultimately translated into higher consumer prices.

3. **Retaliatory Tariffs and Their Inflationary Effects**

   - Countries affected by tariffs often respond with countermeasures. This results in restricted market access and reduced competition, leading to higher domestic prices.
   - *Example*: The European Union imposed tariffs on U.S. agricultural products in response to American tariffs on steel and aluminum. This reduced U.S. export volumes, forcing American farmers to raise domestic prices to compensate for lost international revenue.

4. **Consumer Purchasing Power Decline**

   - As businesses pass on increased costs to consumers, real wages decline, reducing purchasing power. This results in a downward cycle where consumers can afford fewer goods and services, leading to stagflation (a combination of inflation and economic stagnation).

The Indirect Impact of Trade Wars on Inflation

The following observations illustrate how global trade wars might indirectly affect inflation in Australia even in the absence of direct tariff impositions on Australia.

Australia is used in this segment as an illustrative example but the same explanation applies internationally.

Australia like many other countries has a bilateral Free Trade Agreement ("FTA") with the United States. Since 1 January, 2005 there has been no customs duty payable on most US originating goods imported into Australia. Similarly, there has been no customs duty payable on most Australian originating goods imported into the United States.

For the sake of this analysis, assume that the United States did not impose increased tariffs on Australia because of the FTA or for any other geopolitical purpose. Assume further that the US did impose increased tariffs on for example, China. Australia then is not immune to the economic consequences of that trade war between the United States and China.

When the United States imposes tariffs of 10% or 20% on Chinese imports, the cost of goods in the U.S. rises due to these added levies.

In response, China retaliates with similar tariffs on U.S. exports, increasing the cost of American products entering the Chinese market. While Australia is not directly involved in this tariff exchange, the cascading effects of these tariffs can indirectly contribute to inflation within Australia in the following ways:

1. **Increased Cost of Goods from China and the United States**

    - China is a significant manufacturing hub for Australian imports. As Chinese manufacturers (indirectly) may face increased costs due to U.S. tariffs, these costs are passed down to all importing countries, including Australia. Consequently, Australian businesses and consumers face higher prices for Chinese-manufactured goods, contributing to domestic inflation.

    - Similarly, if U.S. manufacturers indirectly face higher costs from Chinese tariffs, their increased production expenses may be transferred to their global customers, including Australia, further driving up import costs.

2. **Disruptions in Global Supply Chains**

    - Global trade wars cause shifts in supply chains as businesses seek alternative markets and suppliers to offset tariff-induced costs. This reallocation leads to inefficiencies, delays, and increased logistical expenses, all of which can filter through to Australian businesses and consumers.

3. **Commodity Price Fluctuations**

    - Australia is a major exporter of raw materials, including iron ore and coal, to China. If China's economy slows due to tariff-induced economic strains, its demand for Australian exports may decline.

A downturn in demand could lead to economic contraction in Australia, reducing business investments and employment growth while maintaining inflationary pressures due to imported cost increases.

While Australia is not a direct participant in tariff escalations between the U.S. and China, its economy is still susceptible to the inflationary repercussions of global trade conflicts.

These indirect effects underscore the interconnected nature of global commerce, where even countries maintaining free trade agreements cannot fully shield themselves from external tariff-driven economic pressures.

Author's Commentary:

The impact of tariffs on inflation, consumer purchasing power, and business strategy is no longer a secondary concern—it has become a central economic issue in the modern trade landscape. While policymakers may impose tariffs to protect domestic industries or correct trade imbalances, their unintended consequence is often a broad inflationary surge that extends far beyond the targeted goods and sectors.

This chapter has illustrated how both direct and indirect inflationary effects manifest when tariffs are introduced. However, the more pressing concern is whether tariff-driven inflation has become an entrenched feature of global commerce.

Are tariffs now an unavoidable driver of long-term price instability, or is there still a path toward mitigating their inflationary effects?

The New Normal: Have Tariffs Become an Inflationary Fixture?

Historically, tariff-induced inflation was seen as a temporary side effect—a transitional cost that businesses and consumers absorbed before the market adjusted. Today, however, the globalization of supply chains and the strategic use of tariffs in economic warfare suggest that tariff-driven inflation is becoming a long-term structural issue rather than a short-term shock.

Three key factors reinforce this shift:

1. **Persistent Global Trade Wars and Retaliatory Cycles**

- Tariffs are no longer isolated policy measures—they have become recurring components of trade disputes, creating extended inflationary pressures.
- The U.S.-China trade war, for example, has not been fully reversed, meaning that the inflationary effects of earlier tariff hikes remain embedded in global pricing structures.
- As new trade conflicts emerge—such as those linked to carbon border adjustments and digital taxation—inflationary pressures are unlikely to subside.

2. **Supply Chain Shifts and Economic Fragmentation**

- Tariffs disrupt global supply chains, forcing companies to relocate production, seek alternative suppliers, and absorb new logistical costs.
- Unlike in previous decades, where trade liberalization reduced costs, modern supply chain restructuring tends to increase prices, reinforcing inflationary trends.
- The emergence of regional trade blocs as an alternative to WTO-led globalization (e.g. CPTPP, RCEP, and U.S.-led reshoring initiatives) is leading to a less efficient but more protectionist global economy, where inflationary pressures may remain high.

3. **Inflationary Policy Loops: Central Banks vs. Trade Protectionism**

- Central banks attempt to control inflation through interest rate adjustments, but tariffs counteract these efforts by continuously driving up import prices.
- Higher interest rates make borrowing more expensive, which slows economic growth—yet tariff-driven price increases continue to affect goods and services, making it harder to achieve price stability.
- This creates an inflationary policy loop, where monetary policy measures are partially undermined by persistent trade protectionism.

If tariffs continue to be used as a primary economic weapon, inflation will no longer be a temporary trade-off—it will become a built-in characteristic of the global economic system.

The Unresolved Dilemma: Trade Stability vs. Inflation Control

Policymakers and businesses face an increasingly difficult balancing act—how to pursue trade stability and economic security without exacerbating inflationary risks.

- Governments must decide whether protecting domestic industries through tariffs is worth the inflationary burden placed on consumers and manufacturers.
- Businesses must adapt to sustained trade uncertainty, using diversified supply chains, price hedging strategies, and automation to minimize inflationary risks.
- Consumers, as the end recipients of inflation, must adjust to higher costs, fluctuating wages, and economic volatility driven by prolonged trade disputes.

While alternative trade policies—such as targeted subsidies, investment incentives, and cooperative trade agreements—could help mitigate tariff-driven inflation, the current trend toward economic nationalism suggests that such solutions remain politically challenging.

Conclusion: Inflation as a Byproduct of a Fragmented Trade Order

The inflationary consequences of tariffs are no longer limited to trade-dependent nations—they impact all economies, including those not directly involved in tariff disputes. As nations increasingly weaponize trade policy, inflation will continue to be a structural consequence of protectionist strategies.

The core question remains: Can global trade institutions adapt to prevent tariffs from becoming a permanent inflationary force, or is the world moving toward an era where trade conflicts and price instability go hand in hand?

This book will continue to explore whether global economic governance can counteract the inflationary effects of tariffs, or whether inflation has now become an inescapable byproduct of modern trade policy.

Chapter 13

Tariffs and Supply Chain Disruptions

Introduction

The global economy relies on complex and highly integrated supply chains that span multiple countries. However, the escalation of tariff wars, particularly between economic superpowers like the United States and China, has disrupted global supply networks, increased costs, and forced businesses to rethink their sourcing strategies.

This chapter explores the key challenges tariffs pose to supply chains, the industries most affected, and how businesses and governments are adapting to these disruptions.

Key Challenges of Tariff-Induced Supply Chain Disruptions

1. **Increased Production Costs**

    - Tariffs raise the cost of imported materials, making production more expensive for manufacturers and ultimately increasing costs for consumers.

2. **Supply Chain Delays and Uncertainty**

    - Sudden tariff impositions disrupt just-in-time (JIT) inventory systems, leading to shortages and inefficiencies.
    - JIT systems rely on seamless and timely deliveries to minimize storage costs. When tariffs are suddenly introduced, businesses face immediate cost increases, supplier bottlenecks, and shortages of critical materials and products.

- Companies must absorb higher costs, pass them on to consumers, or seek alternative suppliers, all of which can have broader economic repercussions.

3. **Geopolitical Risks in Trade Routes**

- Countries retaliate with counter-tariffs, further complicating global trade.
- Recent 2025 U.S. policy announcements have reignited trade tensions, including:
    - 25% tariffs on imports from Canada and Mexico under national security provisions.
    - 10% tariffs on imports from China, targeting key manufacturing inputs.
    - New restrictions on duty-free imports under the de minimis rule, impacting e-commerce giants like Shein and Temu.
    - U.S. "across the board" retaliatory tariffs.
- Economists warn that these tariffs may exacerbate inflation and trigger new rounds of retaliatory measures, further complicating supply chain logistics.

Industries Most Affected by Supply Chain Disruptions

1. Automotive Industry: Rising Costs and Delays

The automotive sector depends on global supply networks, sourcing components from different regions. Tariffs disrupt:

- Parts imports and exports (e.g. engines from Germany, steel from China, semiconductors from Taiwan).
- Manufacturing costs, forcing companies to raise prices or absorb losses.

Case Example: U.S. Steel and Aluminum Tariffs

- The Trump administration imposed a 25% tariff on steel and a 10% tariff on aluminum under Section 232 of the Trade Expansion Act.

- U.S. automakers like General Motors (GM) and Ford reported billions in extra costs, leading to factory closures and layoffs.
- Foreign retaliation: Canada and Mexico imposed counter-tariffs on U.S. auto parts, disrupting North American supply chains.

2. Electronics Industry: Component Shortages and Higher Prices

The electronics industry relies heavily on Asian manufacturers, particularly China, Taiwan, and South Korea. Tariffs increase:

- Chip production costs, affecting companies like Apple, Qualcomm, and Samsung.
- Shipping delays, impacting smartphones, computers, and home appliances.

Case Example: Semiconductor Tariffs and Export Controls

- The U.S. imposed tariffs on Chinese-made semiconductors, exacerbating the global chip shortage.
- China responded by restricting rare earth mineral exports, essential for chip production.
- Companies like Intel and NVIDIA faced higher costs and supply chain bottlenecks.

3. Pharmaceutical Industry: Supply Chain Vulnerabilities

Pharmaceutical supply chains are highly globalized, with active pharmaceutical ingredients (APIs) sourced from different countries. Tariffs disrupt:

- Drug manufacturing, increasing production costs.
- Medical device supply chains, affecting hospitals and healthcare providers.

Case Example: U.S. Tariffs on Chinese Medical Supplies

- During the COVID-19 pandemic, U.S. tariffs on Chinese medical equipment (e.g. face masks, ventilators) delayed crucial shipments.
- The pharmaceutical industry lobbied for exemptions, highlighting the risks of over-reliance on foreign suppliers.

Case Study: Semiconductor Shortages and U.S.-China Tariff Policies

Semiconductors are the backbone of modern technology, powering everything from smartphones to electric vehicles (EVs). However, the U.S.-China trade war disrupted semiconductor supply chains, leading to a global chip shortage.

How the Trade War Exacerbated the Shortage

- 2018: The U.S. imposed a 25% tariff on Chinese semiconductors.
- 2020: The U.S. restricted chip exports to China, affecting Huawei and other firms.
- 2021–2022: China retaliated by limiting rare earth mineral exports, crucial for chip production.
- 2025: The Trump administration tightened controls on semiconductor imports and rare earth materials, escalating supply chain challenges.

Recent U.S. tariff announcements, particularly those targeting Canada, Mexico, and China, are expected to disrupt supply chains across multiple industries. The removal of duty-free trade provisions could further increase costs and restrict market access.

Author's Commentary

Tariffs and sanctions are not merely economic tools; they shape global trade relationships, industrial policy, and geopolitical strategy. Supply chain disruptions are not simply a short-term consequence of tariffs—they represent a fundamental shift in trade dynamics that businesses and governments must anticipate and react.

While nearshoring and diversification have emerged as key strategies for mitigating trade risks, long-term solutions require deeper multilateral cooperation and economic realignment. If protectionist trade policies persist, new economic blocs and regional trade alliances will emerge, reinforcing economic fragmentation.

Author's Key Strategic Recommendations

1. **Encouraging Supply Chain Resilience:** Governments should incentivize regional supply chains and domestic production capacity to reduce reliance on vulnerable trade routes.

2. **Balancing Tariffs with Trade Diplomacy**: While tariffs may serve short-term economic interests, they should be strategically applied to avoid excessive economic retaliation and supply chain fragmentation.

3. **Enhancing Multilateral Trade Mechanisms:** Strengthening WTO dispute resolution frameworks and cooperative trade agreements can help address trade imbalances without escalating trade wars.

4. **Leveraging Technological Innovation**: Investments in automation, AI-driven logistics, and digital supply chain solutions can improve trade efficiency and adaptability.

5. **Preparing for the Future of Trade Warfare**: As economic policies become more protectionist, businesses must adopt long-term risk assessment models to anticipate disruptions caused by tariffs, trade disputes, and geopolitical shifts.

Final Thought

The future of global supply chains depends on how nations balance protectionist policies with economic interdependence. Whether tariffs will lead to self-sufficiency or further economic fragmentation remains uncertain, but what is clear is that businesses and governments must be prepared for a more volatile trade landscape in the years ahead.

Chapter 14

Currency Manipulation and Its Role in Trade Wars

Introduction

Currency manipulation, particularly through deliberate devaluation, plays a significant role in international trade dynamics and can influence tariff policies. This chapter explores how currency devaluation affects tariff policies, examines China's currency devaluation amid U.S. tariff increases, discusses World Trade Organization (WTO) regulations on currency manipulation, and offers policy recommendations to address this complex issue. Additionally, the role of trade-based money laundering (TBML) and its intersection with global trade practices is summarized.

1. How Currency Devaluation Affects Tariff Policies

Currency devaluation involves a country intentionally lowering the value of its currency relative to others. This practice can offset the impact of tariffs by making exports cheaper and imports more expensive, thereby influencing trade balances.

Impact on Tariff Policies:

- **Neutralizing Tariffs:** When a country devalues its currency, its goods become cheaper for foreign buyers, potentially counteracting the effects of tariffs imposed by other nations.

- **Trade Imbalances:** Persistent devaluation can lead to trade surpluses for the devaluing country and deficits for its trading partners, prompting retaliatory tariffs and trade disputes.

- **Competitive Devaluations:** Such actions can trigger a "race to the bottom," where countries competitively devalue their currencies, leading to global economic instability.

A notable example is the **U.S.-China trade relationship**, where currency valuation has been a contentious issue.

2. Historical Context of Currency Wars

Currency wars, also known as competitive devaluations, occur when countries intentionally devalue their currencies to gain a trade advantage. A notable instance is the 1930s Great Depression, when many economies abandoned the gold standard, leading to significant currency devaluations. In modern history, the 1985 Plaza Accord was an agreement among major economies, including the U.S., Japan, Germany, France, and the UK, to intervene in currency markets and prevent unilateral devaluation measures.

3. Case Study: China's Currency Devaluation Amid U.S. Tariff Increases

In August 2019, during escalating trade tensions with the United States, China allowed the yuan to depreciate beyond the 7-per-dollar threshold.

Background:

- **U.S. Tariffs:** The U.S. imposed significant tariffs on Chinese goods, aiming to reduce the trade deficit and address concerns over intellectual property practices.

- **China's Response:** China permitted its currency to weaken, making its exports more competitive despite the tariffs.

Implications:

- **Trade Deficit:** The devaluation helped maintain China's export volumes to the U.S., sustaining the trade imbalance.

- **Market Reactions:** The move led to volatility in global financial markets, with concerns over a potential currency war.

- **Policy Responses:** The U.S. labeled China a "currency manipulator," escalating tensions and leading to discussions on the need for clearer international rules on currency practices.

This case illustrates how currency devaluation can be used to mitigate the impact of tariffs and complicate international trade relations.

4. The Role of the International Monetary Fund (IMF)

While the World Trade Organization (WTO) addresses trade-related issues, the International Monetary Fund (IMF) plays a crucial role in monitoring global currency practices. The IMF's mandate includes overseeing exchange rate policies and identifying instances of manipulation, thereby complementing the WTO's efforts in promoting fair trade. However, the IMF lacks binding enforcement powers and relies primarily on policy recommendations and consultations with member states.

5. WTO Regulations on Currency Manipulation

The WTO does not have explicit rules governing currency values, but certain provisions can be interpreted to address currency manipulation.

Relevant Provisions:

- **GATT Article XV (4):** WTO members should not use exchange rate actions to frustrate the intent of the General Agreement on Tariffs and Trade (GATT).
- **IMF Collaboration:** The WTO defers to the IMF on matters related to exchange rates.

Challenges:

- **Enforcement Limitations:** The WTO relies on the IMF to assess currency practices, but the IMF has limited enforcement capabilities.
- **Dispute Resolution Ambiguity:** There is uncertainty over whether currency manipulation falls within the WTO's dispute settlement mechanism, leading to calls for clearer guidelines.

6. Trade-Based Money Laundering (TBML): The Intersection of Money Laundering and Trade

While money laundering and currency manipulation are separate issues, they intersect in trade-based money laundering (TBML).

A. Understanding TBML

TBML involves the use of international trade transactions to disguise the origins of illicit funds through mispricing, multiple invoicing, and falsely describing goods and services.

B. Impact on Global Trade

- **Economic Distortion:** TBML misrepresents trade data, affecting economic policy decisions.
- **Competitive Disadvantage**: Legitimate businesses struggle to compete with TBML-linked entities.
- **Regulatory Challenges**: The complexity of global trade transactions makes detection difficult.

7. Author's Policy Recommendations

To mitigate the adverse effects of currency manipulation, the following measures are recommended:

1. Strengthen WTO and IMF Collaboration:

- **Enhanced Monitoring:** Improve tracking of exchange rate policies.
- **Clearer Guidelines:** Define and prohibit currency manipulation explicitly.

2. Global Coordination on Currency Stabilization:

- **Multilateral Agreements:** Encourage countries to commit to exchange rate stability.
- **Regular Consultations:** Establish global economic forums for dialogue.

3. **Promote Transparent Central Bank Policies:**

- **Disclosure Requirements:** Require real-time data on foreign exchange interventions.
- **Accountability Mechanisms:** Implement mechanisms to ensure central bank policies do not create unfair trade advantages.

Author's Commentary

Currency manipulation remains one of the most contentious and least regulated trade practices, allowing countries to subtly shift economic advantages in their favor without the visibility of tariffs.

This chapter has demonstrated how currency devaluation influences tariff policies, particularly in the China-U.S. trade dispute, but the broader concern is whether currency manipulation can be effectively regulated in an evolving trade landscape.

Without effective WTO-IMF enforcement mechanisms, currency manipulation will continue to undermine fair trade, fueling retaliatory measures, financial instability, and global trade distortions. If currency devaluation becomes a normalized policy tool, the world risks a perpetual cycle of trade imbalances and economic uncertainty.

The challenge remains: will international institutions adapt, or will currency manipulation remain a permanent, unchecked force in economic warfare?

Part 3
Tariffs – Formulation

Chapter 15

The Influence of Lobbying on Tariff Policy

Introduction

Political lobbying and multinational corporations (MNCs) play a significant role in shaping global trade policy, particularly in the formulation and negotiation of tariffs.

While governments set tariff rates in the interest of economic stability, national security, and international trade agreements, corporate interests often exert considerable influence over these decisions.

Lobbying efforts by powerful industry groups and MNCs can lead to protective tariffs that benefit specific sectors but may also result in market distortions, increased consumer prices, and retaliatory trade measures.

The challenge for policymakers is to balance corporate advocacy with broader national economic interests and international trade obligations.

This chapter explores:

- How political lobbying shapes tariff policy.
- The role of MNCs in influencing trade negotiations.
- Case studies demonstrating corporate influence on tariffs.
- The consequences of lobbying-driven protectionism.
- Potential policy reforms to ensure tariffs serve national interests rather than corporate agendas.

How Political Lobbying Shapes Trade Policy

Lobbying is a primary tool used by industry groups to influence trade policy. Corporations and trade associations employ various strategies to advocate for tariffs that protect their market position:

- Direct lobbying of government officials and trade representatives.
- Public campaigns to sway public opinion in favor of protectionist policies.
- Funding research and think tanks that support their policy positions.
- Grassroots mobilization to create the appearance of widespread support for certain trade measures.

Industries with strong lobbying power can justify tariffs on the grounds of economic security, unfair foreign competition, or national security, even when the overall economic impact may be questionable.

Case Study: The Steel Industry's Influence on U.S. Tariff Policy

The American Iron and Steel Institute (AISI) is a leading advocate for protective tariffs on steel imports. Representing major U.S. steel producers, the AISI has long argued that foreign competitors, particularly from China, engage in unfair trade practices, such as:

- Government subsidies that artificially lower production costs.
- Dumping steel at below-market prices.
- Currency manipulation to gain trade advantages.

As a result of these lobbying efforts, the Trump administration imposed a 25% tariff on steel imports under Section 232 of the Trade Expansion Act of 1962, citing national security concerns.

Economic and Trade Consequences of the Steel Tariffs

- **Retaliatory Tariffs**: China and other affected nations imposed counter-tariffs on U.S. goods, particularly targeting agriculture and manufacturing exports.
- **Higher Costs for U.S. Industries**: Companies reliant on steel imports, such as automotive manufacturers and construction firms,

faced increased production costs, leading to higher consumer prices and reduced profit margins.

- **Limited Job Growth**: Despite expectations, steel tariffs resulted in only modest job increases in the steel industry, while other sectors saw job losses due to retaliatory measures.
- **WTO Disputes**: Several countries challenged the U.S. steel tariffs at the WTO, arguing they violated international trade agreements.

While the tariffs provided relief for U.S. steel producers, the broader economic impact demonstrated the risks of industry-driven protectionism.

The Role of Multinational Corporations in Tariff Negotiations

MNCs operate across multiple jurisdictions and use their financial and political resources to shape trade policies that minimize costs and maximize market access.

Unlike national governments, which must balance economic and political considerations, MNCs focus on maintaining stable global supply chains and reducing tariff burdens on their products.

Key Strategies MNCs Use to Influence Trade Policy

1. **Direct Engagement with Policymakers**

    - MNCs employ lobbyists and legal experts to negotiate trade terms directly with government officials.
    - Example: Boeing and General Motors have lobbied the U.S. government to secure exemptions from tariffs on critical imports.

2. **Industry Coalitions and Trade Associations**

    - MNCs form coalitions with industry peers to present a unified voice in trade negotiations.
    - Example: The U.S. Chamber of Commerce and the National Association of Manufacturers (NAM) advocate for business-friendly tariff policies.

3. **Public Relations and Media Campaigns**

    - Large corporations use media campaigns to influence public opinion on tariffs.

- Example: In response to U.S.-China trade disputes, Apple highlighted how tariffs on Chinese components would increase prices for U.S. consumers.

4. **Political Contributions and Electoral Influence**
   - Many corporations strategically fund political candidates who support their trade priorities.
   - Reports indicate tech giants and major exporters have directed campaign contributions toward lawmakers who oppose protectionist tariffs.

Case Study: Apple and U.S.-China Tariffs

During the U.S.-China trade war (2018–2020), tariffs on Chinese-manufactured components disrupted Apple's global supply chain. Apple actively lobbied for tariff exemptions, arguing that:

- Higher tariffs on Chinese-made parts would increase consumer prices.
- Tariffs would disrupt Apple's supply chain, potentially benefiting competitors like Samsung.
- The U.S. economy benefits from Apple's business model, which supports jobs in software development and retail despite outsourcing production.

Outcome of Apple's Lobbying Efforts

- Partial exemptions were granted for key iPhone components, such as battery display screens.
- Delayed tariff implementation on certain electronic components.

Lessons from the Apple Case

- MNCs leverage economic importance to secure exemptions from protectionist tariffs.
- Government relationships and strategic advocacy are crucial in tariff negotiations.
- Tariff disputes force MNCs to rethink supply chain strategies, including diversifying suppliers or reshoring production.

Consequences of Lobbying-Driven Protectionism

1. **Increased Protectionism and Retaliatory Measures**

    - Lobbying-driven tariffs often trigger retaliatory trade measures, as seen in the U.S.-China steel dispute.
    - Trade wars escalate, increasing costs for businesses and consumers.

2. **Favoritism Towards Specific Industries**

    - Certain industries gain an advantage through tariffs, while others suffer from higher costs.
    - Example: U.S. steel producers benefited from tariffs, but the automotive and construction sectors faced higher input costs.

3. **Regulatory Capture (see below)**

Policy Recommendations

To ensure tariff decisions prioritize national interests over corporate agendas, the following reforms should be implemented:

1. **Enforcing Transparency in Lobbying Activities**

    - Mandatory disclosure of lobbying expenditures and policy proposals.
    - Public databases tracking corporate influence on trade decisions.

2. **Ensuring Tariff Policies Reflect Broader Economic Interests**

    - Independent economic assessments should guide tariff policy decisions.
    - Governments should conduct wider stakeholder consultations before implementing tariffs.

3. **Limiting Undue Corporate Influence**

    - Governments should establish clear boundaries between policymakers and corporate interests, including cooling-off periods for officials transitioning to lobbying roles.

- Stronger ethical guidelines should prevent conflicts of interest in trade policymaking.

Author's Commentary

Political lobbying and multinational corporations significantly influence tariff policy, often leading to protectionist measures that serve corporate interests over broader economic stability.

The U.S. steel tariffs and Apple's response to trade restrictions illustrate the powerful role of corporate advocacy in shaping trade policy.

While lobbying can provide necessary industry insights, excessive corporate influence may lead to "regulatory capture".

Key Features of "Regulatory Capture":

1. **Industry Influence**: Regulators act in favor of the industry they oversee, often due to lobbying, financial incentives, or close relationships.

2. **Revolving Door**: Officials move between jobs in regulatory agencies and the industries they regulate, leading to conflicts of interest.

3. **Policy Bias**: Regulations become overly favorable to industry players, stifling competition or burdening new entrants.

4. **Weak Enforcement**: Regulatory bodies fail to impose meaningful penalties on industry violations, reducing accountability.

5. **Public Harm**: Consumers, taxpayers, or smaller businesses suffer due to ineffective regulation, higher costs, or lower safety standards.

Examples of "Regulatory Capture":

- **Finance:** The 2008 Global Financial Crisis was partly attributed to regulatory agencies being too lenient on Wall Street banks.

- **Pharmaceuticals:** Drug companies influencing regulators to approve medications with insufficient testing.

- **Energy & Environment:** Fossil fuel industries shaping environmental policies to minimize restrictions on pollution.

This concept was extensively discussed by economist George Stigler, who argued that industries often exert pressure on regulators to serve their interests rather than the public good.

"Regulatory capture" principally leads to economic inefficiencies, and escalated trade disputes. Strengthening transparency, accountability, and ethical safeguards are essential to ensuring trade policies serve national and international economic stability rather than private corporate interests.

Chapter 16

The Role of Economic Sanctions in Global Trade

Introduction

Economic sanctions have long been a tool of statecraft, used by governments to exert pressure on foreign nations to change policies or behavior. Statecraft refers to the strategic management of state affairs, particularly in governance, diplomacy, and national security.

Unlike tariffs, which primarily regulate trade and protect domestic industries, sanctions are primarily political tools aimed at achieving national security or geopolitical objectives.

This chapter explores:

- The differences between economic sanctions and tariffs.
- Case studies on U.S. sanctions against Russia and tariffs on China.
- The impact of sanctions on global trade and supply chains.
- The role of international institutions like the WTO in managing sanctions-related disputes.
- Strategic considerations for policymakers to ensure the effective use of economic sanctions.

1. Differences Between Economic Sanctions and Tariffs

Although both sanctions and tariffs impose trade restrictions, they differ significantly in intent, scope, and economic consequences. The table below highlights key distinctions:

Aspect	Economic Sanctions	Tariffs
Primary Goal	Political pressure, national security objectives	Economic protectionism, trade balance correction
Target	Specific entities, countries, or industries	Broad-based trade measures affecting imports
Implementation	Legal restrictions, executive orders	Import/export duties on goods
Economic Impact	Market access restrictions, asset freezes	Increased costs for importers and consumers
International Law	UN resolutions, bilateral agreements	Challenged via WTO dispute mechanisms
Risk of Retaliation	Diplomatic conflicts, counter-sanctions	Retaliatory tariffs from trading partners

While sanctions aim to weaken adversarial nations through financial and trade restrictions, tariffs typically seek to protect domestic industries or correct trade imbalances. However, both measures risk unintended consequences, including supply chain disruptions, inflation, and geopolitical tensions.

2. Case Studies: U.S. Sanctions on Russia vs. U.S. Tariffs on China

A. U.S. Sanctions on Russia

The U.S. has imposed extensive economic sanctions on Russia following geopolitical conflicts, including:

- **2014 Annexation of Crimea**: Initial sanctions targeting Russian banks, energy exports, and government officials.
- **2022 Invasion of Ukraine**: Expanded sanctions on financial institutions, high-tech exports, and military-linked industries.

Key Features:

- **Financial Sanctions**: Russian banks were cut off from SWIFT, restricting international transactions.
- **Energy Restrictions**: Limits on Russian oil and gas exports to Western markets.
- **Asset Freezes**: Russian oligarchs and state-owned enterprises faced asset seizures.
- **Export Controls**: The U.S. restricted Russia's access to semiconductor technology and critical manufacturing equipment.

Impact:

- **Economic Contraction**: Russia's GDP shrank following initial sanctions.
- **Trade Diversion**: Russia deepened economic ties with China and non-Western nations to circumvent Western sanctions.
- **Currency Fluctuations**: The Ruble experienced instability due to restricted access to global financial markets.
- **Energy Market Disruptions**: European nations faced soaring gas prices as Russia retaliated by cutting gas exports.

B. U.S. Tariffs on China

Unlike sanctions, U.S. tariffs on China were implemented primarily for economic reasons, focusing on trade imbalances and intellectual property concerns.

Key Developments:

- **2018 Trade War Escalation**: The U.S. imposed sweeping tariffs under Section 301 of the Trade Act of 1974.
- **Retaliatory Tariffs by China**: Beijing imposed countermeasures on U.S. agricultural products and technology.

Impact:

- **Higher Consumer Prices**: U.S. consumers paid more for electronics, appliances, and automobiles.
- **Trade Diversification**: Businesses sought alternatives in Vietnam, India, and Mexico.
- **Limited Effectiveness**: China adapted by boosting self-sufficiency in key sectors.

3. The Impact of Sanctions on Global Trade

While sanctions are designed to pressure governments, they frequently affect global trade, disrupt supply chains, and cause economic ripple effects.

A. Sanctions on Iran and the Rise of Alternative Trade Systems

- **Oil Export Restrictions**: U.S. sanctions on Iran reduced its oil exports by over 60%.
- **Banking Sanctions**: Iranian banks were cut off from SWIFT, forcing barter trade agreements with China and India.
- **Evasion Tactics**: Iran used ghost ships and cryptocurrency to continue oil exports.

B. Sanctions on Russia and Energy Market Realignment

- **Energy Supply Disruptions**: European nations scrambled for new energy sources after banning Russian oil and gas.
- **Food Security Risks**: Russia, a key wheat exporter, faced sanctions that affected global food prices.
- **Shift to Alternative Payment Systems**: Russia and China expanded their use of non-dollar transactions to bypass restrictions.

4. The WTO and Sanctions: Legal and Institutional Challenges

Unlike tariffs, which fall under WTO jurisdiction, sanctions are often unilateral or multilateral measures imposed for security reasons. However, disputes over trade restrictions frequently arise.

A. WTO Dispute Mechanisms

- **GATT Article XXI (National Security Exception)**: Allows members to impose trade restrictions for security reasons.
- **Key Cases**:
  - *U.S. – Tariff Measures on Certain Goods from China* **(DS543)**: China challenged U.S. tariffs, leading to legal debates over national security claims.
  - *Russia – Measures Concerning Traffic in Transit* **(DS512)**: WTO ruled that national security claims must be justified by genuine threats.

B. Legal Constraints on Sanctions

- **U.S. Law (IEEPA)**: The President can impose economic sanctions but must periodically review their effectiveness.
- **EU Regulations**: The EU imposes sanctions within a legal framework that aligns with international commitments.

Author's Commentary

Sanctions and tariffs are among the most powerful trade policy tools available to governments, yet their effectiveness depends on strategic implementation, compliance with international law, and careful management of global economic consequences.

The growing reliance on sanctions as a form of economic warfare reflects a shift in global trade dynamics. Rather than simply imposing trade restrictions, sanctions are increasingly weaponized to restrict financial markets, freeze assets, and limit technological advancements in targeted nations. However, poorly designed or excessively broad sanctions can have severe unintended consequences, including disrupting supply chains and pushing sanctioned nations toward alternative trading alliances.

Author's Key Strategic Recommendations

1. **Enhancing Multilateral Coordination**: Sanctions should be enforced through global institutions like the WTO, UN, and IMF.

2. **Targeting Sanctions More Precisely**: Sector-specific sanctions avoid harming civilians and destabilizing global markets.

3. **Preventing Sanctions Evasion**: Strengthening financial intelligence-sharing can track and close sanction loopholes.

4. **Balancing Sanctions with Diplomacy**: Sanctions should be part of a broader diplomatic strategy rather than a long-term economic weapon.

Final Thought

Sanctions will remain a dominant force in global trade policy, but their indiscriminate use risks undermining global trade stability. The challenge is to balance economic coercion with diplomatic engagement, ensuring that trade policies achieve their objectives without excessive collateral damage.

Chapter 17

China's Belt and Road Initiative and Its Impact on Trade Wars

Introduction

China's Belt and Road Initiative (BRI), launched in 2013, is an ambitious global development strategy aimed at enhancing trade and investment flows through extensive infrastructure projects. While it promises economic growth for participating countries, the BRI has also sparked geopolitical tensions, particularly with the United States and the European Union.

This chapter explores the BRI's objectives, provides examples of its implementation, assesses its international implications, and examines the potential impact of President Trump's 2025 trade initiatives on the BRI.

1. Understanding the Belt and Road Initiative (BRI)

The BRI seeks to connect Asia with Africa and Europe via land and maritime networks to improve trade and stimulate economic growth. It comprises two main components:

- **Silk Road Economic Belt:** Focuses on linking China to Europe through Central Asia and Russia by land.
- **21st Century Maritime Silk Road**: Aims to connect China to Southeast Asia, Africa, and Europe through sea routes.

As of October 2023, the BRI encompasses 151 countries, accounting for approximately 5.1 billion people and a combined gross domestic product of $41 trillion.

Examples of BRI in Operation

1. **China-Pakistan Economic Corridor (CPEC):** A collection of infrastructure projects in Pakistan, including highways, railways, and energy pipelines, enhancing connectivity between the two nations.

2. **Port of Chancay, Peru:** A $1.3 billion Chinese-built port aimed at facilitating trade between Asia and South America, exemplifying China's expanding influence in Latin America.

3. **Standard Gauge Railway, Kenya:** A $4.7 billion railway project intended to link Nairobi to Mombasa, improving transportation and trade within Kenya. However, financial challenges have stalled its completion.

Benefits for Participating Countries

- **Infrastructure Development:** BRI projects have led to the construction of roads, ports, and railways, facilitating trade and mobility.

- **Economic Growth**: Improved infrastructure can boost local economies by attracting investment and creating jobs.

- **Enhanced Connectivity**: Countries gain better access to global markets, potentially increasing exports and economic integration.

2. International Implications of the BRI

While the BRI offers economic opportunities, it also raises several concerns:

A. Increased Chinese Influence Over Emerging Markets

Through the BRI, China has expanded its presence in regions like Latin America, Africa, and Southeast Asia, often surpassing traditional powers such as the United States in trade partnerships. For instance, China's trade with Latin America has grown significantly, with substantial investments in infrastructure projects.

B. Potential Debt Risks for Participating Countries

Many BRI projects are financed through loans from Chinese institutions, leading to concerns about debt sustainability. Countries like Kenya have faced significant debts due to large-scale infrastructure projects, raising questions about long-term economic viability and potential dependency on China.

C. Concerns Over Trade Dependencies and Monopolies

The extensive reach of the BRI has led to apprehensions about participating countries becoming overly dependent on China for trade and infrastructure, potentially leading to monopolistic scenarios where local industries cannot compete with Chinese enterprises.

3. Impact of President Trump's 2025 Trade Initiatives on the BRI

In January 2025, President Trump announced plans to impose a 10% tariff on Chinese imports, citing concerns over trade imbalances and national security.

Potential Effects on the BRI

- **Shift in Trade Alliances:** U.S. tariffs may prompt countries to strengthen economic ties with China through the BRI, seeking alternative markets and investment sources.

- **Acceleration of BRI Projects:** China might expedite BRI initiatives to counteract the impact of U.S. tariffs, enhancing its global economic influence.

- **Geopolitical Tensions:** Increased U.S. protectionism could heighten geopolitical competition, with countries feeling pressured to align with either the U.S. or China, potentially leading to a more polarized global trade environment.

4. Author's Policy Recommendations

To address the challenges and maximize the benefits of the BRI, the following policy recommendations are proposed:

A. Enhancing Transparency in Global Infrastructure Projects

- **Public Disclosure:** Ensure that all project details, including financing terms and environmental assessments, are publicly accessible to promote accountability.

- **Stakeholder Engagement:** Involve local communities and stakeholders in decision-making processes to ensure that projects meet the needs of the population.

B. **Encouraging Investment from Multiple Stakeholders**

- **Diversified Funding:** Promote investments from various international partners to prevent over-reliance on a single country and to distribute risks more evenly.
- **Public-Private Partnerships:** Leverage private sector expertise and capital to enhance project efficiency and sustainability.

C. **Strengthening Regulatory Frameworks to Prevent Debt Traps**

- **Debt Sustainability Assessments:** Conduct thorough analyses to ensure that countries can manage and repay loans without compromising their economic stability.
- **International Oversight:** Establish global standards and monitoring mechanisms to oversee lending practices and prevent predatory lending.

Author Commentary

The Belt and Road Initiative is one of the most ambitious economic projects of the 21st century, fundamentally altering the landscape of global trade and infrastructure development.

While it brings undeniable economic benefits to participating nations, it also introduces complex political and financial risks that must be carefully managed.

The strategic response of the U.S., particularly with increased tariffs and trade restrictions, reflects broader concerns over China's growing influence.

Going forward, it seems prudent for countries engaging with the BRI to adopt balanced approaches, ensuring that their participation fosters sustainable economic growth while safeguarding their financial and political autonomy.

Transparency, diversified investment, and robust regulatory frameworks will be essential in mitigating risks and maximizing the long-term benefits of this initiative.

Chapter 18

Trade Wars and Potential Resolutions

Introduction

Trade wars have long been a disruptive force in global economic relations, often triggered by protectionist policies, geopolitical tensions, and retaliatory measures. Since the Trump administration's initiation of unilateral tariffs against major economies, the risk of escalating trade conflicts has increased.

The imposition of tariffs on steel, aluminum, and technology products set off a wave of retaliatory measures, particularly between the United States and China, with ripple effects on other trading partners.

With global trade tensions already heightened, predicting the next major trade war is not a speculative exercise but rather an analysis of existing fault lines. This chapter examines the most likely future trade conflicts, explores strategies for de-escalation, and assesses the potential role of the WTO and diplomatic negotiations in resolving these disputes.

Predicting the Next Major Trade War

1. U.S.-China Economic Tensions

Despite multiple rounds of negotiations and temporary ceasefires, U.S.-China trade relations remain fraught with instability. Key unresolved issues include:

- **Tariffs on Chinese Goods:** The U.S. continues to impose Section 301 tariffs on Chinese imports, citing intellectual property theft and unfair trade practices.

- **Chinese Retaliation:** China has responded with tariffs on American agricultural products, particularly soybeans, creating economic hardship for U.S. farmers.
- **Technology and National Security Barriers:** Restrictions on Chinese tech companies (e.g. Huawei and TikTok bans) and U.S. limitations on semiconductor exports continue to fuel tensions.

Potential Escalation?

- Further U.S. sanctions on Chinese tech companies could prompt China to restrict access to rare earth materials, crucial for global electronics production.
- Increased Chinese subsidies in key industries (e.g. electric vehicles and AI technology) could trigger countermeasures from the U.S. and EU.
- A political crisis over Taiwan could result in an economic standoff, with trade restrictions and potential supply chain disruptions.

WTO Implications

The WTO has struggled to mediate U.S.-China disputes due to political gridlock and procedural delays. While WTO dispute resolution mechanisms remain an option, neither country has demonstrated a strong commitment to allowing the organization to resolve their trade conflicts.

2. EU vs. U.S. Disputes Over Digital Taxation

The European Union has been increasingly aggressive in taxing U.S. digital giants such as Google, Amazon, Facebook, and Apple under Digital Services Tax (DST) laws. The U.S. views these taxes as unfairly targeting American firms.

Potential Escalation?

- **Retaliatory U.S. Tariffs:** The U.S. has already threatened to impose tariffs on European luxury goods (e.g. French wines, Italian fashion) in response to DST measures.
- **Tech Trade Barriers:** The EU may respond by imposing data privacy restrictions that limit U.S. firms' ability to operate freely in European markets.

- **Fragmentation of Global Digital Trade Rules:** If unresolved, these disputes could lead to competing regulatory regimes, making international digital trade increasingly complex.

WTO Implications

The WTO lacks a comprehensive digital trade agreement, meaning that bilateral negotiations between the U.S. and the EU will likely take precedence over formal dispute resolution mechanisms.

3. Carbon Tariffs and Emerging Economies

As part of global climate initiatives, the European Union has introduced Carbon Border Adjustment Mechanisms (CBAMs), effectively carbon tariffs on imports from countries with weaker environmental regulations.

Potential Escalation?

- **Developing Countries Retaliate:** Emerging economies, particularly India, Brazil, and Indonesia, perceive carbon tariffs as disguised protectionism and may retaliate with tariffs on European goods.

- **China Challenges CBAM at the WTO:** China, a major exporter of carbon-intensive goods, may bring a case against the EU for violating WTO non-discrimination principles.

- **The U.S. Introduces Its Own Carbon Tariffs:** The Biden administration floated the idea of implementing U.S.-led carbon tariffs, which could trigger conflicts with major fossil fuel-exporting nations. It remains uncertain whether the Trump administration will advance this policy.

WTO Implications

WTO rules on environmental trade measures are vague and underdeveloped, making it difficult to predict how such disputes will be adjudicated. The WTO needs clearer environmental trade guidelines to prevent major conflicts over climate-related tariffs.

Strategies for De-escalating Trade Wars

1. Strengthening Diplomatic Negotiations

While trade disputes are often framed as economic conflicts, they are fundamentally political in nature. Governments must prioritize high-level diplomatic engagement to prevent minor disputes from escalating.

Author's Recommended Diplomatic Strategies

- **U.S.-China Trade Dialogues:** Establishing regular, high-level trade discussions between Washington and Beijing to address tariffs, technology disputes, and supply chain resilience.
- **EU-U.S. Trade Council:** Strengthening transatlantic cooperation to prevent digital taxation disputes from escalating into broader trade wars.
- **Global Climate Trade Agreements:** Encouraging multilateral agreements on carbon pricing to avoid unilateral retaliatory measures.

2. Exploring Structural Reforms in Trade Governance

Revamping the WTO Framework

- The 165 WTO member countries could form a specialized committee to review and modernize trade rules, making them more flexible and responsive to contemporary trade challenges.
- The inclusion of private sector representatives in trade dispute mediation could enhance efficiency and add a commercial perspective to trade agreements.

Enhancing Bilateral and Regional Trade Agreements

- Countries could structure free trade agreements with more commercial terms, similar to corporate contracts, ensuring greater enforceability and flexibility in adapting to changing economic conditions.
- Regional trade agreements such as ASEAN, USMCA, and the African Continental Free Trade Area (AfCFTA) could be expanded to serve as alternatives to WTO mechanisms, offering faster resolution of trade conflicts.

Author's Commentary

Trade wars are not just economic skirmishes; they are deeply political, strategic, and institutional challenges. The U.S.-China trade conflict, EU-U.S. digital tax disputes, and carbon tariffs represent the three most likely trade war scenarios in the coming years.

These trade wars are not merely a matter of tariffs and market access; they are battlegrounds for economic power, strategic influence, and the shaping of global governance.

While traditional diplomatic engagement remains an essential component of international trade, it is increasingly evident that the mechanisms underpinning global commerce are no longer fit for purpose.

The rigid structures of international trade institutions, slow-moving dispute resolution processes, and outdated frameworks often fail to address the complexities of a rapidly evolving global economy.

To ensure a more stable and dynamic trading environment, a reimagining of trade governance is imperative.

One bold proposition is to restructure multilateral and perhaps bilateral trade agreements as commercial contracts rather than diplomatic treaties, embedding clear, structured dispute resolution mechanisms akin to those used in high-value corporate arbitration. Such a shift would reduce dependence on bureaucratic international bodies and introduce greater legal certainty, efficiency, and enforceability in resolving trade conflicts.

Moreover, a more pragmatic approach to trade negotiations should recognize the central role of multinational corporations—not just as market players but as stakeholders in shaping trade policy.

Unlike nation-states, which are often encumbered by political constraints, corporate actors operate with a results-driven focus that could introduce much-needed efficiency, pragmatism, and innovation into trade negotiations. While governments must remain the ultimate arbiters of national economic policy, leveraging corporate expertise and influence in structured negotiations could lead to trade agreements that are more responsive to market realities.

The world now stands at a crossroads. It can choose to persist with outdated mechanisms that are increasingly incapable of managing modern trade complexities, risking further fragmentation and economic inefficiency.

Alternatively, it can embrace a future where trade policy is governed by principles of efficiency, adaptability, and commercial logic, creating a system that is better equipped to handle the geopolitical and technological challenges of the 21st century.

The evolution of global trade governance will determine whether the coming decades are defined by economic cooperation and mutual prosperity or by escalating trade tensions and uncertainty. The need for reform is not just an abstract policy debate—it is a matter of economic survival in an era where power is increasingly measured not by military might alone, but by control over supply chains, market access, and financial systems. The challenge for policymakers is whether they have the vision—and the courage—to adapt to this new reality.

Chapter 19

The Role of Developing Nations in Global Trade Wars

Introduction: What Constitutes a Developing Country?

In international trade discussions, developing countries are generally classified as nations with low to middle-income economies, limited industrialization, and a high dependency on agriculture, raw materials, or low-cost manufacturing exports.

These economies often face challenges such as lower GDP per capita, limited access to advanced technology, weaker infrastructure, and high poverty rates. However, this classification is not rigid and varies depending on economic, social, and political factors.

How Many Developing Countries Are There?

The World Bank, United Nations (UN), and World Trade Organization (WTO) have different ways of classifying countries based on economic and social indicators.

- The World Bank categorizes economies based on Gross National Income (GNI) per capita:
    - Low-income economies (GNI per capita below $1,085)
    - Lower-middle-income economies ($1,086–$4,255)
    - Upper-middle-income economies ($4,256–$13,205)
    - High-income economies (above $13,205)

- The United Nations (UN) classifies 152 countries as developing, with an emphasis on factors such as human development indices, industrial output, and economic stability.
- The WTO does not have a fixed definition, allowing members to self-designate as developing nations, although this classification can be challenged by other members.

As of 2025, there are roughly 140 to 160 developing countries, depending on the criteria used by different international organizations.

How Does a Country Gain Recognition as a Developing Country?

A country gains developing status based on:

1. **Economic Indicators**: Income levels, GDP per capita, industrialization, and trade performance.
2. **Social Development Metrics**: Education, health care, infrastructure, and technological capacity.
3. **International Designation**: Recognition by the United Nations, World Bank, or WTO.

Special Status of Developing Countries in International Trade

Developing countries enjoy preferential treatment under various WTO international trade agreements to help them integrate into the global economy. This status includes:

1. **Special and Differential Treatment (SDT) in WTO Agreements**
    - Longer time frames to implement trade rules.
    - Flexibility in tariff commitments.
    - Technical assistance and capacity-building programs.
2. **Preferential Trade Agreements**
    - Access to Generalized System of Preferences (GSP) programs, allowing duty-free or reduced-tariff access to developed markets (e.g. the EU's Everything But Arms initiative).

3. **Development Aid and Financial Assistance**
    - International Monetary Fund (IMF) and World Bank funding programs specifically designed to support economic development.

Despite these benefits, many developing nations struggle to leverage their special status due to trade wars, limited negotiating power, and external economic shocks, as will be discussed in this chapter.

Challenges Faced by Developing Nations in Trade Wars

1. Vulnerability to Economic Shocks Due to Reliance on Exports

Developing countries often depend heavily on exporting commodities and low-cost manufactured goods. Trade wars can lead to decreased demand for these exports, causing significant economic downturns.

For example, during the U.S.-China trade war, reduced Chinese demand for raw materials from Africa and Latin America severely affected sub-Saharan African economies that export iron ore, soybeans, and crude oil.

2. Limited Power in WTO Negotiations Against Larger Economies

Developing nations often have little leverage in WTO negotiations, as trade rules are shaped primarily by economic superpowers such as the U.S., the EU, and China. Their dependence on foreign aid and trade concessions further weakens their position in disputes.

For example, in WTO tariff disputes, developing nations may struggle to retaliate with countermeasures, unlike larger economies that impose reciprocal tariffs.

3. Difficulty in Navigating Tariff-Driven Supply Chain Disruptions

Trade wars often disrupt global supply chains, making it difficult for developing nations to maintain their roles as suppliers or manufacturers. Higher tariffs imposed by wealthier nations increase production costs and limit access to essential raw materials.

The COVID-19 pandemic magnified this issue, as developing nations faced extreme supply chain vulnerabilities due to trade restrictions.

Case Study: Africa's Response to U.S.-China Tariff Conflicts

The Problem

The U.S.-China trade war negatively impacted African economies that rely on exporting raw materials to China. Lower demand for African commodities such as copper, crude oil, and soybeans caused significant revenue losses.

The Solution: African Continental Free Trade Agreement (AfCFTA)

To reduce dependency on external markets, African nations established the AfCFTA, which:

- Eliminates tariffs on 90% of goods traded within Africa.
- Creates a unified market of 1.3 billion people with a combined GDP of $3.4 trillion.
- Strengthens intra-African trade, reducing reliance on China, the U.S., and the EU.

Ramifications of the Trump Administration's Proposed 2025 Tariffs

In 2025, the Trump administration announced new tariffs on imports from Canada, Mexico, and China, citing national security and economic protectionism.

- 25% tariffs on Canadian and Mexican imports.
- 10% tariffs on Chinese goods.

Impact on Developing Nations

- **Global Economic Slowdown:** Tariff hikes reduce global trade volumes, indirectly affecting developing economies.
- **Trade Diversion**: As major economies shift supply chains, developing nations might lose their export markets.
- **Investment Uncertainty**: Trade wars create instability, deterring foreign investment in developing countries.

Policy Strategies for Developing Nations

1. Diversifying Export Markets to Reduce Economic Dependency

- Reducing reliance on the U.S. and China by expanding trade with regional partners and emerging markets.
- Developing stronger trade ties with South America, Southeast Asia, and the Middle East.

2. Strengthening Trade Alliances with Regional Partners

- Expanding participation in regional trade agreements such as AfCFTA, MERCOSUR, and ASEAN.
- Developing joint economic strategies to counter external economic shocks.

3. Investing in Domestic Industrial Growth to Lessen Reliance on Imports

- Strengthening local manufacturing to reduce dependency on imported goods.
- Encouraging infrastructure investments in energy, technology, and education to drive industrialization.

Author's Commentary: Rethinking the Role of Developing Nations in Trade Wars

Developing nations stand at a critical crossroads in the evolving landscape of global trade wars. While their vulnerability to external shocks is well documented, a reactive posture is insufficient in today's fast-changing economic environment. Instead, developing countries must shift toward a proactive, innovation-driven approach that not only mitigates their economic dependencies but also strategically positions them as indispensable players in global trade.

1. The Need for a 'South-South' Trade Revolution

Historically, developing nations have been excessively reliant on trade with major economic powers such as the U.S., the EU, and China. However, an overlooked yet highly viable alternative is the expansion of South-South trade partnerships—that is, stronger economic ties between developing nations themselves.

A shift in focus towards regional collaboration and collective bargaining could transform the way developing countries engage in trade disputes. The African Continental Free Trade Agreement (AfCFTA) is a promising start, but similar models should be aggressively pursued across Latin America, Southeast Asia, and South Asia. Developing countries must recognize their collective economic weight—representing over 40% of global GDP in purchasing power parity (PPP) terms—and use it as leverage in trade negotiations.

Innovative Strategy:

- The establishment of a Developing Nations Trade Bloc (DNTB) that collectively negotiates tariff reductions and trade privileges with developed economies.

- Introduction of a common currency basket or digital trade currency among developing nations to reduce reliance on the U.S. dollar, thereby mitigating exposure to foreign exchange volatility in trade.

2. Redefining 'Developing' in a Knowledge-Based Economy

The traditional classification of developing nations based on GDP per capita and industrial output is increasingly outdated. In the 21st-century knowledge economy, intellectual capital, digital economies, and technological innovation are redefining economic development. Nations that invest in digital infrastructure, artificial intelligence, fintech, and green technology can bypass traditional industrial dependencies and carve a niche in global trade.

For example, Rwanda's rise as a digital economy hub and India's global dominance in software exports demonstrate that developing nations can transition from commodity-based economies to knowledge-driven economies. Instead of fighting for preferential trade access based on historical classifications, developing nations should proactively redefine themselves as innovation hubs and demand trade privileges based on emerging strengths in technology, renewable energy, and digital services.

Innovative Strategy:

- **Rebranding Developing Nations as 'Innovation Economies':** Governments must aggressively shift their global trade narratives from dependency on aid and raw material exports to highlighting their strengths in emerging digital industries.

- **Technology Trade Pacts**: Creating exclusive partnerships for AI, green energy, and digital banking solutions among developing nations to foster self-reliant growth.

3. From Trade Dependence to Trade Leadership

Rather than accepting trade wars as inevitable disruptions, developing nations should take an active role in shaping global trade rules. Instead of being policy takers, they must become policy makers in global trade forums. The WTO's developing country designation must be reformed to ensure fairer representation of their interests.

Innovative Strategy:

- **A United Developing Nations Voting Bloc at the WTO**: Strengthening voting power by forming a unified coalition to push back against unfair trade policies.

- **Permanent Seats for Emerging Economies in Trade Rulemaking**: Demanding structured representation in global trade organizations where only major economies currently have decision-making power.

4. Beyond Industrialization: The Green Trade Opportunity

Developing nations must move beyond traditional industrialization models and leverage the global shift toward sustainability. The world's leading economies are aggressively pursuing carbon-neutral trade policies, and this presents an opportunity for developing countries to position themselves as green manufacturing hubs.

For example, rather than competing with China in low-cost manufacturing, countries like Vietnam, Kenya, and Brazil could focus on producing sustainable, eco-friendly consumer goods and become leaders in green supply chains.

Innovative Strategy:

- **Carbon Credit Trade Alliances**: Developing nations should monetize their natural resources through carbon trading and sell carbon offsets to major polluting economies.

- **Green Energy-Driven Industrialization**: Instead of replicating fossil-fuel-heavy industrialization models, developing nations should prioritize renewable energy-powered industries that align with future trade regulations.

5. From Victims to Architects of Trade Policy

Trade wars should not be seen as insurmountable threats but as opportunities to redefine economic self-sufficiency. Developing nations must move beyond merely securing preferential trade treatment and actively restructuring their trade strategies to become power players in global commerce.

Instead of merely reacting to tariffs imposed by the U.S. or China, developing nations should employ smart countermeasures, such as:

- **Retaliatory Non-Tariff Barriers (NTBs)**: Using strategic import restrictions on specific industries to counterbalance trade disadvantages.

- **Diversifying Investment Partnerships**: Shifting focus towards investment from emerging players like India, ASEAN, and the Middle East to reduce dependence on traditional Western investors.

Conclusion: Building a Self-Sustaining Trade Future

The global economic landscape is shifting, and developing nations must move away from a dependency mindset toward strategic, self-sustaining trade policies. While WTO agreements and preferential treatments provide some relief, the future belongs to those nations that actively shape their economic destiny through innovation, regional cooperation, and digital transformation.

Rather than being the collateral damage in trade wars, developing countries can reshape their role as architects of global trade—leveraging technology, sustainability, and collective bargaining to redefine their position in international commerce.

Chapter 20

Trade Wars and Economic Nationalism

Introduction

Economic nationalism, characterized by policies that prioritize domestic industries and labor over global economic integration, has seen a notable resurgence in the 21st century.

This shift has led to increasing trade wars among major economies, as nations implement protectionist measures such as tariffs, quotas, and subsidies to safeguard their economic interests.

The implications of these actions are profound, affecting global trade flows, international relations, and the foundational principles of the World Trade Organization (WTO).

The Trump administration's 2025 tariff policies serve as a key example of economic nationalism in action, raising critical questions about the future of free trade and multilateral cooperation.

The Rise of Economic Nationalism in the 21st Century

Several key factors have fueled the resurgence of economic nationalism:

1. Globalization Backlash

Globalization has driven significant economic growth over the past few decades. However, it has also displaced traditional industries and led to job losses in certain sectors, fueling discontent and a demand for greater trade protection.

- *Example:* The decline of U.S. manufacturing jobs in the Rust Belt has been attributed to outsourcing and foreign competition. Once a thriving industrial hub, cities like Detroit and Cleveland have experienced sharp declines in employment as production moved overseas to lower-cost economies. This shift has led to political support for tariffs and trade barriers aimed at reviving domestic manufacturing, exemplified by the Trump administration's "America First" trade policies.

- *Example*: In India, domestic industry groups have pushed for higher import tariffs on electronics and textiles to counter cheap Chinese imports. The government has responded with a "Make in India" initiative, encouraging foreign companies to set up production facilities domestically by offering incentives and imposing tariffs on imported components to bolster local industries.

2. Populist Political Movements

The rise of populist political movements worldwide has initiated policies that emphasize national economic interests over international cooperation. Many of these movements reject global institutions like the WTO and favor bilateral trade deals over multilateral agreements.

- *Example*: The Brexit movement in the UK, driven by concerns over sovereignty and economic self-determination, led to the UK leaving the European Union. This shift allowed the UK to negotiate independent trade agreements but also introduced trade frictions, particularly in key industries like fisheries and agriculture, as businesses adjusted to new regulatory barriers.

- *Example*: In Brazil, nationalist policies have included agricultural subsidies aimed at protecting domestic agribusinesses from international competition. The Brazilian government has introduced protective tariffs on imported grain and meat products, benefiting domestic producers but straining relations with key trading partners such as Argentina and the European Union.

3. Economic Disparities and Protectionism

Rising income inequality has also driven economic nationalism. Governments seeking to support domestic employment and address wealth disparities have turned to trade restrictions and industrial policies that favor local industries.

- *Example*: In France, the Yellow Vest movement emerged in protest against economic policies perceived to favor urban elites. Protestors called for greater protection of French manufacturers, particularly in industries such as steel and automobile production. In response, the French government imposed restrictions on imports from lower-cost economies to protect local jobs.

- *Example*: The United States-Mexico-Canada Agreement (USMCA), which replaced NAFTA, included provisions that increased local content requirements for auto manufacturing. By mandating that a higher percentage of vehicle components be sourced from within North America, the agreement aimed to preserve jobs in the U.S. auto sector while making foreign outsourcing less attractive.

Trade Wars Among Major Economies

Economic nationalism has manifested in numerous trade conflicts, particularly among the world's largest economies.

United States: Protectionist Tariffs Under Trump (2018–2025)

The U.S. has frequently invoked national security and economic fairness to justify high tariffs on imports.

- *Example (2018):* The Trump administration imposed a 25% tariff on steel imports under Section 232 of the Trade Expansion Act of 1962, citing the need to protect the American steel industry from foreign competition. This led to retaliatory tariffs from key trade partners, including Canada, the EU, and China, affecting U.S. exporters.
- *Example (2025):* The Trump administration imposed 25% tariffs on imports from Canada and Mexico, and 10% tariffs on Chinese goods, citing concerns related to illegal immigration and national security. These tariffs led to higher consumer prices for everyday goods, affecting industries such as electronics, automobiles, and agriculture.

China: Retaliatory Tariffs and Economic Countermeasures

China has responded to U.S. trade barriers with its own tariffs and regulatory actions targeting American goods.

- *Example*: China imposed tariffs on U.S. agricultural products, including soybeans and pork, directly impacting American farmers. The move forced U.S. agricultural producers to seek alternative markets, with countries like Brazil filling the void left by diminished U.S.-China trade.

- ***Example***: In response to U.S. semiconductor restrictions, China limited exports of rare earth minerals, essential for the tech industry. This led to supply chain disruptions for U.S. technology firms dependent on Chinese-sourced materials for manufacturing electronic components.

European Union: Selective Protectionism

The EU has faced internal divisions in responding to U.S. tariffs. Some nations seek bilateral agreements, while others advocate for strong countermeasures.

- ***Example***: In response to U.S. steel and aluminum tariffs, the EU imposed retaliatory tariffs on American products, including motorcycles and whiskey. This response led to tension between American exporters and European markets, particularly impacting states reliant on manufacturing and exports.

- ***Example***: The EU's Carbon Border Adjustment Mechanism (CBAM) places tariffs on high-carbon imports, a move criticized by developing countries as a protectionist measure under the guise of environmental policy. Emerging economies argue that the policy disproportionately affects their exports while benefiting European manufacturers.

Protectionist Policies: Tariffs, Quotas, and Subsidies

Nations employ various protectionist trade tools to safeguard domestic industries:

- **Tariffs:** Taxes on imports to make them more expensive and less competitive. ***Example***: The U.S. steel tariffs (2018) increased prices for domestic auto manufacturers, making American-made cars more expensive.

- **Quotas:** Limits on how much of a product can be imported into a country. ***Example***: The EU's quota on Chinese textiles reduced competition for European manufacturers.

- **Subsidies:** Financial aid to domestic industries to help them compete internationally. ***Example***: China's state subsidies for electric vehicle (EV) manufacturers have made BYD and other Chinese automakers global leaders.

Author's Commentary

Economic nationalism, once a relic of the mercantilist past, has surged back into the mainstream, fracturing the global trading order and igniting modern trade wars.

Governments claim these policies shield domestic industries and workers, yet they come at a steep cost—disrupted supply chains, higher consumer prices, retaliatory measures, and deepening geopolitical tensions. The very fabric of globalization, woven over decades, is now fraying under the weight of protectionist fervor.

The Trump administration's 2025 tariffs epitomize this shift, emphasizing how economic nationalism breeds conflict rather than cooperation. In an era where major economies race toward self-sufficiency, the grand experiment of free trade—once hailed as the engine of prosperity—stands at a crossroads.

With the WTO weakened, its authority undermined by major powers, the rules-based order that once governed global commerce is under existential threat.

The central question looms larger than ever: Can international institutions adapt and reassert their role, or has the pendulum swung irreversibly toward a world of unilateral economic brinkmanship? If the latter proves true, the implications are profound: trade will no longer be a stabilizing force in international relations but a weapon wielded in economic warfare.

The age of negotiated trade agreements may soon give way to a chaotic landscape of shifting alliances, punitive tariffs, and strategic decoupling—where economic survival is dictated not by competition, but by coercion.

If history teaches us anything, it is that economic nationalism does not end with trade wars alone. It fuels political isolation, technological fragmentation, and ultimately, conflict. We may not yet be at the precipice, but we are certainly walking the edge.

Book 2
International
Trade Rules & Trade Wars

Part 4: Introduction to International Trade Rules

Chapter 21

Why Trade Wars Need International Rules

Introduction

International trade does not exist in a vacuum. The economic competition between nations—manifested through tariffs, subsidies, and trade barriers—has always been a defining feature of global commerce. However, as trade wars have escalated in complexity and scope, the need for a structured, rules-based system to manage disputes and regulate trade interactions has become imperative. Without such a system, nations risk descending into protectionist retaliation cycles that ultimately harm global economic stability.

Book 1 of this volume explored the role, effects, and formulation of tariffs as a primary instrument of trade policy, including how they have been weaponized in economic conflicts. However, tariffs do not operate in an unregulated environment. Their application is subject to international agreements, legal commitments, and dispute resolution mechanisms—most notably the General Agreement on Tariffs and Trade (GATT) of 1994 and its successor institution, the World Trade Organization (WTO), established in 1995.

This chapter serves as a bridge to Book 2, which explores these agreements' historical evolution. It explains why international rules exist, how they attempt to regulate trade conflicts, and why they remain fragile in the face of geopolitical and economic pressures.

The Necessity of International Trade Rules

1. The Historical Consequences of Unregulated Trade Wars

Trade wars have long been a feature of economic history, but their unregulated escalation has led to devastating consequences. The Smoot-Hawley Tariff Act of 1930 is one of the most infamous examples. Intended to protect American industries, the Act led to retaliatory tariffs from U.S. trading partners, exacerbating the Great Depression and contributing to a collapse in global trade.

A lesson learned from this and other economic disasters of the early 20th century was that nations cannot afford to conduct trade solely based on short-term national interests without regard for global stability. In response, institutions like the International Monetary Fund (IMF), the World Bank, and later the GATT/WTO were established to regulate global trade and prevent economic nationalism from spiraling out of control.

2. The Role of GATT and the WTO in Preventing Trade Wars

The General Agreement on Tariffs and Trade (GATT), first signed in 1947, was created to establish a foundation for stable, predictable trade relationships. It introduced key principles such as Most-Favored-Nation (MFN) treatment and Tariff Bindings, ensuring that trade rules were applied fairly among participating countries. By 1994, the limitations of GATT in handling non-tariff barriers and resolving disputes necessitated the creation of the World Trade Organization (WTO), a more comprehensive body with stronger enforcement mechanisms.

The WTO introduced the Dispute Settlement Understanding (DSU), which provides structured mechanisms to address trade conflicts before they escalate into full-scale economic warfare. Through binding arbitration, retaliatory tariffs within legal limits, and structured negotiation processes, the WTO aims to regulate trade conflicts before they spiral into economic retaliation.

3. The Fragility of International Trade Rules in Modern Conflicts

Despite their intended purpose, WTO agreements and trade regulations have proven fragile in the face of modern trade disputes. The U.S.-China trade war (2018–2020), the collapse of WTO dispute settlement mechanisms due to U.S. opposition, and the rise of unilateral trade sanctions highlight the challenges that institutions like the WTO face in enforcing rules on powerful economies.

4. The 2025 Trump Administration Initiatives and Global Responses

The Trump administration's 2025 trade initiatives have placed unprecedented pressure on the WTO's ability to regulate global commerce. These initiatives include:

- The United States Reciprocal Trade Bill is intended to allow the President to impose tariffs mirroring those placed on U.S. goods by foreign nations.
- The expansion of tariffs on Chinese technology exports, led to a renewed wave of U.S.-China trade hostilities.
- The withdrawal of U.S. support for the WTO Appellate Body, effectively paralyzes that organization's dispute resolution mechanism.

These actions have led to sharp reactions from global trade partners:

- The European Union has condemned the Trump administration's unilateral measures as a threat to multilateral trade stability, warning of retaliatory actions if the WTO is further undermined.
- China has escalated retaliatory tariffs and introduced new export restrictions on rare earth minerals, further straining U.S.-China relations.
- Canada and Japan have pushed for an emergency WTO reform summit to counteract growing disruptions, but consensus remains elusive.

The situation underscores a broader dilemma: can multilateral trade agreements survive the increasing trend toward economic nationalism?

Moving Forward: The Role of Trade Agreements in Managing Conflict

The material that follows in Book 2 examines how GATT and WTO regulations attempt to create a stable framework for global trade, while also exposing their vulnerabilities. This includes commentary on the need for reform in agreements governing tariffs, subsidies, trade-related investment, and dispute resolution.

However, obtaining meaningful reform within a multilateral forum of 165 member countries, each with divergent geopolitical agendas and trade alliances, presents a formidable challenge. The WTO has long struggled to balance the interests of developing nations, economic superpowers, and regional trade blocs.

Key questions to be explored in the following chapters include:

- How do GATT and WTO agreements legally constrain tariff implementations?
- What are the most important WTO agreements, and how do they regulate trade disputes?
- Can WTO reform address the challenges of modern economic nationalism and trade wars?
- What alternative trade frameworks may emerge if WTO dysfunction persists?

By addressing these issues, Book 2 will provide a detailed analysis of how international trade rules function—and whether they remain capable of governing an increasingly fragmented global economy.

Author's Commentary: Rethinking the Future of Trade Governance

The conventional wisdom surrounding international trade rules has long been predicated on the assumption that structured agreements—such as GATT and WTO frameworks—serve as the best mechanisms to contain trade wars. However, as recent economic disputes have demonstrated, these institutions are increasingly ill-equipped to regulate the dynamics of modern trade conflicts.

The underlying issue is not simply a lack of enforcement but rather a fundamental mismatch between 20th-century trade governance and 21st-century economic realities. In an era where supply chains are deeply integrated, yet geopolitical tensions drive economic decoupling, the very concept of "free trade" may require a radical reconceptualization.

One possibility is the emergence of a tiered trade system, where countries voluntarily subscribe to different levels of trade engagement based on reciprocal enforcement capabilities—akin to a trade security council rather than a universal, one-size-fits-all WTO structure.

Another underexplored aspect of trade governance is the potential for AI-driven adjudication in trade disputes. The WTO Dispute Settlement Body is often bogged down by lengthy legal deliberations, bureaucratic inefficiencies, and, more recently, the paralysis of its Appellate Body.

AI and blockchain technologies could revolutionize dispute resolution by creating transparent, automated arbitration systems that track trade agreement violations in real time. An AI-driven dispute settlement mechanism could provide instantaneous rulings based on pre-set legal frameworks, reducing the scope for political interference and economic brinkmanship. While such a system would require international buy-in and the development of machine-readable trade agreements, it could represent the next frontier in global trade governance.

Furthermore, current discourse on trade rules tends to focus heavily on state-to-state conflicts, overlooking the increasingly influential role of multinational corporations in shaping trade outcomes. In many cases, global companies—particularly those in technology, finance, and critical resource sectors—exercise economic leverage that rivals or even surpasses that of nation-states.

If trade rules are to remain relevant, they may need to evolve to include direct enforcement mechanisms against corporate actors who engage in de facto trade wars by controlling key resources, manipulating supply chains, or imposing extraterritorial economic sanctions. This could take the form of a Corporate Trade Accountability Framework (CTAF) that places enforceable obligations on multinational corporations, ensuring they operate within globally agreed trade parameters rather than weaponizing economic power beyond the reach of traditional state-based trade law.

Ultimately, the survival of international trade governance hinges on its ability to evolve beyond the constraints of the post-war economic order. The proliferation of bilateral and regional trade agreements suggests that states are increasingly skeptical of globalized trade governance, preferring tailored, interest-based partnerships.

If the WTO is to remain relevant, it may need to adopt a hybrid model—retaining its role as a global trade custodian but integrating more flexible, modular trade agreements that reflect the fragmented economic landscape. The challenge is no longer just about enforcing trade rules; it is about reimagining a system that can adapt to the forces of economic nationalism, technological disruption, and corporate economic power—all of which threaten to render existing institutions obsolete.

Chapter 22

The Establishment of the World Trade Organization – Challenges in Trade Governance

Introduction

The World Trade Organization (WTO) serves as the foundation of the international trade system, having replaced the General Agreement on Tariffs and Trade (GATT) in 1995.

The WTO's mission is to promote free trade, reduce trade barriers, and create a stable and predictable environment for global commerce. However, its effectiveness has been subject to scrutiny due to institutional stagnation, the complexity of its dispute resolution process, and the rise of unilateral and regional trade policies that challenge its authority.

This chapter explores the historical evolution of the WTO, its legal framework under the Marrakesh Agreement Establishing the WTO, its role in trade governance, and the systemic challenges it faces.

Historical Context: From GATT to the WTO

The origins of the WTO can be traced to post–World War II efforts to establish a multilateral trade system.

The Bretton Woods Conference (1944) sought to create a global economic order, proposing the establishment of an International Trade Organization (ITO) alongside the International Monetary Fund (IMF) and the World Bank.

However, the ITO was never ratified, particularly due to opposition from the United States, leading instead to the creation of GATT in 1947, a provisional agreement that focused on reducing tariffs among its 23 founding members.

Over time, GATT expanded its membership and scope but struggled to address non-tariff barriers, intellectual property rights, and trade in services.

The Uruguay Round (1986–1994), a series of trade negotiations, culminated in the Marrakesh Agreement (1994), which formally established the WTO in 1995, incorporating a broader set of trade rules and a structured dispute settlement system.

The Marrakesh Agreement: Legal Foundation of the WTO

The Marrakesh Agreement consists of 16 articles that define the structure, functions, and scope of the WTO. Some key provisions include:

- **Article I – Establishment of the WTO:** The WTO is officially created as a global institution overseeing trade agreements and resolving disputes.

- **Article II – Scope of the WTO:** The WTO governs a range of trade agreements, including:
    - General Agreement on Tariffs and Trade (GATT 1994) – Trade in goods
    - General Agreement on Trade in Services (GATS) – Trade in services
    - Agreement on Trade-Related Aspects of Intellectual Property Rights (TRIPS) – Intellectual property regulations
    - Dispute Settlement Understanding (DSU) – Rules for resolving trade disputes

- **Article III – Functions of the WTO:**
    - Implementing and administering trade agreements
    - Serving as a forum for trade negotiations
    - Monitoring national trade policies through Trade Policy Reviews (TPRs)
    - Cooperating with institutions like the IMF and World Bank

- **Article IV – Governance Structure of the WTO:**

- o Ministerial Conference: Highest decision-making body (meets every two years)
- o General Council: Handles WTO affairs between Ministerial meetings
- o Dispute Settlement Body (DSB): Oversees trade dispute resolution

Trade Governance and the Role of the WTO

A Stable and Predictable Trading System

The WTO aims to create a predictable global trading environment by ensuring legally binding agreements between its 165 members. This stability seeks to allow businesses to plan investments, facilitates smoother global supply chains, and reduces arbitrary trade restrictions.

Example: A Japanese electronics manufacturer should expect consistent tariff treatment when exporting products to Europe, rather than facing abrupt policy changes or discriminatory tariffs.

However, economic nationalism and unilateral trade policies, such as the U.S.'s 2025 tariff measures, undermine this predictability and question the WTO's ability to enforce stability.

Multilateral Trade Agreements Administered by the WTO

The WTO oversees numerous trade agreements discussed in the following chapters, including:

- GATT 1994 (governing trade in goods)
- GATS (trade in services)
- TRIPS (intellectual property)
- Agreement on Agriculture (AoA)
- Sanitary and Phytosanitary (SPS) Agreement (food safety)
- Technical Barriers to Trade (TBT) Agreement (regulatory standards)
- Trade Facilitation Agreement (TFA) (reducing trade costs)

Despite its role in trade liberalization, the WTO has failed to modernize most of its agreements, with most remaining unchanged since 1947. Many of the 1995 WTO agreements were merely extensions of their 1947 equivalents with additional procedural provisions included. The only major new agreement since 1995 was the 2013 Trade Facilitation Agreement (TFA), highlighting the WTO's inflexibility in adapting to modern economic realities.

Dispute Resolution and Enforcement Challenges

The WTO Dispute Settlement Understanding (DSU) provides a legal framework for resolving trade disputes. However, enforcement remains problematic, as:

1. Only member governments—not businesses—can bring cases
2. Cases take years to resolve, often rendering remedies ineffective
3. Major economies, such as the U.S. and China, frequently ignore WTO dispute resolution outcomes.

Example: The U.S.–EU Airbus-Boeing dispute over aircraft subsidies lasted nearly 20 years, with both sides imposing retaliatory tariffs.

The paralysis of the WTO Appellate Body since 2019, due to the U.S. blocking judicial appointments, has severely weakened the WTO's ability to enforce its rulings, further undermining its credibility. This issue is discussed in greater detail later in this book.

Criticisms and Challenges Facing the WTO

1. **Consensus-Based Decision-Making**: All 165 members must agree on new trade rules, leading to decision paralysis.

2. **Rise of Economic Nationalism:** The U.S., China, and EU increasingly impose unilateral trade measures, bypassing WTO rules.

3. **Developing Countries and Trade Equity:** Developing nations argue that WTO rules favor advanced economies, creating an uneven playing field.

4. **Regional and Bilateral Trade Agreements Undermine the WTO:** The rise of mega-regional trade agreements like the CPTPP and USMCA weakens WTO authority.

5. **Ambiguity in WTO Agreements:** Terms such as "like goods" in trade law are numerous and vague, leading to subjectivity and conflicting legal interpretations.

THE ESTABLISHMENT OF THE WORLD TRADE ORGANIZATION

Case Study: The WTO's Fisheries Subsidies Agreement

The 2022 WTO Fisheries Subsidies Agreement was designed to reduce overfishing by eliminating harmful government subsidies. While praised as a step toward sustainable trade, the agreement:

- Requires ratification by two-thirds (110) of WTO members
- As of 2024, only 86 members have ratified it, delaying implementation

This demonstrates the WTO's difficulty in enforcing global commitments, even when an agreement is widely supported.

Author's Commentary

The WTO was born out of a vision—a rules-based system designed to bring order, predictability, and fairness to global trade. For decades, it succeeded in fostering economic integration and reducing trade barriers. Yet today, that vision is in jeopardy.

The WTO faces an existential crisis, its authority weakened by an era of escalating unilateralism, stalled negotiations, and growing skepticism about the efficacy of multilateral trade governance.

At its core, the WTO's challenge is twofold: it is structurally constrained by a consensus-based decision-making process that hinders reform, and it lacks effective enforcement mechanisms to curb trade disputes before they spiral into economic warfare.

Major economies, once its strongest advocates, now routinely circumvent its frameworks in favor of bilateral and regional agreements, prioritizing strategic self-interest over collective economic stability.

As we move deeper into 2025, the global trading system is increasingly fragmented, with tariff and non-tariff barriers proliferating and the promise of open markets giving way to protectionist instincts.

The WTO must either adapt to these shifting economic realities or risk irrelevance. The question is not merely whether reform is necessary—it is whether the WTO can overcome its own inertia to reclaim its role as the steward of fair and stable trade.

If history is any guide, trade governance does not simply collapse; it erodes until a crisis forces transformation. The WTO stands at that moment of reckoning. Its survival will depend on its ability to evolve—not as a passive arbiter, but as an institution capable of enforcing discipline, fostering genuine cooperation, and restoring confidence in the rules-based trading order.

Otherwise, it will not be globalization that defines the future of trade, but the brute force of economic nationalism.

Chapter 23

Trade Wars: The Fragility of Rules

Introduction: Trade as a Geopolitical Tool

The strategic use of trade policies as instruments of political and economic influence has become an increasingly prevalent feature of international relations. This phenomenon, often described as the "weaponization" of trade, involves the deliberate use of tariffs, trade barriers, and economic sanctions to exert pressure on other nations.

A prime example of this strategy is China's approach to trade policy, which frequently aligns with its broader geopolitical objectives. Recent disputes involving China, Australia, and the United States highlight how trade measures are employed not only as economic instruments but also as diplomatic and coercive tools.

Under the Trump administration in 2025, the United States has escalated the use of tariffs as both a punitive and strategic weapon, shaping global trade dynamics in unprecedented ways. This chapter examines the weaponization of trade through key case studies, explores broader patterns in trade strategies employed by global powers, and evaluates international responses to economic coercion. Additionally, it considers legal frameworks under the World Trade Organization (WTO) and the implications of such strategies on global trade stability.

The Trump Administration's 2025 Trade Policy: Tariffs as a Weapon

Since returning to office in 2025, President Donald Trump has expanded his previous trade war tactics, now employing tariffs not only as economic leverage but as a fundamental tool of geopolitical strategy. Unlike traditional trade policies aimed at reducing deficits and protecting domestic industries, Trump's renewed tariff measures serve as a bargaining chip in diplomatic negotiations, border security enforcement, and ideological clashes with rival economies.

Key 2025 Tariff Measures and Their Implications

- **Reciprocal Tariff Strategy:** The administration has implemented a broad "reciprocal tariffs" doctrine, ensuring that any country imposing higher tariffs on U.S. exports faces an equivalent tariff on its own goods entering the American market. This measure, particularly targeting the European Union and China, has caused friction in transatlantic relations and raised fears of retaliatory measures.

- **Steel and Aluminum Tariffs:** The reintroduction of a 25% tariff on steel and aluminum imports, including from traditional allies such as Canada and Mexico, aims to boost American manufacturing. However, industries reliant on these materials, including the automotive and construction sectors, warn of rising costs that could dampen economic growth.

- **Canadian and Mexican Tariffs Linked to Immigration Enforcement:** In a radical move, Trump has tied trade policy to border security, imposing 25% tariffs on all imports from Canada and Mexico, citing national security concerns related to illegal immigration and drug trafficking.

- **China and Comprehensive Import Tariffs:** A sweeping 10% tariff on all imports from China, imposed under national security provisions, marks the most aggressive step in the ongoing U.S.-China economic conflict. Beijing swiftly retaliated with tariffs of 10% to 15% on American exports, escalating tensions and disrupting supply chains.

These aggressive tariff measures illustrate the administration's belief that trade is no longer just an economic tool but a crucial component of national security and diplomatic influence. The rapid expansion of tariffs raises concerns over economic destabilization, increased consumer costs, and the potential for a full-scale global trade war.

The Australian Experience: Trade as a Political Weapon

China's imposition of punitive tariffs and import restrictions on Australian products underscores the use of trade as a retaliatory mechanism. Three major cases exemplify this strategy:

1. **Barley (DS598):** In 2020, China imposed anti-dumping and countervailing duties on Australian barley, alleging unfair trade practices. The move severely disrupted Australia's agricultural exports and was widely perceived as retaliation for Australia's call for an independent inquiry into the origins of COVID-19.

2. **Wine (DS602):** Similarly, China levied duties as high as 218.4% on Australian wine exports, citing anti-dumping concerns. The measure effectively excluded Australian wine from the Chinese market, demonstrating how tariffs can be wielded to inflict economic damage on targeted sectors.

3. **Australia's Anti-Dumping Measures (DS603):** China responded by challenging Australia's anti-dumping duties on Chinese products such as wind towers and railway wheels. A WTO panel ruled in China's favor on some aspects in 2024, illustrating the reciprocal nature of trade disputes and the contested methodologies used in anti-dumping investigations.

Economic and Strategic Ramifications of Trade Conflicts

The weaponization of trade policies extends beyond tariffs and anti-dumping measures. Broader economic disruptions emerge as nations employ trade as a geopolitical tool:

1. **Technology and Supply Chain Dependencies:**
   - The U.S.-China trade conflict has directly affected global semiconductor supply chains. The U.S. has restricted China's access to advanced microchips, forcing Chinese firms to invest heavily in domestic production. Apple, Dell, and other major technology companies have begun shifting manufacturing to Vietnam and India to mitigate risks associated with trade wars.

2. **Energy Security and Trade Disruptions:**
   - The Russia-Ukraine conflict demonstrated how geopolitical tensions can disrupt global energy trade. European reliance on Russian gas was significantly curtailed following the imposition of sanctions, leading to a rapid shift toward alternative energy sources such as LNG imports from the United States.
   - Similarly, tensions in the South China Sea threaten major shipping routes that facilitate global trade. Any military confrontation in the region could significantly increase global shipping costs and disrupt the movement of critical goods.

3. **Financial Market Instability:**
   - Trade wars often result in currency devaluations, market volatility, and inflationary pressures. When the U.S. imposed tariffs on Chinese goods in previous disputes, financial markets reacted negatively, with stock indices experiencing turbulence due to uncertainty over prolonged economic conflicts.
   - Economic nationalism and protectionist policies encourage inward-looking trade strategies, which can exacerbate supply chain shortages and reduce global economic efficiency.

Legal Context: GATT Articles XX and XXI as Justifications for Tariffs

The General Agreement on Tariffs and Trade (GATT), which forms the legal backbone of the WTO, generally prohibits unilateral tariff increases beyond agreed limits. However, Articles XX and XXI provide exceptions under which tariffs can be justified:

- **Article XX (General Exceptions):** Allows WTO members to impose trade restrictions for non-economic reasons, such as environmental protection or national security. However, case law has ruled that such measures must not be applied in a discriminatory or arbitrary manner.
- **Article XXI (National Security Exemption):** Permits nations to take trade actions necessary to protect their essential security interests. However, WTO rulings (e.g. Russia–Ukraine Transit Dispute, 2019) have set precedents that limit the unrestricted use of this exemption.

TRADE WARS: THE FRAGILITY OF RULES

Author's Commentary

The increasing weaponization of tariffs marks a profound transformation in global trade policy. Historically used as economic safeguards to protect domestic industries, tariffs are now increasingly leveraged as geopolitical instruments, blurring the line between economic strategy and political coercion.

This shift has been particularly evident in the U.S.-China trade conflict, where successive tariff escalations have disrupted global supply chains and fueled economic uncertainty.

Similarly, European Union trade policies targeting technology exports to China and Russia's counter-sanctions on Western economies exemplify how trade measures are being repurposed for broader strategic objectives.

As trade policy becomes more deeply entwined with geopolitical maneuvering, the risk of economic fragmentation grows. The emergence of regional trade blocs, such as the Comprehensive and Progressive Agreement for Trans-Pacific Partnership (CPTPP) and China's Belt and Road Initiative (BRI), reflects an attempt to secure economic advantages in an increasingly unpredictable trade landscape.

Yet, these realignments also raise concerns about supply chain vulnerabilities, retaliatory measures, and the long-term erosion of multilateral trade norms.

The WTO, traditionally the guardian of global trade rules, faces mounting pressure to adapt to this new reality.

Recent disputes over steel and semiconductor tariffs, for instance, have exposed the organization's limitations in enforcing trade agreements when economic nationalism overrides institutional mechanisms.

Without meaningful reforms, the WTO risks losing credibility, particularly as powerful economies increasingly sidestep its arbitration framework in favor of unilateral action or bilateral agreements.

Future reforms must strengthen the WTO's dispute resolution process, ensuring it remains a neutral arbiter capable of addressing both traditional trade concerns and emerging challenges, such as digital trade barriers and climate-related tariffs.

The resilience of global trade will depend not only on institutional reform but also on the willingness of policymakers to uphold a rules-based system—rather than allowing economic coercion to dictate international commerce.

Chapter 24

Leveraging 2025 Technology in the Administration of WTO Agreements

Introduction

As global trade becomes increasingly complex, new technologies are emerging to improve efficiency and transparency in the administration of WTO agreements. However, many people may not be familiar with these technologies, such as blockchain, artificial intelligence (AI), and the Internet of Things (IoT).

Additionally, several WTO agreements, such as the Agreement on Pre-shipment Inspection (PSI), the Agreement on Trade-Related Aspects of Intellectual Property Rights (TRIPS), the Sanitary and Phytosanitary (SPS) Agreement and Technical Barriers to Trade (TBT) Agreement are vital to global trade but could benefit from technology modernization.

To help readers understand these topics more easily, brief explanations of key terms are provided throughout this chapter.

While the benefits of these technologies are clear, a major hurdle remains: who will drive their implementation? The WTO consists of 165 member countries, each with different economic priorities, levels of technological advancement, and geopolitical interests. Funding constraints, lack of interest often from developing nations, geopolitical tensions, and the absence of a central authority willing to push for technological adoption make implementation challenging.

This chapter explains these agreements and the role new technologies could play in enhancing them, while also addressing the difficulties of implementation.

Key Technological Concepts Explained

Blockchain

Blockchain is a secure digital ledger technology that records transactions across multiple computers so that the record cannot be changed retroactively. This makes it a powerful tool for trade, where trust, transparency, and security are crucial.

Smart Contracts

These are self-executing contracts where the terms are written directly into code. Once predefined conditions are met (such as goods being delivered), the contract executes automatically thereby removing the need for intermediaries.

Artificial Intelligence (AI)

AI refers to computer systems that can perform tasks that typically require human intelligence, such as analyzing data, recognizing patterns, and making predictions. In trade, AI can detect fraud, optimize supply chains, and automate compliance monitoring.

Big Data Analytics

Big Data refers to the vast amounts of information generated in modern commerce. AI tools analyze this data to provide insights that can help businesses and policymakers make informed trade decisions.

Internet of Things (IoT)

IoT refers to physical objects embedded with sensors and connected to the internet, allowing them to collect and share data. In trade, IoT is useful for tracking shipments, monitoring storage conditions, and improving customs processes.

The Role of Blockchain in International Trade

Blockchain technology has emerged as a transformative force in the realm of cross-border trade. Its decentralized and immutable ledger system ensures secure and verifiable transactions, addressing many inefficiencies and risks associated with traditional trade processes.

Enhancing Transparency and Trust

- Blockchain creates a tamper-proof record of trade transactions, significantly reducing the risk of fraud, corruption, and document manipulation.
- All stakeholders, including importers, exporters, banks, customs authorities, and shipping companies, can access a single, verified source of truth, fostering greater trust in the trade ecosystem.

Smart Contracts for Trade Facilitation

- Smart contracts, which are self-executing agreements embedded in blockchain, can automate compliance with WTO agreements by ensuring trade obligations are met in real time.
- For instance, an exporter can receive payment automatically upon confirmation of goods delivery, eliminating delays and disputes.

Reducing Paperwork and Trade Costs

- Traditional trade relies heavily on paper-based processes, such as letters of credit and bills of lading, which are slow and costly.
- By digitizing trade documentation, blockchain reduces administrative burdens, accelerates customs clearance, and minimizes human errors.

Enhancing Trade Finance

- Blockchain enables financial institutions to verify transaction authenticity instantly, reducing risks associated with fraud and delayed payments.
- Trade finance solutions, such as blockchain-based letters of credit and supply chain financing, improve liquidity and accessibility for businesses.

AI and Big Data Analytics in WTO Administration

Artificial intelligence and big data analytics can further enhance the efficiency of WTO agreements by providing real-time insights into trade flows, policy impacts, and market trends.

Predictive Analytics for Trade Policy Optimization

- AI-driven analytics can assess the impact of WTO agreements on different economies, helping policymakers make informed decisions.
- Predictive modeling can identify potential trade disputes before they escalate, allowing for proactive resolution.

Automating Compliance Monitoring

- AI-powered monitoring tools can detect non-compliance with trade agreements, reducing the burden on regulatory agencies.
- Automated systems can flag discrepancies in trade documentation and alert relevant authorities, ensuring swift action.

The Internet of Things (IoT) and WTO Agreements

IoT technology is revolutionizing trade logistics and compliance by providing real-time tracking and monitoring of shipments.

Real-Time Shipment Tracking

- IoT devices embedded in shipping containers provide real-time data on location, temperature, and condition of goods.
- This enhances trade efficiency by ensuring compliance with regulatory requirements and reducing losses due to spoilage or mishandling.

Smart Ports and Automated Customs Processing

- IoT-enabled smart ports utilize automated scanning and data-sharing to expedite customs clearance.
- Reduced reliance on manual inspection improves efficiency while ensuring adherence to WTO trade facilitation agreements.

Challenges and Considerations

Despite the promising benefits, several challenges must be addressed for widespread adoption:

Interoperability Issues

- Different blockchain networks may not communicate seamlessly, requiring standardization efforts.
- Efforts should be made to integrate disparate systems for a more cohesive trade infrastructure.

Legal and Regulatory Uncertainty

- Many countries lack clear regulations governing blockchain-based trade processes.
- Greater international cooperation is required to establish a unified regulatory framework.

Adoption Barriers

- High initial costs and resistance from traditional trade players may hinder adoption.
- Educating stakeholders on the benefits of technology integration can facilitate smoother transitions.

Author's Commentary: The Need for Leadership in WTO Reform

The administration of WTO agreements in the 21st century faces a paradox. The challenge is not an absence of viable technological solutions but rather the entrenched resistance to their adoption.

The WTO, an institution designed to regulate and facilitate international trade, has access to cutting-edge advancements such as blockchain for supply chain transparency, artificial intelligence for dispute resolution, and the Internet of Things (IoT) for real-time trade monitoring.

Yet, despite the clear benefits, progress remains sluggish due to bureaucratic inertia, political fragmentation, and a lack of institutional leadership.

The integration of technology into global trade governance is not a theoretical exercise; it is an urgent necessity. The inefficiencies and opacities within WTO administration create unnecessary trade barriers, increase compliance costs, and weaken the ability of developing nations to participate equitably in global markets.

The digital transformation of trade regulation—through smart contracts, AI-driven tariff monitoring, and enhanced data-sharing protocols—offers the potential to reduce corruption, improve enforcement, and foster greater predictability in trade relationships.

However, the political will to drive these changes remains conspicuously absent. Member states, each with its own economic agendas and regulatory preferences, are reluctant to cede control over aspects of trade governance to automated and transparent systems. Meanwhile, the WTO Secretariat lacks the authority to unilaterally implement reforms, leading to a stagnation that benefits entrenched interests over systemic progress.

To address these challenges, the WTO must establish a dedicated technological oversight body—a permanent institution tasked with the phased implementation of digital trade governance. This body should operate with a clear mandate, empowered to:

- **Develop and enforce global standards** for the integration of AI, blockchain, and IoT in trade regulation.
- **Collaborate with international financial institutions** to provide technical and financial support to developing nations, ensuring equitable access to digital trade infrastructure.
- **Create structured incentives** to encourage member states to embrace technology-driven regulatory mechanisms.
- **Act as a neutral arbiter** in disputes related to digital trade implementation, preventing powerful economies from dictating terms at the expense of smaller nations.

Without proactive leadership and a structured framework for digital transformation, the modernization of WTO agreements will remain an abstract ideal rather than an operational reality.

The technological tools to enhance global trade governance already exist; the failure to implement them is a failure of institutional resolve. In an era where digital innovation is reshaping global commerce at an unprecedented pace, the WTO can no longer afford to be a passive observer.

It must act decisively, leveraging 2025 technology to fortify its role as the cornerstone of fair and efficient global trade.

Part 5
General Agreement on Tariffs and Trade 1994 – The Foundations of International Trade

Chapter 25

Non-Tariff Barriers to Trade

The evolution of global trade policy has, in recent years, highlighted the complex interplay between tariffs and non-tariff barriers (NTBs) in shaping international commerce.

The United States' robust trade policies in 2025 have drawn international attention due to their significant impact on most of the 165 World Trade Organization (WTO) member countries. The escalation of trade tensions, often described as "trade wars," is not solely predicated on the imposition of tariffs but increasingly centers on the strategic use of NTBs.

At the heart of the United States' recalibration of trade policies is the acknowledgment that trade imbalances are not exclusively caused by foreign tariffs but also by various NTBs employed by trading partners.

The introduction of the United States Reciprocal Trade Bill by Congressman Riley M. Moore on January 24, 2025, underscores the U.S. government's intent to combat what it perceives as unfair restrictions on its exports.

President Trump's Agenda 47, which prioritizes reciprocal trade measures, identifies NTBs as a significant impediment to achieving what his administration terms a "level playing field." While the bill remains under congressional consideration, parallel efforts by the Office of the U.S. Trade Representative (USTR) and the Department of Commerce to scrutinize foreign tax policies, including value-added taxes (VAT) and digital services taxes (DST), reflect the administration's proactive approach to countering these perceived disadvantages.

Many of the 165 WTO member countries utilize in one form or the other each of the following non-tariff barriers to trade. Whether they do so or not in the context of what the Trump administration has referred to as a "level playing field" will be the subject of much discussion, anxiety and retaliatory action by WTO member countries over the ongoing years.

Defining Non-Tariff Barriers

Non-tariff barriers encompass a broad range of regulatory and administrative measures imposed by governments that restrict trade without directly levying tariffs. These barriers can take many forms, including:

1. **Import Quotas**: Limitations on the quantity of goods that can be imported within a specific period. For example, Japan has historically imposed strict quotas on rice imports to protect its domestic agricultural sector, significantly limiting market access for foreign producers.

2. **Licensing Requirements**: Many countries require importers to obtain special licenses, which can be restrictive and time-consuming. China's complex licensing requirements for certain high-tech products, such as semiconductors, serve as a barrier to U.S. and European firms seeking to enter the Chinese market.

3. **Sanitary and Phytosanitary (SPS) Measures**: Regulations concerning food safety and animal and plant health, which may act as disguised restrictions on trade. The European Union's strict SPS measures on hormone-treated beef have effectively excluded U.S. beef producers from the European market for decades.

4. **Technical Barriers to Trade (TBTs)**: Standards and regulations that specify product requirements in terms of safety, quality, or environmental impact. For instance, India's new safety certification requirements for electronic goods have posed significant hurdles for foreign manufacturers, delaying entry into the Indian market.

5. **Subsidies and State Support**: Financial support provided by governments to domestic industries, distorting competition. The European Union's subsidies to its agricultural sector under the Common Agricultural Policy (CAP) have long been criticized for disadvantaging agricultural exporters from developing nations.

6. **Foreign Tax Policies**: The imposition of VAT and DST by various countries is increasingly viewed by the U.S. as a method of discrimination against American businesses. France's DST, for instance, disproportionately affects U.S. technology firms such as Google, Amazon, and Facebook, triggering retaliatory measures from Washington.

7. **Administrative Delays and Bureaucratic Procedures**: Complex customs procedures, excessive documentation requirements, and slow processing times serve as significant impediments to trade. Brazil, for example, has been criticized for its notoriously lengthy customs clearance procedures, which add costs and uncertainty for importers.

8. **Local Content Requirements**: Mandates requiring a certain percentage of a product to be sourced domestically. Indonesia's regulations requiring companies in the oil and gas sector to prioritize domestic suppliers over foreign firms exemplify this form of trade restriction.

9. **Government Procurement Preferences**: Policies that favor domestic firms in public tenders and contracts. The U.S. Buy American Act prioritizes American-made goods in federal procurement, limiting opportunities for foreign firms to compete.

Case Studies of NTBs in Action

Case Study 1: The European Union's Carbon Border Adjustment Mechanism (CBAM)

The European Union has introduced the Carbon Border Adjustment Mechanism (CBAM), a policy designed to impose carbon tariffs on imported goods based on their carbon footprint. While officially a climate change initiative, CBAM acts as a de facto non-tariff barrier by increasing costs for exporters from countries with less stringent environmental regulations, particularly affecting industries in developing nations.

Case Study 2: India's Restrictions on E-Commerce Platforms

India's evolving e-commerce regulations have created significant hurdles for foreign firms, particularly U.S. giants like Amazon and Walmart-owned Flipkart. Restrictions on inventory control and mandatory compliance with data localization laws have constrained the ability of foreign e-commerce platforms to operate effectively in the Indian market, favoring domestic competitors.

Case Study 3: China's Cybersecurity Laws

China's cybersecurity regulations, which mandate that foreign technology firms store data locally and undergo security reviews before operating in the country, have been seen as a significant non-tariff barrier. These policies have effectively hindered market entry for U.S. firms, particularly in cloud computing and software services, by imposing additional compliance burdens.

Legal and Economic Implications

The widespread use of NTBs presents substantial challenges for global trade governance. Many NTBs violate the principles established under the General Agreement on Tariffs and Trade (GATT), particularly the commitment to national treatment and non-discrimination. However, countries often justify these measures on public policy grounds, such as consumer safety, environmental protection, or national security.

From an economic perspective, NTBs contribute to inefficiencies by distorting markets, raising costs for consumers, and limiting competition. While intended to protect domestic industries, NTBs often lead to retaliatory measures, exacerbating trade tensions.

The current U.S. approach, particularly its reciprocal tariff strategies, risks triggering countermeasures from trading partners, potentially leading to prolonged disputes within the WTO framework.

Author's Commentary

As global trade dynamics evolve, the role of NTBs has become both a tool of economic strategy and a focal point of international disputes. Unlike conventional tariffs, NTBs encompass a broad array of restrictions—ranging from licensing requirements, subsidies, and regulatory standards to local content rules and quotas—that often operate under the guise of public policy objectives such as environmental protection, health and safety, or national security.

However, these barriers can function as de facto protectionist measures, distorting markets, restricting access, and creating significant friction in international commerce.

Recent developments, such as the U.S. Reciprocal Trade Bill and increased scrutiny over foreign tax policies, illustrate how NTBs are not merely technical trade issues but instruments of economic leverage.

Countries, particularly major economies like the United States, China, and the European Union, frequently use NTBs as geopolitical tools, imposing restrictions to advance strategic interests rather than simply to correct market inefficiencies. For instance, China's export restrictions on rare earth minerals and the European Union's carbon border adjustment mechanism (CBAM) exemplify how NTBs are being weaponized under the rationale of sustainability or national interest.

The WTO, while theoretically designed to mitigate unfair trade practices, has struggled to address NTBs effectively due to their complex and often opaque nature. The organization's dispute resolution framework remains ill-equipped to deal with new-age trade barriers, many of which do not fit neatly into traditional definitions of protectionism. This is evident in the WTO's inability to decisively rule on disputes related to environmental and digital trade restrictions, where countries argue that NTBs serve legitimate non-commercial purposes.

Furthermore, while NTBs can protect domestic industries and address genuine concerns like consumer safety and environmental sustainability, they also invite retaliation, leading to an escalation of trade conflicts.

The ongoing U.S.-China trade tensions, for example, have seen both nations implementing NTBs under the pretext of security concerns, effectively bypassing WTO rules. Similarly, the European Union's restrictive standards on agricultural imports, ostensibly based on health and safety regulations, have been criticized as a form of economic protectionism that disproportionately affects developing economies.

The path forward for WTO members is fraught with challenges. While the ideal goal is to balance legitimate regulatory concerns with free and fair trade, the reality is that without substantial reform of WTO rules and governance, these barriers will continue to be a major disruptor of global trade.

The WTO's dispute settlement system, once the backbone of international trade order, requires urgent modernization to account for emerging forms of trade restrictions, digital trade complexities, and environmental trade policies.

Ultimately, non-tariff barriers represent both a challenge and an opportunity—a challenge because of their potential to fragment global markets, but also an opportunity for nations to rethink the fundamental governance of international trade. The question remains: can global trade governance adapt quickly enough to address these modern barriers, or will the increasing reliance on NTBs signal the erosion of a truly rules-based trading system?

Chapter 26

GATT – The Evolution of GATT and Its Analytical Framework

Introduction

The General Agreement on Tariffs and Trade (GATT) has been the foundation agreement of the global trade system since its inception in 1947.

Emerging from the ruins of World War II, GATT was designed to promote economic cooperation and reduce barriers to international trade, aspiring towards a rules-based trading system that prioritizes transparency, predictability, and fairness in global markets.

A fundamental aspect of understanding GATT and its evolution into the World Trade Organization (WTO) lies in the analytical tools developed to interpret and apply its principles. The GATT Analytical Index and the WTO Analytical Index provide comprehensive resources for interpreting international trade rules, resolving disputes, and formulating policy.

This chapter introduces these critical research tools, highlighting their importance in trade law, their applications, and their underutilization by domestic law firms, which often fail to recognize their relevance in cross-border trade disputes.

1.1 Historical Background

The creation of GATT was a pragmatic and political response to the economic chaos of the interwar years, particularly the Great Depression of the 1930s. Protectionist measures such as the U.S. Smoot-Hawley Tariff Act (1930) exacerbated global economic instability, demonstrating the dangers of economic isolationism.

In the aftermath of World War II, the international community sought to prevent a return to trade protectionism. While the proposed International Trade Organization (ITO) never materialized due to U.S. political opposition, GATT emerged as a practical alternative.

Initially signed by 23 countries, GATT provided a provisional framework for trade liberalization—one that would eventually evolve into the WTO in 1995.

1.2 GATT's Analytical Framework: The GATT Analytical Index

The GATT Analytical Index: Guide to GATT Law and Practice (1947–1994) serves as the definitive resource for understanding GATT's legal and procedural framework during its first five decades. Published by the GATT Secretariat, this index compiles:

- Legal interpretations by contracting parties.
- Dispute settlement decisions and panel rulings.
- Working group discussions that shaped GATT's evolution.

For researchers, practitioners, and policymakers, the GATT Analytical Index is an indispensable resource in navigating the complexities of GATT law and its foundational principles.

1.3 Expanding the Framework: The WTO Analytical Index

The establishment of the WTO in 1995 marked a major transformation in global trade governance. With this shift, the need for expanded legal interpretation grew, leading to the development of the *WTO Analytical Index.*

This resource builds upon the *GATT Analytical Index*, extending its scope to cover all WTO agreements and jurisprudence.

Key Features of the WTO Analytical Index:

- Comprehensive commentary on agreements such as the General Agreement on Trade in Services (GATS) and the Agreement on Trade-Related Aspects of Intellectual Property Rights (TRIPS).
- Analysis of dispute settlement decisions, including panel and Appellate Body rulings, offering insights into legal interpretations of WTO agreements.

- Coverage of institutional and procedural developments within the WTO framework, providing clarity on WTO governance structures.

Unlike the GATT Analytical Index, the WTO Analytical Index is regularly updated, reflecting jurisprudential developments and addressing emerging trade challenges.

1.4 The Importance of Analytical Tools in Trade Law

Both the GATT and WTO Analytical Indices serve as critical resources for understanding international trade law. These tools provide a structured approach to navigating:

- Legal texts and trade agreements.
- Dispute settlement reports.
- Member obligations under WTO law.

Their applications are particularly valuable in:

- Dispute Resolution: Providing precedents and interpretations that inform trade dispute adjudication.
- Policy Formulation: Assisting policymakers in drafting trade laws aligned with international obligations.
- Academic Research: Supporting scholars analyzing the evolution of trade rules and their global impact.

Despite their importance, it is observed that very few domestic law firms worldwide have access to or awareness of these resources. As a result, they often fail to incorporate international precedents when advising clients on cross-border trade disputes.

Instead, most legal practitioners rely solely on domestic law and of course this is understandable. But in so doing, those legal practitioners are ignoring an important if not critical alternative repository of analytical commentary and WTO precedents which often directly impact on domestic disputes. It is suggested that those advising corporations on cross-border disputes should have regard to the insights contained within these analytical tools.

1.5 Relevance to Contemporary Trade Issues

The principles enshrined in GATT and expanded upon in the WTO framework remain highly relevant to today's trade challenges. However, issues such as:

- Digital trade and e-commerce regulations.
- Environmental sustainability and trade policies.
- The rise of regional trade agreements and their interaction with WTO rules.

illustrate the need for more flexible and adaptive trade governance.

While the *GATT and WTO Analytical Indices* provide a historical record of trade jurisprudence, they do not necessarily address the rapidly evolving nature of global commerce. This raises concerns about the WTO's ability to modernize its legal framework in response to new economic realities.

Author's Commentary

The GATT Analytical Index and its WTO counterpart serve as the intellectual backbone of the multilateral trading system, providing a structured synthesis of decades of legal and procedural developments.

These resources have not only guided policymakers and legal practitioners but have also played a pivotal role in shaping trade jurisprudence, ensuring that the principles of transparency, predictability, and fairness remain central to international commerce.

By distilling vast legal precedents and dispute resolution mechanisms, these analytical frameworks empower stakeholders to navigate the complexities of international trade law with clarity and confidence.

However, while these tools remain indispensable in resolving disputes and informing trade policy, their historical orientation presents a fundamental limitation. As the global economy undergoes rapid transformation—driven by technological advancements, environmental imperatives, and shifting geopolitical alignments—the reliance on past jurisprudence alone is unlikely to provide sufficient guidance for emerging challenges.

The rise of digital trade, climate-related trade policies, and the increasing use of non-tariff barriers demands a more adaptive, forward-looking approach that extends beyond the scope of traditional legal interpretations.

For the WTO to remain a relevant and effective institution, policymakers, legal scholars, and trade negotiators must move beyond passive reliance on existing analytical tools and actively advocate for continuous legal reform within the multilateral framework.

While the GATT and WTO legal indexes offer a critical foundation, they must be complemented by modernized trade disciplines, proactive regulatory adaptations, and a more dynamic dispute resolution system capable of addressing contemporary economic realities.

If the WTO fails to modernize, it risks becoming a custodian of outdated trade principles rather than a leader in shaping the future of global commerce. The multilateral system must evolve not only in response to crises but through proactive institutional adaptation, ensuring that it continues to serve as the cornerstone of equitable, rules-based international trade.

In this sense, the GATT Analytical Index and its WTO successor must not be viewed as static repositories of past wisdom but as living instruments that should be continuously refined to reflect the shifting contours of global trade.

Ultimately, the future of the multilateral trading system depends on its ability to strike a delicate balance between historical continuity and legal innovation. By embracing reform, modernization, and inclusivity, the WTO can reaffirm its role as the primary architect of global trade governance—ensuring that the analytical frameworks it has built over decades remain not just relevant, but indispensable, in the evolving landscape of international commerce.

Chapter 27

Most-Favored Nation Principle – Foundation Principle of GATT

The Most-Favored-Nation (MFN) principle, enshrined in Article I of the GATT, is one of the foundational pillars of the global trading system. The wording within Article 1 is the very first trade rule agreed upon approximately 80 years ago.

This principle generally mandates that any trade advantage granted by one member to another must be extended to all other members, ensuring non-discrimination and promoting fairness in international trade.

Understanding the MFN Principle

The MFN principle seeks to ensure equality among trading partners by requiring that any preferential treatment given to one country—such as reduced tariffs, favorable quotas, or other trade advantages—is automatically extended to all of the other 165 WTO members. In simple terms, it prevents countries from favoring one trading partner over others, thereby supposedly fostering a level playing field.

For example:

- **Scenario 1:** If Country A lowers its tariffs on steel imports from Country B, the same tariff rate must apply to steel imports from all other WTO members, regardless of whether they are major trading partners or competitors.

- **Scenario 2:** Suppose a country negotiates a lower tariff on bananas from a specific country. Under the MFN principle, this reduced tariff must be extended to all other WTO members importing bananas.

Historical and Legal Context

The principle of MFN dates back to early bilateral trade agreements but gained global prominence with the establishment of GATT in 1947. Article I of GATT explicitly codifies the MFN obligation, stating that any "advantage, favor, privilege, or immunity" granted to products of one country must immediately and unconditionally be extended to like products of all other members.

This principle was reaffirmed and expanded under the World Trade Organization (WTO) framework established in 1995. The WTO Analytical Index provides a detailed interpretation of Article I, illustrating its practical application through case law and trade practices.

Key Cases Illustrating the MFN Principle

1. **EC – Bananas III (WT/DS27/AB/R)**: This landmark case involved the European Communities' preferential treatment of bananas from former colonies in Africa, the Caribbean, and the Pacific. The Appellate Body found that such preferences violated the MFN principle because they discriminated against bananas from Latin American countries, highlighting the necessity of treating all members equally in trade relations.

2. **Canada – Auto's (WT/DS139/AB/R)**: This case dealt with Canada's preferential treatment of certain automotive imports based on origin. The Appellate Body ruled that such practices contravened the MFN obligation, reinforcing the requirement for non-discriminatory treatment of like products from all WTO members.

3. **Indonesia – Certain Measures Affecting the Automobile Industry (WT/DS54, 55, 59, 64)**: In this dispute, the European Communities, Japan, and the United States challenged Indonesia's National Car Program, which provided tax and tariff benefits to certain car manufacturers based on local content and origin criteria. The WTO Panel found that these measures violated the MFN principle under Article I:1 of GATT 1994, as they discriminated between imported products based on their country of origin. This case underscores the MFN principle's role in preventing origin-based discrimination.

4. **Colombia – Indicative Prices and Restrictions on Ports of Entry (WT/DS366/R)**: This case involved Colombia's use of indicative prices

for customs valuation and restrictions on ports of entry for certain textiles, apparel, and footwear. Panama, the complainant, argued that these measures violated the MFN principle by discriminating against imports from specific countries. The Panel concluded that Colombia's measures were inconsistent with Article I:1 of GATT 1994, as they did not accord immediately and unconditionally to like products originating in Panama the same treatment granted to like products from other countries.

5. **Russia – Tariff Treatment of Certain Agricultural and Manufacturing Products (WT/DS485/R):** In this dispute, the European Union challenged Russia's tariff rates on certain products, alleging that they exceeded Russia's bound rates and were applied in a discriminatory manner. The Panel found that Russia had applied higher tariffs to products from the European Union compared to those from other countries, thereby violating the MFN principle under Article I:1 of GATT 1994. This case highlights the importance of adhering to bound tariff commitments and the MFN obligation to ensure non-discriminatory treatment in trade.

Exceptions to the MFN Principle

While the MFN principle is central to the GATT/WTO system, it is not absolute. Key exceptions include:

- **Preferential Trade Agreements (PTAs):** Article XXIV of the GATT permits the formation of customs unions or free trade areas, provided they cover substantially all trade and do not raise barriers to non-participants. For instance, the European Union's internal trade rules fall under this exception (see later on this topic).

- **Generalized System of Preferences (GSP):** Developed countries may grant preferential tariff rates to developing countries under specific schemes to promote economic development (see later the difficulties associated with identifying a developing country).

- **National Security Exceptions:** Article XXI allows members to deviate from MFN obligations when trade measures are necessary for national security purposes. No doubt the Trump administration will be relying on this exemption for its 2025 tariff threats.

Practical Implications

The MFN principle was intended to promote predictability and fairness in the global trading system by:

- **Reducing Trade Barriers:** Ensuring that any reduction in tariffs or other barriers benefits all members equally.
- **Enhancing Market Access:** Guaranteeing that countries cannot selectively block or favor certain trading partners.
- **Promoting Economic Stability:** Encouraging a consistent and transparent trading environment.

Challenges and Criticisms

Despite its benefits, the MFN principle faces challenges:

- **Regionalism vs. Multilateralism:** The rise of regional trade agreements, such as the Comprehensive and Progressive Agreement for Trans-Pacific Partnership (CPTPP), often bypasses MFN obligations, creating fragmented trade rules. In other words the provision is dated and easily circumvented by FTA's.
- **Implementation Issues:** Developing countries may struggle to enforce MFN provisions due to limited resources or capacity constraints.
- **Trade Remedies:** Measures like anti-dumping duties and safeguards can lead to temporary deviations from MFN commitments, creating tensions between fairness and protectionism.
- **Is the MFN principle dated:** With the proliferation of regional trade agreements it is a reasonable question to ask whether the MFN principle is relevant in 2025 when it is so easily circumvented.

Authors comment

The Most-Favored-Nation principle has often been described as a cornerstone of international trade, embodying the spirit of equality and non-discrimination. By ensuring that trade advantages are universally shared, it strives to foster a fair and predictable global trading environment.

However, as foreshadowed, the principle was created over a century ago at a time when Free Trade agreements were rare. As of January 2025, some sources have estimated that there were approximately 400 free trade agreements in force worldwide.

This number includes both bilateral and multilateral agreements as well as non-reciprocal trade arrangements. The exact count is probably variable depending on the source and the inclusion criteria for different types of trade agreements. Nevertheless, even if the number is half that reported the point remains that countries are favoring these types of bilateral or regional agreements over the multilateral GATT or WTO agreements.

Balancing the GATT principle with evolving trade dynamics and exceptions poses ongoing challenges. Through cases like *EC—Bananas III, Canada—Autos, Indonesia—Automobiles, Colombia—Indicative Prices, and Russia—Agricultural Tariffs*, the principle's application has been refined or even undermined. This illustrates that countries do not have the same high regard for this GATT principle as they perhaps did 80 years ago when international trade dynamics were profoundly different.

Chapter 28

Tariff "Bindings" – Article II of GATT

Article II of the GATT establishes the concept of what has become known as "tariff bindings" or "bound tariffs".

Put simply, each WTO member is required as a condition of membership to voluntarily "bind" its tariff rates applicable on each imported product thereby undertaking that it will not increase its tariffs above those "bound" tariff rates for each respective product.

The "bound" tariff rates on each potential imported product must be submitted by each country in what Article II describes as "a Schedule."

Each WTO member country therefore has submitted to the WTO as a condition of membership its Schedule of bound tariff rates relating to each item of commerce. For example, country X might have within its Schedule that it will not increase tariff rates on motor cars beyond 15%. Then it might have in the same schedule that it will not increase tariff rates on: metal lathes beyond 10%; hacksaws 5%; plastic buckets 3%; spectacles 7%.

Once country X submits its Schedule of bound rates to the WTO, then it is obliged under Article II of the GATT to not impose duty rates beyond those bound rates.

By way of a further relevant example, the United States will have previously lodged a Schedule of different commodities to the WTO specifying what the maximum tariff rates or bound rates it has agreed will apply on each line of commerce imported into the United States.

This mechanism is supposed to underpin the predictability and stability of the global trading system but is very topical because on February 13, 2025 President Donald Trump, mandated the Office of the U.S. Trade Representative (USTR) and the Department of Commerce to conduct a comprehensive review of foreign tax policies, including value-added taxes (VAT) and digital services taxes (DST), which are perceived to disadvantage U.S. exporters.

The outcome of this review is intended to inform potential reciprocal tariff measures designed to counteract these perceived imbalances.

This approach raises significant legal and economic concerns, particularly regarding the United States' commitments under Article II of the GATT which relevantly prohibits member countries from imposing tariffs beyond their bound rates, except through formal renegotiation processes.

The proposed US reciprocal tariffs, if implemented unilaterally in response to foreign domestic taxes, could well contravene these obligations, as they don't seem to fall within the general exceptions outlined in Article XX or the national security exceptions in Article XXI (see later). This observation however is speculative and the legitimacy of any US increased tariffs will be contingent on the reasons provided for their imposition.

While often overlooked in public discourse, tariff bindings are foundational to ensuring that countries adhere to negotiated commitments on tariff rates.

This chapter explores the workings of Article II, explains its implications and particularly its current relevance and finally, provides case studies to better explain its application.

Understanding Tariff Bindings

At its core, Article II requires GATT/WTO members to adhere to maximum tariff rates (or "bound" rates) for specific products as agreed upon during trade negotiations. These bindings are listed in each member's "schedule of concessions", creating legally enforceable limits on the tariffs a country can impose on imports of those products.

In practical terms:

- **Binding Commitment:** A country cannot increase its tariff rates beyond the bound levels specified in its schedule without renegotiation.

- **Predictability:** By setting these ceilings, Article II fosters a predictable trading environment, which is essential for businesses and investors.

- **Flexibility within Bounds:** Countries retain the freedom to set lower tariffs or provide duty-free treatment as long as they do not exceed the bound rates.

The Historical and Legal Framework of Article II

The principle of tariff bindings originated in the early 20th century during efforts to stabilize trade relations following World War I. Under GATT 1947, the concept became a formalized commitment to ensure countries did not unilaterally raise tariffs to protectionist levels, a practice that had contributed to economic disarray during the Great Depression.

According to leading trade scholars like John H. Jackson in *The World Trading System: Law and Policy of International Economic Relations*, tariff bindings are a vital constraint on the ability of governments to respond unpredictably to domestic political pressures. Jackson emphasizes that these constraints are key to promoting long-term economic growth and trust between nations. However, it seems in 2025 this aspiration is just that!

Misconceptions about Tariff Increases

The general public often misunderstands how tariff rates can be increased despite the constraints of Article II. Proposals such as those made by U.S. President Donald Trump to raise tariffs highlight this confusion.

While bound tariffs set limits, governments can still impose additional duties using mechanisms outside the direct scope of Article II, such as:

- **Anti-Dumping Duties:** Imposed under the Agreement on Implementation of Article VI of GATT (Anti-Dumping Agreement) to counteract unfair trade practices.

- **Safeguard Measures:** Applied temporarily to protect domestic industries from sudden import surges under the Agreement on Safeguards.

- **Countervailing Duties**: Levied to offset subsidies provided to foreign producers that harm domestic industries.

These measures are not considered violations of tariff bindings if they conform to WTO rules.

When China or the United States threaten to raise tariffs it is generally done through one or other of these exemptions to Article II rather than raise tariffs above their "bound" rates. So an anti-dumping duty might be imposed rather than an increased import duty.

Key Case Studies on Article II

1. *Thailand—Customs and Fiscal Measures on Cigarettes from the Philippines (WT/DS371/R):* This dispute involved Thailand's tariff treatment and customs valuation of imported cigarettes from the Philippines. The panel found that Thailand had violated its tariff binding commitments by applying duties that effectively exceeded its bound rates. This case underscored the importance of adhering to tariff schedules and highlighted the interplay between customs practices and Article II obligations.

2. *Thailand—Taxes on Imported Alcoholic Beverages (WT/DS313):* This case focused on Thailand's discriminatory tax measures on imported whiskey and other alcoholic beverages. Although not a direct Article II violation, the dispute underscored how measures ostensibly outside tariff bindings, such as internal taxes, could still breach broader GATT principles, including those indirectly linked to tariff commitments.

3. *Argentina—Import Measures (WT/DS438/444/445):* Argentina's measures requiring importers to balance their imports with exports and make certain investments in Argentina were challenged. The case demonstrated how practices that indirectly affect the application of tariffs could fall afoul of Article II by creating barriers inconsistent with bound commitments.

Implications for Global Trade

It is said that tariff bindings under Article II are integral to the stability of the multilateral trading system. They supposedly:

- **Enhance Trust:** By committing to predictable tariff rates, countries create an environment conducive to international trade and investment.

- **Reduce Uncertainty:** Businesses benefit from knowing that tariff rates will not arbitrarily increase.

- **Balance Flexibility and Discipline:** Article II allows governments some policy space while ensuring they cannot exceed agreed limits without renegotiation.

Challenges and Criticisms

Despite its benefits, Article II faces challenges:

- **Circumvention Risks:** Practices such as imposing excessive customs fees or non-tariff barriers can undermine the spirit of tariff bindings. In other words there are many other tariff and nontariff barriers to trade that countries can and do utilize.

- **Complexity in Enforcement**: Disputes often arise over technicalities, such as customs valuation or tariff classification.

- **Public Misunderstanding**: Policymakers and the public often underestimate the constraints and implications of Article II, leading to unrealistic expectations about tariff policy.

- **What's in a name?** Some countries impose additional taxes at the time of importation but call them domestic taxes (like excise) rather than tariff rates. This raises the issue of what constitutes a domestic tax. This question is addressed elsewhere in this document.

Conclusion

Article II of GATT, while less publicized than other provisions, has historically (at least until 2025) played a crucial role in shaping the global trading system. By preventing arbitrary tariff increases and fostering predictability, this measure underpins the trust and stability that international trade requires.

However, as cases like *Thailand—Cigarettes and Thailand—Whiskey* illustrate, the effective application of Article II depends on meticulous adherence to commitments and vigilance against circumvention.

Author's Commentary

At its core, Article II of the GATT establishes a crucial principle in global trade governance: a member's bound tariffs act as a ceiling rather than a floor, meaning they can be lowered unilaterally but not raised beyond agreed commitments without formal renegotiation. This mechanism was designed to curb unpredictable tariff escalations, ensuring stability and reducing the risk of retaliatory trade conflicts.

However, while this principle remains embedded in WTO legal frameworks, its practical relevance is diminishing in an era where major economies frequently sidestep their obligations through alternative mechanisms.

The contemporary trade landscape has seen a shift away from tariff commitments as rigid constraints to a more flexible, opportunistic approach where governments reinterpret or circumvent WTO disciplines to suit their economic and geopolitical strategies.

In particular, major economies—including the United States, China, and the European Union—have increasingly relied on regulatory instruments such as anti-dumping duties, safeguard measures, and retaliatory trade policies to achieve their commercial objectives without directly violating Article II.

This shift is not accidental; it reflects the growing perception that rigid tariff bindings are impractical in a world of evolving trade priorities. In the past, tariffs were primarily economic instruments, used to regulate competition and revenue.

Today, they are increasingly leveraged as geopolitical tools, deployed as bargaining chips in trade negotiations, national security strategies, and retaliatory trade wars. The U.S.-China trade tensions illustrate this new reality, where tariff commitments have become more of a diplomatic convenience than a binding economic constraint.

An example of this evolving trade policy approach is the February 2025 directive by the U.S. government, mandating the Office of the U.S. Trade Representative and the Department of Commerce to conduct a comprehensive review of foreign tax policies.

While presented as a policy assessment, this move is widely interpreted as a prelude to imposing retaliatory tariffs against countries whose VAT systems or digital service taxes are perceived as unfairly disadvantaging U.S. exports. Such actions reflect a broader trend where tariff commitments are no longer viewed as absolute constraints but as flexible components of a state's economic strategy.

Similarly, China's trade policies have demonstrated a selective application of tariff obligations, using export controls, import restrictions, and state subsidies to manage its trade relationships while technically remaining within WTO parameters.

The European Union's Carbon Border Adjustment Mechanism (CBAM) presents another example of how tariff-equivalent measures are being designed to bypass traditional WTO rules while still exerting economic pressure on trading partners.

These developments raise critical questions about the relevance of Article II in a world where WTO obligations are selectively observed or openly disregarded.

The more frequently countries seek alternative means to adjust tariffs without engaging in formal renegotiations, the weaker the credibility of the WTO's foundational trade disciplines becomes. If a rule exists but is no longer meaningfully enforced, its value to the global trading system must be reconsidered.

This does not mean that Article II should be abandoned entirely, but it does suggest that a modernization of WTO tariff rules is urgently needed. If tariff bindings are to remain a cornerstone of the WTO framework, clearer rules on permissible adjustments, more robust enforcement mechanisms, and a greater commitment from major economies to uphold their obligations will be essential.

The future of Article II will be determined not by its legal text but by the willingness of WTO members to uphold its principles.

If leading economies continue to sidestep their commitments through regulatory maneuvering and discretionary trade measures, then Article II risks becoming a relic of a bygone trade era rather than an effective tool for stabilizing international commerce.

Rather than allowing this principle to erode through neglect, WTO members must either reinforce its application through meaningful reforms or formally acknowledge the need for its revision. If a rule is no longer respected by key participants, maintaining it in its current form serves little purpose beyond highlighting the WTO's diminishing influence.

The exemptions to Article II obligations—including those permitted under Articles XX and XXI of the GATT 1995—are explored in a later chapter, where their growing role in shaping modern trade policy is further examined.

Chapter 29

"National Treatment" Principle – Article III of GATT

Article III of the GATT addresses the issue of discrimination by member countries, requiring them to treat imported and domestic products equally once the goods have entered their market.

This chapter explores the key principles underlying Article III, focusing on the distinctions between paragraphs 2 and 4 within Article III, the types of measures covered, and the interpretation of its provisions through case law and commentary.

Overview of Article III

The purpose of Article III is to prevent members from using internal taxes, regulations, or other measures to protect domestic industries.

It embodies the principle of "national treatment," which ensures that imported products are not subjected to treatment less favorable than that accorded to domestic goods. The article aims to avoid indirect protectionism, ensuring fair competition between imported and domestic products.

Key Provisions of Article III

Paragraph 2: Internal Taxation

The WTO obligations imposed by this Article of the GATT are particularly relevant in light of the United States mandate of 13 February, 2025 to the Office of the U.S. Trade Representative (USTR) and the Department of Commerce to conduct a comprehensive review of foreign tax policies, including value-added taxes (VAT) and digital services taxes (DST), which are perceived to disadvantage U.S. exporters.

The outcome of this review is intended to inform potential reciprocal tariff measures designed to counteract these perceived imbalances.

This initiative aligns with President Trump's broader "Fair and Reciprocal" trade plan, which seeks to overhaul existing trade relationships by imposing tariffs that mirror those levied on U.S. goods by other nations.

The administration argues that such measures are necessary to address trade deficits and rectify what it perceives as unfair trade practices, including the application of consumption-based taxes like VAT and DST by trading partners.

The proposed US reciprocal tariffs, if implemented unilaterally in response to foreign domestic taxes, could contravene its WTO obligations for the reasons explained more fully elsewhere in this book but generally speaking, the imposition of US tariffs for the purposes outlined above do not fall within the general exceptions outlined in Article XX or the national security exceptions in Article XXI of the GATT.

Moreover, the US administration's focus on VAT and similar taxes seems to overlook the fact that these domestic tax structures in other non-US WTO member countries are standard fiscal tools employed by numerous countries and are typically designed to be neutral in their trade effects.

For example, exports from countries with VAT systems often receive rebates, ensuring that the tax does not disadvantage foreign consumers, including those in the United States. Therefore, using the existence of such taxes as a justification for imposing additional U.S. tariffs seems to lack any substantive legal basis under WTO trade rules.

Dealing with discriminatory domestic taxes

It is possible and often probable however that domestic taxes (like VAT, GST, excise, carbon taxes and the like) are used to provide a competitive edge for domestic products relative to the like imported product.

For example, if an excise tax at the rate of 5% is imposed on domestically made whiskey, then it is possible that the country might also impose a 15% import duty on imported whiskey. That is permissible and often happens. However, that same country might then, in addition, impose a 20% "excise" on that imported whiskey perhaps at some later time like at the time of distribution or delivery.

"NATIONAL TREATMENT" PRINCIPLE – ARTICLE III OF GATT

Under WTO rules the imposition of a 5% tax on a domestic product and a 20% tax on a like imported product is discriminatory for which there is a WTO remedy in that it is a breach of the rules within Article III of the GATT.

The utilization by the United States of this existing WTO trade rule (described below) would seem to provide a better outcome than the imposition of additional tariffs by the United States.

The obvious consequences of such imposition of additional tariffs by the United States are retaliatory tariffs. If the United States therefore is concerned that these domestic taxes are discriminatory then it should be aware there is already within the WTO rules a provision addressing this very issue. It is Article III of the GATT.

Elements of Article III of the GATT

Paragraph 2 of Article III prohibits discriminatory taxation of imported goods. It has two distinct components:

1. **First Sentence:**

   - This provision states that imported products "shall not be subject, directly or indirectly, to internal taxes or other internal charges of any kind in excess of those applied, directly or indirectly, to like domestic products."

   - It establishes a clear prohibition against applying higher taxes to imported goods than to domestic like goods.

   Case Law Example: Japan—Alcoholic Beverages II (WT/DS8/AB/R)

   - In this case, Japan imposed higher taxes on imported alcoholic beverages compared to domestic ones, such as shochu. The Appellate Body held that this violated the first sentence of Article III:2 because the imported and domestic products were "like products" and the tax differential protected domestic production.

   Illustrative Example: Consider a country that imposes domestic taxes (like VAT) on imported bottled water at a rate of 20% while taxing domestic bottled water at only 5% VAT. Such a disparity would constitute a violation of the first sentence because the products are considered "like" and the higher tax burdens the imported goods unfairly.

2. **Second Sentence:**
   - This provision addresses "directly competitive or substitutable products." It prohibits internal taxes applied in a way that affords protection to domestic production, even if the products are not "like" but compete in the same market.

Case Law Example: Korea—Alcoholic Beverages (WT/DS75/AB/R)
   - Korea applied lower taxes to soju, a domestically produced beverage, than to imported alcoholic beverages like whiskey and vodka. The Appellate Body found that the products were directly competitive and substitutable, and the tax differential violated the second sentence of Article III:2 by affording protection to domestic products.

Illustrative Example: Imagine a government imposing a high excise tax on imported orange juice while applying a lower tax on locally produced apple juice. Although orange juice and apple juice are not "like products," they may be directly competitive or substitutable, making such tax discrimination a violation of the second sentence.

Paragraph 4: Internal Regulations

Paragraph 4 prohibits discriminatory internal laws, regulations, and requirements affecting the sale, offering for sale, purchase, transportation, distribution, or use of imported goods. It states:

"The products of the territory of any contracting party imported into the territory of any other contracting party shall be accorded treatment no less favorable than that accorded to like products of national origin in respect of all laws, regulations, and requirements affecting their internal sale, offering for sale, purchase, transportation, distribution, or use."

Key Elements of Paragraph 4:

- **Like Products:** Imported and domestic products must be considered "like products" for the provision to apply.

- **No Less Favorable Treatment:** Imported products must not be disadvantaged in their ability to compete in the domestic market.

Case Law Example: United States—Clove Cigarettes (WT/DS406/AB/R)

- The United States prohibited the sale of clove cigarettes, which were primarily imported, while allowing the sale of menthol cigarettes, a predominantly domestic product. The Appellate Body held that this measure violated Article III:4 because it accorded less favorable treatment to imported products.

Illustrative Example: Suppose a country bans the use of certain food additives in imported canned goods while allowing their use in domestically produced canned goods. Such a regulation would likely violate Article III:4 because it imposes an unfair disadvantage on imported products.

Differences Between Paragraphs 2 and 4

- **Scope**: Paragraph 2 focuses on internal taxes and charges, while paragraph 4 addresses internal regulations and laws affecting the sale and distribution of products.

- **Standard of Comparison**: Paragraph 2 applies to "like products" and "directly competitive or substitutable products," whereas paragraph 4 is limited to "like products."

- **Objective**: Paragraph 2 aims to prevent discriminatory taxation, while paragraph 4 ensures that regulations and laws do not disadvantage imported goods in their marketability.

Article III of GATT is badly outdated

Article III seeks to balance the sovereign right of countries to regulate their economies with the need to prevent protectionism. It is evident from the provision's detailed wording that it reflects the careful negotiation of competing interests.

Despite this obvious observation, that detailed consideration was made approximately 80 years ago and it is strongly suggested that Article III requires immediate revision.

The authority for this opinion is the announcement by the Trump administration to conduct inquiries into the domestic taxation and regulatory measures of the United States trading partners impacting on US exports. This review includes non-tariff barriers like domestic taxes and regulations impacting on US exports.

Another suggested reason for reform of Article III is that without effective enforcement of Article III, the tariff bindings required by Article II are rendered meaningless.

Traditional Challenges and Criticisms

- **Interpretation of "Like Products":** Determining what constitutes "like products" or "directly competitive and substitutable products" often leads to disputes, as seen in cases like Japan—Alcoholic Beverages II. For example, is a front-end washing machine "like goods" to a "top loader" washing machine. These types of questions are myriad and are often answered subjectively.

- **Regulatory Autonomy:** Countries sometimes view Article III as a constraint on their ability to pursue legitimate regulatory objectives, such as public health or environmental protection.

- **Enforcement Complexity**: The detailed assessments required in disputes under Article III make enforcement challenging, particularly for developing countries with limited resources.

Author's Commentary: Rethinking the National Treatment Principle in a New Economic Order

The principle of "National Treatment" in Article III of the GATT has long been regarded as a cornerstone of fair trade, preventing domestic regulations and taxation from being weaponized as covert protectionist measures. However, the fundamental premise upon which Article III was built—that domestic and imported goods should be treated equally—may be increasingly inadequate in an era where economic nationalism, digital trade, and corporate influence reshape the global trading landscape.

The original framers of the GATT did not—and could not—anticipate a world where value is often embedded in data, intellectual property, and digital services rather than just in physical goods. This raises an important question: can the existing framework of Article III still function effectively in an age of digitalized commerce and shifting global trade power?

One critical shortcoming of Article III is its focus on tangible goods rather than the broader economic structures that dictate trade advantages. In contemporary trade disputes, domestic preferences and disadvantages are often embedded within legal, financial, and technological systems that go beyond straightforward taxation or regulatory barriers.

For instance, a nation's data privacy laws or artificial intelligence regulations could create significant market distortions that implicitly favor domestic firms while penalizing foreign competitors. Under the current framework of Article III, such digital and regulatory trade barriers are largely outside the scope of enforcement, raising the need for an expanded interpretation or even an overhaul of the provision.

A potential solution could involve the creation of an "Article III+" framework that incorporates not just goods but also digital trade regulations, ensuring that national treatment is extended to the new frontiers of global commerce.

Another underexplored aspect of Article III is its failure to adequately address the rise of state-subsidized industries and the blurring of lines between public and private economic interests. In many cases, governments do not need to impose direct discriminatory taxation on foreign goods when they can instead subsidize their domestic industries to achieve the same protectionist result.

Countries like China have demonstrated how state-backed enterprises can circumvent traditional notions of market competition by leveraging government resources to gain an unfair advantage. This is often achieved by circumventing the outdated WTO prohibitions about subsidies.

The GATT framework, including Article III, was designed for an era of classical economic liberalism, where trade distortions were primarily tariff-based rather than state-directed. A more sophisticated revision of Article III could introduce a "competitive neutrality" test—requiring not only equal treatment in taxation and regulation but also ensuring that state interventions do not function as de facto protectionist measures that undermine the principle of fair competition.

Finally, the traditional interpretation of "like products" in Article III has become increasingly outdated, as modern consumer behavior and technological advancements redefine market competition. In the past, determining whether two goods were "like" was largely a matter of physical characteristics, end uses, and market positioning.

While the interpretation of the adjective "like" seems straightforward enough at first instance, there are considerable difficulties associated with how the term is interpreted. This difficulty is exacerbated by the use of the term "like" in two different senses in paragraphs 2 and 4 respectively of Article III of the GATT. Moreover, this same problem is further exacerbated by the use of the same term "like" in other Articles of the GATT (like Article VI of the GATT) where it is interpreted in a different way than it is interpreted in Article III.

In the current economic climate, factors such as environmental sustainability, ethical sourcing, and digital compatibility perhaps should play a critical role in consumer preferences. For example, can a factory-farmed chicken be considered "like" an organic, free-range chicken? Is a fossil fuel-powered car truly "like" an electric vehicle? If the purpose of Article III is to ensure fair competition, then it may be time to rethink whether the rigid historical definition (via precedents) of "like products" and "like goods" still serves this goal.

A more dynamic approach could be adopted, one that takes into account shifting consumer trends, technological advancements, and sustainability concerns. This would not only modernize Article III but also align it with broader global policy goals, such as climate change mitigation and ethical supply chain management.

In conclusion, while the principle of National Treatment remains essential to the integrity of international trade, its current form is becoming increasingly inadequate in addressing modern economic realities. The digital economy, state-backed market distortions, and evolving definitions of "like products" all present challenges that Article III was never designed to manage.

If the WTO wishes to preserve the relevance of its trade governance system, a fundamental rethinking of Article III may be necessary—one that goes beyond its historical role in preventing discriminatory taxation and regulation and instead ensures that the foundational principles of fair competition remain viable in a rapidly evolving global economy.

Chapter 30

Emergency Action Exemptions – Articles XX & XXI of GATT

Introduction

Articles XX and XXI of the General Agreement on Tariffs and Trade (GATT) provide essential flexibility for member states, allowing them to address extraordinary circumstances while maintaining the integrity of the global trading system.

These provisions enable World Trade Organization (WTO) members to implement measures necessary for public policy objectives such as environmental protection and national security, even when such measures might otherwise violate trade commitments.

One of the fundamental obligations under WTO rules is that member states must not raise tariffs above their agreed ("bound") rates, as established under Article II of GATT. However, Articles XX and XXI allow for exceptions to these commitments under specific conditions.

The significance of these provisions has come under renewed scrutiny in light of the Trump administration's 2025 tariff policies, including:

- Increased tariffs imposed on multiple WTO members.
- A February 13, 2025 directive to the U.S. Trade Representative and the Department of Commerce to conduct a comprehensive review of foreign tax policies—particularly value-added taxes and digital services taxes—which are perceived to disadvantage U.S. exporters. The outcome of this review may lead to reciprocal tariffs by the U.S.

It is highly likely that the U.S. will invoke Articles XX and XXI to justify these tariff hikes despite its bound tariff obligations under Article II of GATT. This chapter explores the implications of these provisions, relevant case law, criticisms, and potential reforms.

Article XX: General Exceptions

Article XX allows WTO members to implement trade restrictions for legitimate public policy objectives. However, these exceptions must meet two key conditions:

1. **The Chapeau (Introductory Clause):** Measures must not constitute arbitrary or unjustifiable discrimination or be a disguised restriction on international trade.

2. **Specific Subparagraphs:** Measures must fall under one of the following general categories:

    - Protecting public morals (subparagraph a).
    - Protecting human, animal, or plant life or health (subparagraph b).
    - Conservation of exhaustible natural resources (subparagraph g).

Case Law Examples

- *Brazil—Retreaded Tires (WT/DS332):* Brazil banned imports of retreaded tires to reduce environmental harm. While the WTO upheld the measure under Article XX(b) (public health), it found that Brazil's selective application violated the chapeau's requirement to avoid arbitrary discrimination.

- *United States—Shrimp (WT/DS58/AB/R):* The U.S. restricted shrimp imports to protect endangered sea turtles. The WTO ruled the measure valid under Article XX(g) (conservation of natural resources) but found it discriminatory in its implementation.

Illustrative Example

A government bans imports of products containing hazardous chemicals to protect public health. If the measure is scientifically justified and applied consistently, it may qualify under Article XX(b). However, if it disproportionately targets specific trading partners, it may be deemed unjustifiable discrimination under the chapeau.

Criticism: Potential for Abuse in Public Policy Justifications

One controversial WTO case is *Australia—Plain Packaging (WT/DS435/441)*, where tobacco companies challenged Australia's plain packaging laws. The WTO upheld the measure under Article XX(b) (public health), but critics argued that it unfairly targeted branding without fully banning tobacco sales.

Article XXI: Security Exceptions

Article XXI grants WTO members significant discretion to implement trade measures for national security reasons. However, this discretion is subject to some limitations.

Key Features

- **Self-Judging Nature**: Members determine whether a situation qualifies as a national security concern.
- **Categories of Measures**: Article XXI applies to:
    - Trade restrictions on fissionable materials or nuclear policy.
    - Trade related to arms and military supplies.
    - Actions taken during wartime or "emergency situations in international relations."

Case Law Examples

- *Russia—Transit Restrictions (WT/DS512):* Ukraine challenged Russia's restrictions on transit trade. Russia invoked Article XXI, claiming national security concerns. The WTO ruled that while security exceptions are broad, members must demonstrate a rational connection between security measures and the emergency invoked.
- **U.S. Steel and Aluminum Tariffs (2022):** The U.S. imposed 25% tariffs on steel and 10% tariffs on aluminum, citing national security concerns. Canada, Mexico, and the EU challenged the tariffs as protectionist. The WTO ruled against the U.S., stating that security exemptions cannot be used arbitrarily.

Illustrative Example

A country restricts the export of rare earth minerals essential for military technology, citing national security. If challenged, it would need to prove the measure's legitimate connection to national defense.

Differences and Interconnections Between Articles XX & XXI

Aspect	Article XX (General Exceptions)	Article XXI (Security Exceptions)
Purpose	Allows exceptions for policy objectives	Protects national security interests
Discretion	Requires justification under the chapeau	Grants broad discretion but subject to WTO scrutiny
Duration	Can be indefinite but must be justified	Can be indefinite but must show necessity

Criticisms and Proposed Reforms

Criticism 1: Potential for Abuse of Security Exceptions

- Countries may invoke Article XXI to justify protectionist policies under a national security pretext. ***Example***: The U.S. steel tariffs case demonstrated how governments could impose economic measures under national security rationales without clear military threats.

Proposed Reform:

- Require stronger WTO oversight to prevent abuse.
- Mandate transparency when invoking Article XXI.

Criticism 2: Weak WTO Enforcement Mechanisms

- The WTO issues rulings, but compliance remains voluntary.
- The U.S. refusal to comply with the WTO ruling on steel tariffs highlights the lack of enforcement power.

Proposed Reform:

- Introduce automatic penalties for violations.
- Strengthen WTO dispute resolution mechanisms.

Criticism 3: Elected Governments vs. WTO Rulings

- WTO rulings can override democratically enacted policies. ***Example***: A country bans genetically modified foods for public health reasons. If the WTO overturns the ban, elected officials may have no recourse.

Proposed Reform:

- Allow greater deference to national policies where a legitimate policy objective exists.
- Introduce public interest exemptions in WTO dispute resolution.

Author's Commentary: The Strategic Weaponization of GATT's Emergency Exemptions

Articles XX and XXI of GATT were originally conceived as necessary safeguards—designed to balance the principles of free trade with sovereign policy objectives such as environmental protection, public health, and national security. However, these provisions are increasingly becoming instruments of economic warfare rather than mere exemptions.

The world has moved far beyond the economic realities of 1947, yet the language of these articles remains largely unchanged, providing ample opportunity for strategic manipulation by powerful economies. If the WTO does not evolve to address the modern exploitation of these provisions, the very concept of a rules-based global trade system may be eroded beyond repair.

One of the greatest vulnerabilities of Articles XX and XXI is the unchecked discretion they afford member states. The self-judging nature of Article XXI, in particular, allows governments to invoke national security concerns with minimal scrutiny, transforming what should be a rare exemption into a blunt protectionist tool.

The most alarming consequence of this trend is the emergence of a **"national security arms race"** in global trade—where states retaliate against economic measures by invoking their own security-based restrictions. If the U.S. continues to impose unilateral tariffs under the guise of national security, its trading partners will inevitably follow suit, citing similar justifications for their own protectionist policies.

A precedent has already been set in the Russia—Transit Restrictions case, where the WTO, while ruling that Article XXI cannot be abused arbitrarily, still left open a broad interpretation of what constitutes an "emergency in international relations." The risk is that this vagueness will become an invitation for widespread abuse, leading to economic fragmentation rather than cooperation.

A more radical solution to this problem is the introduction of time-bound security exemptions under Article XXI. Currently, a nation can impose a trade restriction indefinitely under the justification of national security. However, should an exemption that disrupts global trade really be permitted without periodic review? A **sunset clause** could be introduced to require WTO members invoking Article XXI to periodically justify the continued necessity of their security measures.

If a national security concern is genuinely pressing, a country should have no difficulty reaffirming its case every few years. Such a mechanism would prevent abusers where states impose protectionist measures under security pretenses, only to leave them in place indefinitely.

Additionally, the notion of "public policy exemptions" under Article XX is ripe for reinterpretation. The cases of environmental and health-based trade restrictions, such as the *U.S.—Shrimp* and *Australia—Plain Packaging* disputes, reveal an unresolved tension between trade liberalization and legitimate public interest regulations.

One underexplored avenue is the idea of a tiered justification system within Article XX, where different categories of exemptions require different levels of proof. For example, environmental or public health justifications could be subject to an expedited review process with lower evidentiary burdens, whereas trade restrictions that are clearly protectionist in nature—such as taxation measures favoring domestic producers—should require a much stricter test. Such a framework would introduce nuance into an otherwise rigid system, allowing for legitimate regulatory concerns while maintaining trade discipline.

Finally, if the WTO wants to remain relevant, it must recognize that its greatest weakness is not in the rules themselves but in their lack of enforceability. The refusal of the U.S. to comply with WTO rulings on steel and aluminum tariffs is just the latest example of the institution's impotence in the face of economic superpowers.

EMERGENCY ACTION EXEMPTIONS – ARTICLES XX & XXI OF GATT

A potential reform is the introduction of automatic countermeasures—where, if a WTO panel finds a violation of Articles XX or XXI, pre-authorized retaliatory measures could be triggered without the need for separate litigation or diplomatic negotiation. This would significantly raise the stakes for countries considering the abuse of emergency exemptions, making it clear that economic unilateralism comes with a tangible cost.

In an increasingly volatile global economic order, Articles XX and XXI will either evolve to become functional safeguards for genuine emergencies, or they will continue to serve as the legal loopholes that justify trade wars. The direction taken will define whether the WTO remains a credible institution or becomes a relic of a bygone era of trade governance.

Chapter 31

Free Trade Agreements – Article XXIV of GATT

Introduction

Free trade agreements (FTAs) have become a defining feature of the global trading system, allowing countries to foster deeper economic ties while bypassing the complexities of multilateral negotiations under the World Trade Organization (WTO).

Article XXIV of the General Agreement on Tariffs and Trade (GATT) provides the legal foundation for these agreements by carving out an exception to the Most-Favored-Nation (MFN) principle enshrined in Article I.

According to Article XXIV:8(b) of GATT, a Free Trade Area is defined as:

"… A free-trade area shall be understood to mean a group of two or more customs territories in which the duties and other restrictive regulations of commerce… are eliminated on substantially all the trade between the constituent territories in products originating in such territories."

Based on this definition it is reported that there are over 400 FTAs currently in place. An interesting observation is that the legal basis for FTAs does not mention FTAs. Rather, what is permissible involves the elimination of duties and "…other restrictive regulations of commerce…" within a free trade area (whether that be in the territory of only 2 WTO members or within some regional territory where there may be for example 12 WTO members).

It is assumed that the elimination of duties and other restrictive regulations of commerce is best done through an agreement, and those agreements have become known as FTAs.

Article XV anticipates such agreements but does not call them FTAs.

For example, paragraph 4 of Article XXIV relevantly provides that "… The contracting parties recognize the desirability of increasing freedom of trade by the development, through voluntary agreements, of closer integration between the economies of the country's parties to such agreements."

They also recognize that the purpose of a… "free trade area should be to facilitate trade between the constituent territories and not to raise barriers to the trade of other contracting parties with such territories…"

This chapter explores the purpose, requirements, legal interpretations, and challenges surrounding Article XXIV, referencing key case law, authoritative commentary, and real-world implications of FTAs within the evolving global trade environment.

Purpose and Function of Article XXIV

The MFN principle, a cornerstone of GATT, requires WTO members to extend any trade advantage granted to one member to all others equally. This ensures non-discrimination in global trade. However, the reality of securing agreement among 165 WTO members makes achieving comprehensive multilateral liberalization exceedingly difficult.

The most significant expansion of the GATT system (1947) came with the formation of the WTO (1995), incorporating agreements on services and intellectual property. Since then, only one multilateral agreement, the Trade Facilitation Agreement (TFA, 2013), has been successfully implemented.

To circumvent multilateral gridlock, Article XXIV permits countries to form regional and bilateral trade areas, allowing smaller groups of nations to advance trade liberalization independently of WTO-wide consensus.

Legal Requirements for FTAs Under Article XXIV

To ensure that FTAs and customs unions do not undermine the multilateral trading system, Article XXIV imposes strict requirements:

1. **Substantially All Trade**: FTAs and customs unions must eliminate barriers on "substantially all trade" between the members. Selective liberalization is prohibited to prevent trade distortions.

2. **No Higher Barriers to Non-Members**: Tariffs and restrictions against non-members cannot be increased beyond pre-agreement levels, ensuring that regional integration does not disadvantage other WTO members.

3. **Reasonable Implementation Timeline**: Agreements must be implemented within a "reasonable period," generally not exceeding 10 years, unless exceptional circumstances justify a longer transition.

4. **WTO Notification and Review**: All FTAs and customs unions must be notified to the WTO and subjected to a compliance review, ensuring consistency with Article XXIV.

Addressing the MFN Principle in Article I

Article XXIV permits preferential treatment within FTAs, which contradicts the MFN principle in Article I. However, GATT explicitly permits these exceptions if they meet the legal criteria above. This exception acknowledges that regional integration often acts as a stepping stone toward broader multilateral liberalization.

It is an interesting observation to note carefully the scope and intention of the above 4 strict requirements. It seems that WTO members are permitted to agree either bilaterally or regionally on whatever international trade initiatives might be beneficial to them so long as: "…the duties and other restrictive regulations of commerce… are eliminated on substantially all the trade between the constituent territories in products originating in such territories…"

The only other additional substantive prerequisite imposed on WTO members formulating an FTA is that they do not increase duty rates on non-members to that FTA.

It seems then that the contracting parties to an FTA are free to negotiate within the confines of that FTA any legal or administrative measure which facilitates trade between the constituent territories, provided it does not raise barriers to the trade of other contracting parties with such territories.

This freedom to negotiate is enormous and, it is submitted, it is not properly utilized by WTO members who tend to link too closely each chapter of their respective FTAs to the antiquated WTO agreements.

For example, the dispute resolution provisions in most FTAs follow the diplomatic consensus methodology of the WTO dispute resolution provisions which are ineffective.

Case Law Interpretation of Article XXIV

Case Study: Türkiye—Textiles (WT/DS34/AB/R)

- Türkiye, as part of a customs union with the European Union, imposed quantitative restrictions on textile imports from non-EU countries.
- India challenged these restrictions under Article I (MFN principle).
- The WTO Appellate Body ruled that deviations from MFN must be "necessary" for customs union formation.
- Türkiye's restrictions failed this test, underscoring the stringent compliance requirements of Article XXIV.

Illustrative Examples of FTAs and Compliance with Article XXIV

1. **Comprehensive and Progressive Agreement for Trans-Pacific Partnership (CPTPP)**: CPTPP eliminates tariffs on nearly all trade, meeting the "substantially all trade" requirement.

2. **United States-Mexico-Canada Agreement (USMCA)**: Replacing NAFTA, USMCA modernizes trade rules, particularly on digital commerce and environmental standards, ensuring compliance with Article XXIV.

3. **European Union (EU) as a Customs Union**: The EU's integration model is the deepest example of economic union, but WTO cases like *EC—Bananas III* highlight challenges in proving full compliance with Article XXIV.

Challenges and Criticisms of Article XXIV

1. **Risk of "Spaghetti Bowl" Effect**: The proliferation of overlapping FTAs with differing rules of origin creates complex regulatory burdens for businesses and distorts supply chains.

2. **Selective Liberalization Weakens Multilateralism**: By allowing preferential treatment, FTAs undermine the WTO's core principle of non-discrimination, fragmenting global trade governance.

3. **Enforcement and Compliance Issues**: Many FTAs fail to meet the "substantially all trade" threshold, leading to disputes over selective

trade liberalization. ***Example*: Turkey—Textiles** demonstrates how WTO members often violate Article XXIV's intent.

4. **Weak WTO Oversight**: The WTO's review process is inadequate, allowing some FTAs to escape rigorous scrutiny.

5. **FTAs Are Only Agreements—They Can Be Broken**: Unlike binding WTO agreements, FTAs depend on political will. *Example*: The 2025 U.S. tariff hikes on Canada and Mexico demonstrate that even established FTAs like USMCA can be unilaterally violated.

Author's Commentary

Article XXIV of GATT provides the primary legal foundation for the formation of FTAs, aiming to promote regional trade integration while preventing discriminatory practices against non-members. However, the practical effectiveness of FTAs remains severely undermined in 2025 due to their lack of enforceability, reliance on outdated WTO obligations, and the slow, consensus-driven nature of their dispute resolution processes.

A fundamental problem with modern FTAs is their fragility—countries can unilaterally withdraw, ignore obligations, or manipulate trade terms without facing immediate consequences.

This is largely because most FTAs do not include binding enforcement mechanisms, nor do they incorporate trade disputes within commercial dispute resolution frameworks. Instead, FTAs rely on state-to-state consultations that are often driven by diplomatic negotiations rather than legal certainty.

The result is a system where trade disputes become political bargaining chips rather than legal matters that require resolution in a structured and predictable manner.

A serious reconsideration of both the drafting and enforcement of FTAs is now essential. The real stakeholders in FTAs are not governments but importers and exporters—businesses that engage in international commerce and require a clear, enforceable system to resolve disputes efficiently. To achieve this, FTAs must move away from diplomatic consensus models and towards legally binding, commercially structured dispute resolution mechanisms.

The following reforms would address the core weaknesses of FTAs by ensuring stronger enforcement, reducing uncertainty, and treating disputes as commercial legal matters rather than political negotiations.

1. Enhanced Dispute Resolution Outside the WTO Framework

One of the most pressing reforms needed is the development of binding dispute resolution mechanisms outside of the WTO framework, modeled on international commercial arbitration and investment dispute settlement procedures.

- **Why WTO Dispute Resolution Fails for FTAs:** WTO dispute mechanisms are slow, bureaucratic, and consensus-driven, meaning that disputes are often resolved in ways that are politically expedient rather than legally consistent.
- **FTAs Should Mirror Commercial Dispute Resolution**: Rather than relying on diplomatic consultations and political mediation, FTA disputes should be treated as contractual disputes between economic stakeholders (i.e., traders, importers, and exporters). This would allow faster resolution, enforceable rulings, and commercial certainty.
- **Use of International Arbitration Mechanisms**:
    - FTAs should establish independent arbitration panels with authority to issue binding rulings, similar to commercial arbitration under institutions such as ICSID (International Centre for Settlement of Investment Disputes) or the ICC (International Chamber of Commerce).
    - These panels should consist of trade law experts rather than government-appointed representatives, ensuring that decisions are based on legal merit rather than political considerations.
    - Enforcement of Decisions: Dispute rulings must be enforceable through neutral international legal frameworks, ensuring that FTA obligations are not merely aspirational but legally binding.

By shifting FTA disputes into a structured, legally enforceable system, trade conflicts could be resolved in months rather than years, reducing economic uncertainty for traders.

2. Stronger WTO Review Mechanisms for FTA Compliance

- A dedicated WTO panel should be established to monitor whether FTAs comply with Article XXIV and ensure that they genuinely promote trade liberalization rather than fostering protectionist trade blocs.

- More stringent reporting obligations should be introduced, requiring regular assessments of whether FTAs are functioning as intended, with non-compliant agreements subject to penalties.

3. **Harmonization of "Rules of Origin" to Reduce Trade Distortions**

- Many FTAs include conflicting rules of origin, making compliance complex and costly for traders. A move toward standardized rules of origin across agreements would simplify trade, reduce administrative costs, and minimize trade manipulation.
- A single, globally recognized framework for rules of origin should be developed under WTO oversight to ensure greater consistency and transparency.

4. **Binding Enforcement Mechanisms for FTA Violations**

- FTAs should include penalties for non-compliance, ensuring that governments cannot simply ignore their obligations without consequences.
- Enforcement mechanisms should allow for automatic retaliatory measures or financial compensation when a party fails to uphold its trade commitments.
- Dispute settlements should involve direct input from private-sector stakeholders rather than being solely left to government negotiators.

5. **Mandatory Sunset Clauses and Periodic Reviews of FTAs**

- FTAs should not be indefinite agreements but should include periodic reviews (e.g. every five or ten years) to ensure they remain aligned with modern trade realities.
- Re-evaluation should be mandatory, with mechanisms to adjust obligations based on evolving economic conditions.

6. Drafting FTAs as Enforceable Commercial Contracts

- FTAs should be drafted with clear, legally enforceable language rather than broad, aspirational commitments.
- Instead of replicating WTO obligations, FTAs should define specific obligations and responsibilities in a way that mirrors commercial contracts.
- Vague, non-binding provisions—such as those found in the intellectual property chapter of the Australia-China FTA—should be replaced with precise legal terms that allow for meaningful enforcement.

FTAs must evolve beyond their current state of fragility, where commitments are vague, enforcement is weak, and dispute resolution is inefficient. The real stakeholders in these agreements are not governments but traders—importers, exporters, and businesses—that rely on predictable trade rules to operate efficiently.

The fundamental shift needed is to treat FTA disputes as commercial disputes rather than political disagreements. By adopting enhanced dispute resolution mechanisms outside the WTO framework, integrating binding enforcement measures, and structuring FTAs more like commercial contracts, international trade agreements can become more predictable, enforceable, and effective (See later chapter).

Without such reforms, FTAs will continue to operate as fragile diplomatic instruments rather than robust legal frameworks. Their future relevance depends on moving away from outdated consensus-driven models and embracing mechanisms that reflect the realities of modern commerce.

The following chapter provides some suggested options to improve the drafting of FTAs

Chapter 32

The Inadequacies of Free Trade Agreement Dispute Resolution Mechanisms

Introduction: The Systemic Flaws in Trade Dispute Resolution

International trade disputes should be resolved through rules-based mechanisms that ensure predictability and fairness. However, the dispute resolution provisions embedded in FTAs have proven to be ineffective, failing to provide timely, enforceable resolutions—particularly against major economies that choose to disregard their obligations.

While FTAs are supposed to facilitate trade liberalization, their dispute resolution mechanisms largely mirror the World Trade Organization's (WTO) Dispute Settlement Understanding (DSU), which is slow, politically driven, and lacks effective enforcement tools.

As a result, FTAs often fail to protect businesses, traders, and exporters from discriminatory or retaliatory trade measures, rendering these agreements largely symbolic rather than legally robust.

This chapter will examine the fundamental weaknesses of FTA dispute resolution mechanisms, exploring how their reliance on diplomatic consensus, drawn-out legal procedures, and lack of binding enforcement provisions has left traders vulnerable to arbitrary trade restrictions. Key case studies will illustrate how major economies exploit these weaknesses, and recommendations will be proposed to improve FTA dispute settlement systems.

FTA Dispute Resolution: A System Designed to Fail?

Most FTA dispute resolution mechanisms are modeled on the WTO's DSU, which follows a structured, multi-stage process:

1. **Consultations**: Parties must first attempt to resolve disputes diplomatically.

2. **Panel Proceedings**: If consultations fail, a panel of trade experts is established to adjudicate the dispute.

3. **Appellate Review**: Either party may appeal the ruling, leading to further delays.

4. **Implementation & Compliance**: If the losing party refuses to comply, the winning party may impose retaliatory measures.

Key Failures of FTA Dispute Resolution

- **Lack of Automatic Enforcement**: There are no mandatory penalties for non-compliance, allowing major economies to selectively adhere to rulings.

- **Lengthy and Bureaucratic Process**: Even simple disputes can take years to resolve, making them impractical for businesses needing timely relief.

- **Political Influence**: Dispute panels often favor powerful economies, leaving smaller countries with little recourse.

- **Limited Remedies for Traders**: Retaliatory tariffs are often the only recourse, which do not compensate businesses for economic harm.

These systemic failures make FTA dispute resolution mechanisms highly ineffective in ensuring compliance and protecting the rights of businesses engaged in international trade.

Case Studies: How Major Economies Exploit Weak FTA Dispute Resolution Systems

Case Study 1: U.S. Non-Compliance with USMCA Rulings on Canadian Dairy Imports

- The United States-Mexico-Canada Agreement (USMCA) panel ruled in favor of the U.S. in a dispute over Canadian dairy restrictions.

- Canada only made minor adjustments without fully complying—yet faced no direct consequences. ***Key Takeaway***: FTAs lack automatic enforcement mechanisms, allowing selective compliance.

THE INADEQUACIES OF FTA DISPUTE RESOLUTION MECHANISMS

Case Study 2: China's Retaliatory Trade Measures Against Australia Despite an FTA

- Despite the China-Australia Free Trade Agreement (ChAFTA), China imposed trade restrictions on Australian coal, wine, and barley due to political tensions in 2020.
- Australia had no effective FTA enforcement mechanism and had to rely on slow-moving WTO litigation. *Key Takeaway*: FTAs do not prevent economic coercion or provide rapid dispute resolution.

Case Study 3: U.S. Disregard for WTO Ruling on Australian Aluminum

- Australia won a WTO case against U.S. anti-dumping tariffs on aluminum in 2020.
- The U.S. ignored the ruling, leaving Australia with no leverage beyond ineffective retaliatory tariffs. *Key Takeaway*: Retaliatory tariffs are not a viable enforcement mechanism, particularly for smaller economies.

Reforming FTA Dispute Resolution Mechanisms

To make FTAs commercially viable, they must move beyond the WTO model and adopt binding, enforceable dispute settlement systems that deliver swift and predictable remedies for businesses.

1. Legally Binding Arbitration with Commercial Enforcement

- FTA disputes should be resolved through independent arbitration panels modeled on commercial arbitration frameworks like ICSID (International Centre for Settlement of Investment Disputes).
- Rulings must be final and enforceable, eliminating indefinite appeals and political negotiations.

2. Automatic Financial Penalties for Non-Compliance

- FTAs should include monetary penalties for violations, ensuring that compliance is not discretionary. *Example*: If a country fails to implement an adverse ruling, it should be required to compensate affected industries automatically.

3. **Compensation Funds for Affected Traders**

    - FTAs should establish compensation funds to protect businesses from economic harm caused by unfair trade practices. ***Example***: If a country imposes illegal tariffs, affected businesses should receive direct financial compensation without waiting for lengthy litigation.

4. **Faster Resolution Timelines**

    - FTA disputes should be resolved within months, not years, ensuring businesses receive timely remedies.
    - Fixed timelines for dispute resolution must be built into FTA provisions.

Author's Commentary: The Illusion of Free Trade Without Real Enforcement

The failure of FTA dispute resolution mechanisms is not just a legal flaw—it is a fundamental threat to the credibility of modern trade agreements. While FTAs are marketed as providing businesses with certainty and predictability, their dispute resolution provisions often amount to little more than diplomatic formalities, easily ignored or delayed by economically dominant nations.

In practice, FTAs serve as political instruments rather than genuine legal contracts, offering weak assurances that are regularly circumvented when politically expedient. If FTAs are to have any real meaning in the future, their dispute resolution mechanisms must be entirely restructured to remove diplomatic interference and impose automatic, enforceable penalties on violators.

A key problem is that FTA disputes operate on the flawed assumption that countries will comply in good faith. Yet history has demonstrated that major economies, particularly the United States and China, will often disregard adverse rulings, knowing that smaller economies lack the power to enforce compliance.

This reality exposes an uncomfortable truth: without real enforcement mechanisms, FTAs are not agreements at all—they are aspirations. If an agreement lacks practical consequences for non-compliance, then it is effectively voluntary, and a voluntary dispute resolution system is useless in a world where economic interests drive state behavior.

Even more concerning is the growing trend of countries simply walking away from FTAs altogether or choosing to ignore their provisions when politically or economically convenient.

THE INADEQUACIES OF FTA DISPUTE RESOLUTION MECHANISMS

The U.S. withdrawal from the Trans-Pacific Partnership (TPP) under the Trump administration demonstrated how a major economy can abandon a comprehensive trade pact overnight, leaving smaller nations scrambling to salvage what remains of their economic commitments.

Similarly, China's repeated imposition of politically motivated trade restrictions on Australia—despite a standing FTA—highlights the reality that agreements are only respected when it suits national interests. In such cases, dispute resolution mechanisms are rendered meaningless because the violating country simply refuses to participate in the process, leaving affected nations with no meaningful recourse other than prolonged diplomatic protests or ineffective WTO litigation.

A more radical approach would be to shift trade dispute enforcement from state-centric mechanisms to business-centric remedies. Instead of forcing nations to impose retaliatory tariffs—an approach that punishes domestic consumers as much as foreign violators—FTA dispute resolution could be reimagined to provide direct compensation to businesses and industries harmed by unfair trade practices.

For example, if an FTA ruling determines that a country has imposed illegal trade restrictions, affected exporters should receive automatic financial compensation, deducted from the violating country's trade-related financial transactions, rather than waiting for governments to negotiate compliance. This would shift the focus of trade enforcement away from political leverage and toward commercial accountability.

Additionally, FTAs should incorporate pre-agreed enforcement mechanisms that function without requiring litigation. One possibility is the creation of "compliance reserves"—where signatory nations deposit funds into an FTA-administered account, which can be automatically allocated as compensation in the event of a violation.

If a country breaches its FTA obligations, its compliance reserve could be debited in favor of affected businesses, providing immediate financial redress without prolonged political negotiations. This approach would introduce real consequences for non-compliance while removing the reliance on ineffective diplomatic processes.

Ultimately, FTAs must evolve from being mere political statements to becoming enforceable economic contracts. The global economy is too complex, and trade disputes too frequent, for outdated, ineffective resolution mechanisms to remain the norm. If major economies can walk away from agreements with impunity, or simply ignore dispute resolution rulings when it is inconvenient, then FTAs are little more than symbolic arrangements.

The survival of the free trade system depends on rethinking enforcement—not just tweaking procedures—so that dispute resolution is fast, automatic, and business-focused rather than state-controlled. If such reforms are not implemented, FTAs will continue to serve as little more than hollow promises, routinely broken with impunity by the most powerful players in global commerce.

Part 6
WTO 1995 –
Global Trade Governance and Regulations

Chapter 33

The WTO Dispute Settlement Understanding

Introduction: A Pillar of Global Trade Governance

The World Trade Organization (WTO) Dispute Settlement Understanding (DSU) is often hailed (particularly by the WTO) as the "crown jewel" of the multilateral trading system. It is intended to provide a structured, rules-based mechanism for resolving trade disputes between WTO member nations.

While it has contributed significantly to global trade stability, the DSU has also faced criticism for delays, perceived inefficiencies, and insufficient enforcement mechanisms. This chapter explores the history, scope, content, and procedural aspects of the DSU. Illustrative examples, statistics, and commentary are included.

History of the WTO Dispute Settlement Understanding

The DSU evolved from the dispute resolution procedures under the General Agreement on Tariffs and Trade (GATT) 1947. Under GATT, dispute settlement lacked formal enforcement, as decisions required unanimous approval—a major flaw that often rendered rulings ineffective.

Recognizing these deficiencies, the Uruguay Round negotiations (1986–1994) culminated in the establishment of the WTO in 1995, introducing the DSU to provide a more structured and binding dispute resolution system.

Scope and Content of the DSU

The DSU applies to disputes arising under all WTO agreements, including those on goods (GATT), services (GATS), and intellectual property (TRIPS). It outlines a comprehensive process for dispute resolution, encompassing consultations, panel proceedings, appellate review, and implementation of rulings. Interestingly it does not automatically cover disputes under bilateral or regional free trade agreements.

Procedural Insights: Timeframes and Extensions

The DSU sets specific timeframes for each stage of the dispute resolution process to ensure prompt settlement. However, these timeframes are often extended due to procedural complexities and the intricate nature of cases.

- **Consultations:** Intended to be completed within 60 days. Approximately 40% of disputes are resolved at this stage, highlighting its effectiveness in preventing prolonged litigation.

- **Panel Proceedings:** Panels are expected to issue reports within six months, extendable to nine months in complex cases. However, about 75% of panel proceedings exceed the six-month target, with an average duration of 10 to 12 months.

- **Appellate Review:** The Appellate Body aims to conclude reviews within 60 to 90 days. In practice, appeals often take longer due to the complexity of cases and resource constraints, with an average duration of 150 to 180 days.

- **Total Dispute Resolution Time:** On average, disputes take 2 to 3 years to resolve from the initial request for consultations to the final Appellate Body ruling.

Effectiveness of Sanctions

The DSU permits trade sanctions as a last resort when a member fails to comply with rulings. However, these sanctions face significant criticism:

- **Limited Deterrence:** Sanctions are often insufficient to compel compliance, particularly for large economies that can absorb the impact. For example, in the U.S.-Foreign Sales Corporation case, the European Union authorized retaliatory tariffs against the United States, but the measures had limited impact on U.S. compliance.

- **Economic Imbalance:** Retaliation tends to disproportionately harm smaller economies, as they lack the leverage to impose meaningful sanctions.

Appeals Process: Duration and Frequency

The appeals process is a critical component of the DSU, allowing parties to seek review of panel reports on legal grounds. While the DSU stipulates a 60 to 90-day timeframe for appellate review, in practice, appeals often take longer due to the complexity of cases and resource constraints. Moreover, the frequency of appeals has increased over the years, reflecting members' desire for thorough legal scrutiny but also contributing to delays in dispute resolution.

The Role of the WTO Appellate Body

The WTO's Dispute Settlement Understanding (DSU) was historically considered one of the most effective mechanisms for resolving international trade disputes. It provided a structured, two-tiered system where disputes between member states could be resolved through binding arbitration. The Appellate Body, established in 1995, was the highest authority in WTO dispute resolution, ensuring consistency in legal interpretations and preventing unilateral retaliatory actions.

The Paralysis of the Appellate Body

Despite its success in adjudicating hundreds of trade disputes, the WTO Appellate Body ceased to function effectively in December 2019 when the United States blocked the appointment of new judges. The Appellate Body requires a minimum of three judges to hear a case, but with retirements and U.S. obstruction of new appointments, the body was rendered incapacitated.

This paralysis has had significant implications for global trade governance:

- **Trade disputes remain unresolved:** Countries can still file cases, but without a functioning appellate system, there is no final ruling.

- **Increased unilateral retaliatory measures:** With no legal consequences, states have increasingly imposed retaliatory tariffs without waiting for WTO adjudication.

- **Legal uncertainty in international trade:** The lack of appellate oversight weakens the legitimacy of WTO rules and makes it harder for businesses and governments to predict trade outcomes.

Temporary Solutions: The MPIA

In response, the Multi-Party Interim Appeal Arbitration Arrangement (MPIA) was created in 2020 by a group of WTO members, including the European

Union, Canada, and China, as a temporary substitute for the Appellate Body. However, its effectiveness remains limited because:

- The United States and other major economies have not joined it, reducing its authority.
- It lacks the enforceability mechanisms that made the original Appellate Body so powerful.

The Geopolitical Roadblocks to Restoration

Efforts to revive the WTO Appellate Body face significant geopolitical challenges:

- **The U.S. stance on dispute resolution**: The United States, across multiple administrations, has maintained that the Appellate Body overreached its mandate and wants reforms before allowing new appointments.
- **Divergent member state interests**: While many WTO members advocate for the restoration of the Appellate Body, they have conflicting priorities on how to reform it.
- **Rise of alternative dispute mechanisms**: With the DSU's paralysis, countries are increasingly turning to regional trade agreements (RTAs) and bilateral negotiations to resolve disputes, further weakening the WTO.

Trends in WTO Disputes (2015–2023)

An analysis of WTO dispute data from 2015 to 2023 reveals the following trends:

- **Number of Disputes:** The annual number of disputes initiated has shown a downward trend over the examined period, though this observation needs to be balanced against the impact of the COVID-19 pandemic. It may reasonably be anticipated that the number of applications under the DSU will increase dramatically in the near future as a consequence of the 2025 tariff wars.
- **Resolution Outcomes:** A significant proportion of disputes are resolved during consultations, reflecting the effectiveness of early engagement. However, for cases proceeding to panels and appeals, the

timeframes have extended beyond the DSU's stipulated periods. In short these extended periods are unacceptable in that they profoundly impact on commercial dealings.

- **Geographical Distribution:** There has been a notable increase in disputes involving countries from Africa, the Middle East, the Commonwealth of Independent States (CIS), and Asia, indicating a shift in the geographical distribution of WTO disputes.

Case Studies: Recent Australia-China Disputes

1. **Australia–Barley Dispute (2021–2023):** Australia challenged China's anti-dumping and countervailing duties on barley, alleging WTO violations. In 2023, both nations reached a mutually agreed solution, with China lifting the duties following an expedited review.

2. **Australia–Wine Dispute (2021–2024):** Similar to the barley case, China imposed tariffs on Australian wine, leading to a WTO dispute. In 2024, China agreed to remove these tariffs, allowing the re-entry of Australian wine into the Chinese market.

3. **China–Steel Products Dispute (2022–2024):** China successfully challenged Australian anti-dumping measures on steel products. The WTO ruled in favor of China, with Australia adjusting its measures accordingly.

Author's Commentary

The WTO Dispute Settlement Understanding (DSU) was designed to provide a structured, rules-based mechanism to resolve trade disputes among member states. However, the system has increasingly shown its limitations, particularly in its failure to accommodate the real stakeholders of global trade—importers and exporters—who often bear the brunt of non-compliance with WTO obligations. It would be convenient if the WTO could consider the following suggestions:

Ensuring Procedural Fairness for Affected Traders

One of the fundamental flaws of the DSU is that it largely operates as a state-to-state mechanism, leaving traders and businesses with little say in disputes that directly affect them. Procedural fairness should be extended to include affected importers and exporters, ensuring they have standing to be heard in relevant cases. This reform would align the DSU more closely with real-world commercial disputes, where affected parties have direct legal recourse.

The DSU Lacks Effective Enforcement Mechanisms

The DSU's reliance on diplomatic pressure and the threat of retaliatory tariffs makes it an ineffective deterrent for trade violations. The biggest consequence for a country found in breach of WTO obligations is the embarrassment of an adverse ruling, which many governments are willing to ignore. Without meaningful penalties, compliance remains optional rather than mandatory. Stronger, automatic sanctions should be incorporated into DSU rulings, ensuring that violators face immediate consequences.

Binding Alternative Dispute Resolution (ADR) as a Solution

A more effective DSU framework would emphasize alternative dispute resolution (ADR) mechanisms that produce binding outcomes. Currently, WTO dispute resolution is slow, politically driven, and often yields non-binding results. ADR, if properly integrated, could:

- Reduce case resolution times significantly, providing timely remedies.
- Remove excessive bureaucracy, making rulings commercially actionable.
- Provide a binding outcome that ensures compliance.

By adopting ADR models akin to commercial arbitration, the WTO could streamline dispute resolution and make compliance legally binding rather than subject to diplomatic discretion.

Upholding International Trade Rules: Enforce or Abandon

The underlying philosophy of these proposed reforms is simple: international trade rules must either be upheld or abandoned. If countries continue to disregard WTO obligations without repercussions, the legitimacy of the multilateral trading system will erode. To prevent this:

1. Non-compliance should trigger immediate enforcement measures, such as financial penalties or trade restrictions.

2. Countries unwilling to adhere to WTO rulings should be required to withdraw from the organization, rather than benefiting from its trade advantages while ignoring its rules.

Immediate Actions for Reform

While comprehensive DSU reform will take time, immediate steps can and should be taken to enhance enforcement and fairness. The WTO, perhaps in collaboration with the International Chamber of Commerce, should conduct an urgent review of:

- The feasibility of integrating ADR into DSU procedures.
- The implementation of financial penalties for non-compliance.
- Expanding access to dispute resolution for affected traders.

Additionally, WTO members should be encouraged to explore non-WTO ADR processes as a viable alternative to formal panel procedures, ensuring disputes are resolved faster and more efficiently.

A More Effective WTO Dispute Settlement System

The DSU provides a comprehensive legal framework for resolving trade disputes, but its delayed processes, weak sanctions, and exclusion of key stakeholders make it inadequate for modern global trade. Without significant reforms, the WTO risks becoming an institution where rules are routinely breached without consequence. The author strongly urges that WTO members prioritize DSU reform to create a system that is enforceable, efficient, and responsive to commercial realities.

Part 7
WTO Trade Protection Tools

Chapter 34

Agreement on Safeguards

International trade agreements aim to create stable and predictable conditions for global commerce, but they also recognize that sudden and unforeseen import surges can cause significant harm to domestic industries.

To address such economic emergencies, two critical legal frameworks within the World Trade Organization (WTO) provide mechanisms for imposing safeguard measures: Article XIX of the General Agreement on Tariffs and Trade (GATT) and the WTO Agreement on Safeguards.

These frameworks allow countries to implement temporary trade restrictions to mitigate economic disruptions while maintaining overall trade liberalization principles.

Article XIX of GATT: The "Safeguards Clause"

Article XIX, often called the "safeguards clause," permits WTO members to take emergency action when a sudden surge in imports causes or threatens to cause serious injury to a domestic industry. The key provisions of Article XIX include:

1. **Serious Injury Requirement**: A country must demonstrate that increased imports have caused or threaten to cause significant overall impairment to a domestic industry.

2. **Unforeseen Developments**: The import surge must result from unexpected circumstances that were not anticipated during trade negotiations.

3. **Proportional and Temporary Measures**: Safeguard actions must be temporary, non-discriminatory, and proportional to the injury.

Countries implementing safeguards must also compensate affected trading partners or risk retaliatory measures.

Case Study: United States – Steel Safeguards (WT/DS248) In 2002, the United States imposed tariffs on steel imports to protect domestic producers. However, the WTO Appellate Body ruled that the U.S. had failed to establish a causal link between the import surge and the alleged injury, violating Article XIX.

Case Study: Argentina – Footwear Safeguards (WT/DS121) In 1997, Argentina imposed safeguard measures on imports of footwear. The European Communities challenged the measures, arguing that Argentina failed to demonstrate "unforeseen developments" as required by Article XIX. The WTO Appellate Body ruled against Argentina, stating that the evidence was insufficient, and the measures were inconsistent with WTO rules.

Example: If a country experiences a rapid increase in textile imports due to unforeseen technological advancements abroad, it may impose temporary quotas under Article XIX to stabilize the industry while implementing modernization efforts.

The WTO Agreement on Safeguards

The WTO Agreement on Safeguards, adopted as part of the WTO framework, builds upon Article XIX by establishing detailed procedural rules and transparency requirements for implementing safeguard measures. Key features of the Agreement include:

1. **Investigation and Notification**: Countries must conduct thorough investigations and notify WTO members before implementing safeguard measures.

2. **Serious Injury and Causation Standards**: The Agreement requires clear evidence linking increased imports to serious injury, preventing countries from using safeguards arbitrarily.

3. **Non-Discriminatory Application**: Safeguard measures must apply to all import sources rather than targeting specific countries.

4. **Time Limits and Progressive Liberalization:** Safeguard measures must be temporary, and countries must gradually remove restrictions over time.

Case Study: United States – Definitive Safeguard Measures on Steel Imports (DS248) The United States' steel tariffs in 2002 were challenged under the Agreement on Safeguards. The WTO found that the U.S. failed to demonstrate unforeseen developments and serious injury, leading to the termination of the measures.

Case Study: Korea – Dairy Safeguards (WT/DS98) In 1996, Korea imposed safeguard measures on dairy product imports, citing serious injury to its domestic dairy sector. The WTO Panel and Appellate Body found that Korea had not conducted a proper investigation and had failed to meet the requirements under the Agreement on Safeguards, leading to the measures being struck down.

Example: Suppose a developing country sees a sudden influx of cheap agricultural imports that harm local farmers. Under the WTO Agreement on Safeguards, it can impose temporary tariffs but must provide evidence of injury and notify the WTO.

Comparing Article XIX and the WTO Agreement on Safeguards

Feature	Article XIX (GATT)	WTO Agreement on Safeguards
Scope	General provision allowing safeguards	Detailed rules governing safeguard implementation
Injury Requirement	Requires "serious injury" due to unforeseen developments	Requires clear causation and procedural transparency
Time Limits	Temporary but no strict time limits	Maximum duration of safeguard measures and gradual removal required
Notification	Not explicitly required	Mandatory notification and consultation with WTO members
Compensation	Encouraged but not strictly enforced	Requires compensation or risk retaliatory measures

Author's Commentary

The Agreement on Safeguards, embedded in Article XIX of GATT (1947), was originally intended to provide a structured relief mechanism for domestic industries facing serious injury from import surges. However, its application has become increasingly contentious due to legal ambiguities, procedural difficulties, and the risk of protectionist misuse.

One of the most complex aspects of safeguard measures is the requirement that they be applied only in response to "unforeseen developments." Given that globalization and trade liberalization inherently lead to increased competition, determining what qualifies as an "unforeseen" import surge is often a matter of legal interpretation rather than economic reality. This ambiguity is illustrative of the interpretation challenges within the Agreement which frequently lead to disputes between WTO members.

Defining Injury and the "Threat" Standard

A further complication is the requirement that a country must demonstrate a "threat of serious injury" to its domestic industry before imposing safeguards. The challenge lies in the subjective nature of the threat assessment—what constitutes a real threat? Is an increase in imports alone sufficient? The difficulty of proving causation creates uncertainty for governments and businesses alike, leading to inconsistent applications of safeguards across different cases.

The Preference for Alternative Trade Remedies

Rather than navigating the rigorous legal and evidentiary hurdles of safeguards, many WTO members prefer alternative trade remedies such as anti-dumping duties and countervailing measures. These mechanisms face fewer procedural barriers and allow for more targeted trade restrictions, which makes them politically more attractive and legally easier to sustain.

Unlike safeguards, which must be applied on a non-discriminatory basis, anti-dumping and countervailing duties can be directed at specific countries, allowing for greater flexibility in trade defense strategies.

The Procedural Burdens of Safeguards

Governments seeking to implement safeguards must navigate an extensive series of procedural and evidentiary requirements that often make their use impractical. Some of the key challenges include:

- Establishing a direct link between increased imports and industry harm, despite multiple external factors influencing economic performance.
- Securing WTO approval and undergoing mandatory review processes, which can limit the duration and scope of safeguard measures.

- Preventing safeguards from becoming de facto protectionist tools, ensuring compliance with WTO disciplines and avoiding trade retaliation.

Safeguards remain an important, albeit underutilized tool in international trade. However, their credibility depends on transparent application and adherence to WTO rules.

While some members argue that the safeguard mechanism should be reformed to make it more accessible, others contend that loosening the requirements could encourage protectionist behavior. Balancing these concerns is critical to maintaining the legitimacy of safeguards as a trade remedy.

Going forward, WTO members must evaluate whether the existing framework adequately serves modern trade realities or whether refinements are needed to enhance clarity and procedural efficiency. Without careful oversight, the risk remains that safeguards could either be misused for protectionist purposes or become entirely obsolete due to their impracticality.

Safeguards should function as a legitimate tool for temporary relief rather than a permanent trade barrier. They should ensure that they support fair competition rather than distorting global trade.

Chapter 35

The Anti-Dumping Agreement and Article VI of GATT

1. Introduction

In the complex and often adversarial landscape of international trade, one of the most contentious issues is the practice of *dumping*, wherein a company or country exports a product at a price lower than its domestic market price.

This practice, while potentially beneficial to consumers in the short term, can lead to market distortions, harming domestic industries in the importing country. As a response, governments have implemented *anti-dumping (AD) laws* to impose duties and counteract what they perceive as unfair trade practices.

These laws operate under the broader framework of the World Trade Organization (WTO), specifically through the Anti-Dumping Agreement (ADA) and Article VI of the General Agreement on Tariffs and Trade (GATT) 1947.

However, anti-dumping law is a dated concept that, in its current form, has remained largely unchanged for approximately 80 years. When first introduced over a century ago, it was poorly understood, and it remains riddled with subjectivity in both its application and justification.

Many argue that the concept of anti-dumping is outdated and should be replaced. This chapter suggests an alternative to anti-dumping law should be modern competition law principles, particularly those addressing the *misuse of market power* at a country level.

This issue is explored in greater detail in another chapter of this book, but this chapter highlights how anti-dumping laws, despite their robustness in international enforcement, fail to meet the needs of a modern, dynamic global trading system.

2. The Anti-Dumping Agreement and Article VI of GATT

While Article VI of GATT 1947 laid the foundation for addressing dumping, its brevity led to significant misunderstandings and inconsistencies in its application. The ADA, introduced during the Uruguay Round negotiations, provides a detailed legal framework for investigating, determining, and applying anti-dumping measures.

Key Aspects of Article VI of GATT:

- Recognizes the right of members to levy anti-dumping duties on dumped products that cause injury to domestic industries.
- Provides general principles but lacks detailed guidance on procedural and evidentiary requirements.

Key Aspects of the Anti-Dumping Agreement (ADA):

- Elaborates on Article VI by setting out comprehensive procedural rules for initiating and conducting investigations, determining dumping margins, and imposing duties.
- Ensures transparency, fairness, and consistency in the application of anti-dumping measures.

Despite these provisions, the ADA remains highly subjective in its enforcement, with many determinations relying on arbitrary calculations of dumping margins and injury assessments that lack economic rigor.

The growing argument for eliminating anti-dumping laws in favor of competition law reflects concerns over the inherent discretion in AD rulings and their potential misuse for protectionist purposes.

3. Mechanisms of Dumping and Anti-dumping Measures

Dumping is typically identified through the primary criterion:

Price Discrimination: A firm sells the "like" product at a lower export price to a foreign market than in its domestic market. In these circumstances, it is possible subject to some other considerations discussed below for an importing country to impose a dumping duty on that type of particular imported goods by reference to the following formula:

Dumping duty ("DD") = Domestic price in the exporting country ("NV") - Export price ("EP")

$$DD = NV - EP$$

$$\$20 = \$100 - \$80$$

The ADA outlines several key procedural elements:

1. **Determination of Dumping (Article 2)**: Defines normal value as the price of the product in the domestic market of the exporter, allowing adjustments for differences in taxation and physical characteristics.

2. **Injury and Causation (Article 3)**: Requires evidence that dumped imports cause material injury to domestic industry, considering volume effects, price effects, and overall economic impact.

3. **Investigation Procedures (Article 5)**: Stipulates that investigations must be based on sufficient evidence of dumping, injury, and causal links, ensuring fair participation of all interested parties.

4. **Imposition of Anti-Dumping Duties (Article 9)**: Ensures that duties do not exceed the dumping margin and encourages the use of lesser duties where adequate to eliminate injury.

4. Dumping and Trade Wars

While anti-dumping duties are often justified as tools for ensuring fair trade, they have increasingly become instruments of economic warfare. Countries (on behalf of their domestic manufacturers) strategically use anti-dumping investigations and duties to target imports from geopolitical adversaries, escalating trade conflicts.

Notably, during the U.S.-China trade war, a series of anti-dumping duties were imposed on Chinese steel, aluminum, and technology products, triggering retaliatory tariffs.

Similarly, tensions between Russia and Western economies have resulted in trade barriers that go beyond traditional economic concerns, intertwining anti-dumping measures with broader geopolitical strategies.

Sanctions and restrictions on Russian energy exports, for instance, have been met with countermeasures affecting European agricultural and industrial imports.

5. The Inherent Subjectivity of Anti-dumping Measures

A fundamental criticism of anti-dumping measures is their inherent subjectivity. The process of determining dumping margins, assessing material injury, and establishing causal links between imports and domestic industry performance is fraught with discretionary decision-making.

Unlike competition law, which is based on well-defined economic principles, anti-dumping measures often rely on politically motivated assessments that distort markets rather than correct genuine market failures.

This subjectivity has led to significant disputes at the WTO, as seen in:

- *Australia—Anti-Dumping Measures on A4 Copy Paper (WT/DS529)*
- *United States—Definitive Anti-Dumping and Countervailing Duties on Certain Products from China (WT/DS379)*
- *European Communities—Anti-Dumping Duties on Imports of Cotton-Type Bed Linen from India (WT/DS141)*
- *China—Anti-Dumping Measures on Stainless Steel Tubes from Japan and the EU (WT/DS518)*

Each of these cases highlighted the difficulty in ensuring fairness and consistency in anti-dumping determinations, reinforcing the argument that a shift toward competition law principles would lead to more predictable and economically rational trade policies.

6. Strategic and Economic Consequences of Anti-dumping Measures

The effectiveness of anti-dumping measures is a subject of extensive economic research. While these duties can provide temporary relief to domestic industries, they often lead to unintended consequences, including:

- **Trade Diversion:** Imports from the targeted country decline, but other exporters fill the gap, nullifying the protective effects.
- **Higher Consumer Prices:** As anti-dumping duties raise import costs, consumers and businesses relying on imported goods face higher prices.
- **Retaliation and Trade Wars:** The targeted country may impose countermeasures, escalating economic tensions and reducing overall trade.

THE ANTI-DUMPING AGREEMENT AND ARTICLE VI OF GATT

Author's Commentary

The Anti-Dumping Agreement and Article VI of GATT have provided a structured legal framework for addressing dumping and its alleged injurious effects for over 80 years. While these measures were originally designed to counter unfair trade practices, they have increasingly been employed as instruments of strategic trade policy, often serving protectionist interests rather than promoting genuine competition. This raises fundamental concerns about the legitimacy, economic rationale, and broader implications of anti-dumping duties in contemporary international trade.

A key issue with the current anti-dumping regime is its inherent subjectivity. The determination of dumping margins and injury thresholds frequently relies on discretionary methodologies, which can be influenced by domestic political and economic pressures.

As a result, anti-dumping measures are prone to misuse, operating as de facto protectionist barriers rather than as safeguards against genuinely distortive trade practices. Moreover, in an era of globalized supply chains and sophisticated market structures, the traditional concept of dumping—predicated on simplistic cost comparisons and price discrimination—has become increasingly obsolete.

Rather than perpetuating a system that is susceptible to manipulation and economic inefficiency, the author advocates for a paradigm shift in trade regulation. The appropriate response to concerns about unfair competition should be grounded in modern competition law principles, particularly through the regulation of market power abuse.

By addressing anti-competitive behavior directly, rather than relying on blunt trade remedies, competition law offers a more precise and economically coherent approach to fostering fair and efficient markets.

The continued reliance on anti-dumping duties is an anachronism in a global economy where success should be determined by market forces rather than artificial trade remedies. As such, the author contends that anti-dumping laws have outlived their practical utility and should be phased out in favor of a legal and economic framework that upholds competitive neutrality. This shift would not only enhance the integrity of international trade but also mitigate the distortions and retaliatory trade conflicts that anti-dumping measures often provoke.

A detailed exploration of the author's proposed alternative framework is provided in a separate chapter, where the discussion focuses on mechanisms for ensuring fairness in international trade without resorting to outdated and strategically misused anti-dumping provisions.

Chapter 36

The Agreement on Subsidies and Countervailing Measures (SCM Agreement)

Introduction

The Agreement on Subsidies and Countervailing Measures (SCM Agreement) is a fundamental component of the World Trade Organization (WTO) framework, designed to regulate subsidies and countervailing measures to prevent trade distortions.

Given that Article II of GATT limits tariff increases, WTO members often resort to countervailing duties to neutralize the effects of subsidized imports, ensuring a level playing field in international trade.

This chapter explores the scope, function, and enforcement of the SCM Agreement, its impact on trade, and the complexities of its implementation, supported by case law and critical analysis.

Objectives and Scope of the SCM Agreement

The SCM Agreement serves several critical functions:

- **Defining Subsidies**: Establishing the criteria for what constitutes a subsidy under WTO law, encompassing financial contributions by governments that confer a specific benefit to businesses.

- **Prohibiting Certain Subsidies**: Prohibiting subsidies that are explicitly contingent on export performance or domestic content requirements, as these distort global trade.

- **Regulating Permissible Subsidies**: Setting parameters for acceptable subsidies, ensuring compliance with international trade rules.

- **Providing Remedies**: Enabling members to impose countervailing duties to neutralize the adverse effects of unfairly subsidized imports.

These provisions aim to promote fair competition while acknowledging the complex role of subsidies in national economies.

Case Study: *European Communities – Export Subsidies on Sugar*

A key case that illustrates the application of the SCM Agreement is *European Communities – Export Subsidies on Sugar* (DS265, DS266, DS283), initiated in 2003 by Australia, Brazil, and Thailand. The dispute centered on the European Communities' (EC) practice of exceeding its scheduled commitments on sugar export subsidies, in violation of WTO rules.

WTO Findings:

- The WTO Panel ruled that the EC had breached Articles 3.3 and 8 of the Agreement on Agriculture.
- The Appellate Body upheld these findings, confirming that the EC's export subsidies exceeded quantity commitment levels and violated WTO obligations.

This case underscores the critical role of WTO enforcement mechanisms in ensuring compliance with subsidy commitments and the potential consequences of non-compliance.

Categories of Subsidies Under the SCM Agreement

The SCM Agreement classifies subsidies into three broad categories:

- **Prohibited Subsidies**: These include export subsidies tied to performance and local content subsidies requiring domestic over imported goods. These are outright banned due to their trade-distorting effects.

- **Actionable Subsidies**: These subsidies, while not outright prohibited, can cause adverse effects on other WTO members, such as injury to domestic industries or significant distortions in trade.

- **Non-Actionable Subsidies (Expired)**: Previously, certain subsidies for research and development and environmental protection were allowed under specific conditions, but these provisions are no longer in force.

THE AGREEMENT ON SUBSIDIES AND COUNTERVAILING MEASURES

Countervailing Measures and Enforcement

The countervailing measures provided under the SCM Agreement aim to neutralize the effects of unfair subsidies. For a member state to impose countervailing duties, the following criteria must be met:

- **Investigation Requirement**: A thorough investigation must establish the existence and impact of a subsidy.

- **Determination of Injury**: The investigation must demonstrate that the subsidy **materially injures** the domestic industry.

- **Proportionality**: Any countervailing duty imposed must be commensurate with the value of the subsidy, preventing overreach and ensuring fair trade practices.

Author's Commentary: Rethinking the SCM Agreement

The SCM Agreement, while designed to regulate subsidies, is increasingly inadequate in addressing the expanding role of government investment in private sector growth. The author argues that a modern trade framework must balance regulation with economic realities.

The Case for Government Subsidies

Subsidies are often justified for reasons beyond trade competition:

- **Economic Stability**: Government investment helps protect jobs, stabilize industries, and stimulate economic activity.

- **National Security**: Strategic industries such as defense and energy require subsidies to reduce external dependencies.

- **Technological Innovation**: Research subsidies drive breakthroughs in renewable energy, healthcare, and AI, benefiting societies at large.

The Need for Reform

A rigid prohibition of subsidies fails to acknowledge that not all subsidies are inherently distortive. Instead, reforms should:

- Distinguish between harmful subsidies and strategic investments.
- Introduce clear exemptions for sectors like green energy, public health, and national security.

- Improve dispute resolution timelines to prevent legal attrition warfare.
- Create a transparent pre-approval mechanism for subsidies to provide clarity before implementation.

Balancing Trade Fairness with Economic Sovereignty

At its core, the SCM Agreement must reconcile fair trade principles with national economic sovereignty. While unchecked subsidies can distort markets, governments must retain the flexibility to support critical industries, research, and crisis management.

Conclusion

The SCM Agreement, though well-intentioned, remains burdened by ambiguity, rigid structures, and prolonged legal disputes. A reformed SCM framework must prioritize clarity, fairness, and efficiency, allowing global trade to adapt to modern economic challenges without undermining economic growth and strategic national interests.

Until such reforms materialize, the SCM Agreement will continue to serve more as a battleground for economic power struggles than a genuine tool for fair trade regulation.

Chapter 37

The Agreement on Import Licensing

Background and Objectives

Import licensing is a key regulatory tool that governments use to control the movement of goods across their borders. It typically requires importers to obtain official approval before bringing goods into a country.

While such measures can serve legitimate public policy goals—such as protecting public health, national security, or environmental concerns—import licensing also has the potential to distort trade when misapplied.

The WTO Agreement on Import Licensing Procedures (AILP) was established in 1995 as part of the Uruguay Round negotiations. It seeks to ensure that import licensing does not become an unnecessary trade barrier.

The agreement builds upon GATT 1994 principles by setting out clear rules on licensing procedures, promoting transparency, predictability, and fairness in international trade.

Scope and Coverage

The AILP applies to all import licensing systems maintained by WTO members, whether automatic (merely requiring registration) or non-automatic (requiring specific approval). The agreement imposes key obligations, including:

1. **Preventing Trade Distortions**: Licensing must not restrict trade more than necessary.

2. **Promoting Transparency**: Members must notify the WTO and publish their licensing rules.

3. **Ensuring Non-Discrimination**: Licensing procedures must apply uniformly to all trading partners under the Most-Favored-Nation (MFN) principle.

4. **Facilitating Trade**: Procedures should be simple, predictable, and processed in a timely manner.

Case Study: Argentina – Measures Affecting the Importation of Goods (DS438)

A practical example of WTO enforcement on import licensing is the case of *Argentina – Measures Affecting the Importation of Goods* (DS438). In 2012, the European Union, the United States, and Japan initiated a dispute against Argentina, claiming that its import licensing system violated WTO agreements.

Key Issues

1. **Non-Automatic Licensing**: Argentina required prior approval for imports, applying discretionary restrictions that lacked transparency.

2. **Trade-Related Requirements**: Importers were subject to additional obligations, such as balancing imports with exports or investing in local production.

Panel Findings

The WTO panel ruled that Argentina's measures violated the AILP by:

- **Lacking Transparency**: Rules were not published promptly, creating uncertainty.

- **Applying Discretionary Practices**: Licensing decisions were unpredictable and potentially discriminatory.

- **Imposing Unnecessary Restrictions**: Measures functioned as de facto trade barriers.

Outcome: Argentina was required to reform its licensing practices to align with WTO rules. This case illustrates the importance of transparency, fairness, and predictability in import licensing procedures.

THE AGREEMENT ON IMPORT LICENSING

Key Provisions of the Agreement

AILP establishes guidelines for import licensing, covering the following areas:

1. **Automatic Import Licensing (Article 2)**

   - Used primarily for monitoring trade.
   - Must not restrict imports and approvals must be granted within 10 working days.

2. **Non-Automatic Import Licensing (Article 3)**

   - May be required for policy reasons (e.g. public health, security).
   - Must be transparent, with clearly defined approval criteria.
   - WTO members must notify the organization about such measures.

3. **Transparency Requirements (Article 1)**

   - Licensing rules must be publicly available and regularly updated.

4. **Timeliness and Simplicity**

   - Automatic licenses: processed within 10 days.
   - Non-automatic licenses: processed within 30 to 60 days, depending on complexity.

Case Law Analysis

1. *United States – Restrictions on Tuna Imports*

   - The U.S. imposed licensing rules restricting tuna imports due to environmental concerns.
   - WTO ruled that while environmental policies were valid, the licensing created unnecessary trade barriers, violating AILP.

2. *India – Quantitative Restrictions on Imports*

   - India's broad use of licensing was found non-transparent and restrictive.
   - WTO required India to reform its licensing system to improve predictability for exporters.

3. ***European Union – Measures Affecting Steel Imports***
   - The EU's automatic licensing for steel was challenged for excessive documentation requirements.
   - WTO emphasized that licensing should facilitate trade, not obstruct it.

Challenges and Future Considerations

While AILP has been effective in promoting fair trade, several challenges remain:

1. **Limited Scope**: The agreement does not fully address modern digital trade and services.

2. **Transparency Deficiencies**: Some members fail to notify or publish licensing rules on time.

3. **Capacity Constraints in Developing Countries**: Many nations struggle with compliance due to weak institutions.

4. **Technological Lag**: Import licensing is often paper based, creating delays.

Author's Suggested Reforms:

Reforming the Import Licensing Regime

Given the changing nature of international trade, a re-evaluation of the WTO Agreement on Import Licensing Procedures is warranted. The author suggests that the following reforms would assist all stakeholders:

1. **Broaden the Scope**: Expand the AILP to cover digital trade, cross-border data flows, and services-related licensing.

2. **Enhance Transparency**: Strengthen notification and publication requirements to ensure licensing rules are clear and accessible.

3. **Promote Digital Integration**: Introduce electronic licensing systems to modernize processes and reduce inefficiencies.

4. **Support Developing Nations**: Provide capacity-building assistance to help developing countries comply with WTO licensing rules.

5. **Periodic Review Mechanism**: Implement regular AILP reviews to adapt to emerging trade challenges.

Author's Commentary

The WTO Agreement on Import Licensing Procedures plays a critical role in ensuring that licensing measures facilitate, rather than hinder, international trade. However, challenges persist, particularly regarding transparency, non-automatic licensing, and compliance. Disputes such as Argentina (DS438) highlight the importance of vigilance in preventing the misuse of licensing systems.

To keep pace with evolving trade realities, reforms should focus on digital integration, transparency, and expanding the scope of the agreement. Strengthening monitoring mechanisms and assisting developing nations in compliance will enhance the effectiveness and fairness of global trade practices.

By modernizing the import licensing framework, WTO members can ensure that the system remains a tool for trade facilitation rather than an impediment to economic growth.

Part 8
Investment, Intellectual Property & Trade Measures

Chapter 38

The Agreement on Trade-Related Aspects of Intellectual Property Rights (TRIPS)

The TRIPS is one of the most comprehensive international agreements on intellectual property (IP) rights.

Concluded during the Uruguay Round of trade negotiations, TRIPS established a global framework for IP protection, enforcement, and dispute resolution under the auspices of the World Trade Organization (WTO).

This chapter examines the content, goals, and scope of the TRIPS, along with illustrative examples from case law and commentary.

Overview and Objectives of TRIPS

TRIPS was introduced to address disparities in intellectual property protection across WTO member nations and to harmonize standards within the multilateral trading system. Its objectives, outlined in Articles 7 and 8, include:

- **Promotion of Innovation:** Encouraging technological innovation and the dissemination of knowledge.
- **Economic Development:** Contributing to the mutual advantage of producers and users of technological knowledge.
- **Balance of Rights and Obligations:** Ensuring IP rights do not obstruct public policy objectives such as public health and nutrition.

Scope of TRIPS

TRIPS covers a wide range of intellectual property rights, setting minimum standards for their protection and enforcement:

1. **Copyright and Related Rights (Articles 9-14):**
   - Protects literary, artistic, and scientific works, including computer programs and databases. **Example**: The Berne Convention standards are incorporated, requiring protection of moral and economic rights of authors.

2. **Trademarks (Articles 15-21):**
   - Protects distinctive signs, including brand names, logos, and slogans.
   - Requires renewable registration for an initial term of at least seven years.

3. **Geographical Indications (Articles 22-24):**
   - Protects indications that identify goods as originating in a specific region, such as "Champagne" or "Darjeeling."
   - Case Example: The EU—Geographical Indications case reinforced that geographical indications must not unfairly discriminate against products from non-originating regions.

4. **Patents (Articles 27-34):**
   - Requires protection of inventions that are new, involve an inventive step, and are industrially applicable.
   - Allows exceptions, such as for public health, under certain conditions.
   - Case Example: Canada—*Pharmaceutical Patents (WT/DS114)*: Canada's regulatory review exception was challenged by the EU as a violation of patent rights. The WTO upheld Canada's measures, highlighting permissible exceptions under TRIPS for public interest.

5. **Industrial Designs (Article 25-26):**
   - Protects aesthetic and functional aspects of products. ***Illustration***: Furniture designs that combine artistry and functionality are covered, provided they meet the originality criteria.

6. **Undisclosed Information (Trade Secrets) (Article 39):**

    - Protects confidential business information from unfair competition. ***Illustrative Example:*** Protection of proprietary formulas, such as the Coca-Cola recipe, demonstrates the importance of trade secrets in maintaining competitive advantage.

7. **Integrated Circuits (Article 35-38):**

    - Protects layout designs of integrated circuits.
    - This provision is particularly relevant in the technology sector.

Case study to help understand TRIPS:

To provide a better understanding of the different types of intellectual property (IP) under TRIPS, the case of *European Communities – Protection of Trademarks and Geographical Indications for Agricultural Products and Foodstuffs* (DS174) serves as an illustrative example.

This dispute highlights key aspects of TRIPS, including trademarks and geographical indications (GIs), offering insight into how these IP rights are governed.

Background

In 2003, the United States initiated a dispute against the European Communities (EC), alleging that the EC's regulation for the protection of geographical indications (GIs) for agricultural products and foodstuffs violated its obligations under the TRIPS Agreement and the General Agreement on Tariffs and Trade (GATT) 1994.

The U.S. claimed that the EC's GI protection regime discriminated against non-EC products and inadequately protected pre-existing trademarks.

Key Issues

1. **National Treatment Principle:** The U.S. argued that the EC's GI regulation breached the national treatment obligation under Article 3 of TRIPS and Article III of GATT 1994 by affording less favorable treatment to non-EC products and producers.

2. **Coexistence of GIs and Trademarks:** A central contention was whether a GI could be registered and protected in the EC even if it conflicted with a pre-existing trademark. The U.S. asserted that the

EC's regime failed to adequately safeguard prior trademark rights, as mandated by TRIPS Article 16.1.

3. **Procedural Fairness**: The U.S. also criticized the transparency and fairness of the EC's GI registration procedures, arguing it did not provide adequate opportunities for objections from interested parties outside the EC, contrary to TRIPS Article 41.2.

Panel Findings

In 2005, the WTO Panel issued its report addressing the key issues:

- **National Treatment**: The Panel found the EC's GI regulation inconsistent with the national treatment obligation, as it imposed additional requirements on non-EC GIs that were not applied to EC GIs, resulting in less favorable treatment for foreign products.

- **Coexistence of GIs and Trademarks**: The Panel concluded that the EC's regime insufficiently protected pre-existing trademark rights. By allowing the registration of GIs that could conflict with existing trademarks without adequate safeguards against consumer confusion, the EC violated TRIPS Article 16.1.

- **Procedural Fairness**: The Panel determined that the EC's GI registration procedures lacked transparency and failed to provide equal opportunities for objections from non-EC countries, breaching TRIPS Article 41.2.

Outcome

In response to the Panel's findings, the EC amended its GI protection regime to address the identified inconsistencies with the TRIPS Agreement.

This case highlights the delicate balance required in protecting geographical indications while safeguarding trademark rights and the importance of fair and transparent IP procedures.

Key Takeaways

1. **National Treatment and Non-Discrimination**: WTO members must ensure their IP protection systems do not discriminate against foreign products or producers, adhering to the national treatment principle enshrined in TRIPS and GATT 1994.

2. **Balancing GIs and Trademarks**: Regulating the coexistence of geographical indications and trademarks is essential to protecting the rights of trademark holders while recognizing the value of GIs. Measures must prevent consumer confusion and maintain the integrity of both forms of IP.

3. **Transparent and Fair Procedures:** IP registration processes must be transparent and allow participation and objections from all interested parties, regardless of their country of origin, to ensure fairness and compliance with TRIPS obligations.

This case is a good example of how TRIPS addresses diverse aspects of intellectual property and the complexities of harmonizing IP rights in the context of international trade.

Enforcement of IP Rights

TRIPS establishes detailed provisions on enforcement to ensure compliance:

- **Civil and Administrative Procedures:** Members must provide judicial remedies, including injunctions and damages.

- **Border Measures**: Allows customs authorities to suspend the release of infringing goods.

- **Criminal Procedures:** Requires criminal penalties for willful trademark counterfeiting or copyright piracy.

Case Example: *China—Intellectual Property Rights* (WT/DS362): The United States challenged China's enforcement of IP laws, arguing insufficient measures to prevent piracy and counterfeiting. The WTO found that while China's enforcement met minimum TRIPS standards, certain practices required improvement.

TRIPS and Public Policy

TRIPS provides flexibility for members to address public policy objectives:

- **Compulsory Licensing (Article 31):**
    - Permits governments to authorize the use of patents without the patent holder's consent under specific conditions, such as national emergencies.

- o **Example:** During the HIV/AIDS crisis, countries like South Africa and India used compulsory licensing to access affordable generic drugs.

- **Transition Periods:**
  - o Developing and least-developed countries were granted extended timelines to implement TRIPS provisions.
  - o **Illustration:** The pharmaceutical sector in least-developed countries benefited significantly from delayed implementation, allowing continued access to generic medicines.

- **Doha Declaration (2001):**
  - o Affirmed that TRIPS should not prevent members from taking measures to protect public health, particularly in accessing essential medicines.

Dispute Resolution Under TRIPS

As part of the WTO framework, TRIPS disputes are subject to the Dispute Settlement Understanding (DSU). Notable cases include:

1. **India—Patents (WT/DS50):** The United States challenged India's failure to establish a "mailbox" system for patent applications during its transition period. The WTO panel ruled against India, emphasizing the need to implement TRIPS obligations within the stipulated timelines.

2. **Australia—Plain Packaging (WT/DS435/441):** Tobacco companies challenged Australia's plain packaging laws as a violation of trademark rights under TRIPS. The WTO upheld Australia's measures, affirming the public health exception.

3. **US—Section 211 Appropriations Act (WT/DS176):** The WTO ruled that a U.S. law restricting trademark rights related to Cuban entities was inconsistent with TRIPS, emphasizing the need to respect international trademark protections.

Author's Commentary on TRIPS

The TRIPS Agreement is both a milestone and a millstone in global trade governance. It introduced intellectual property (IP) into the multilateral trading system, covering copyright and related rights, trademarks, geographical indications, industrial designs, patents, layout-designs of integrated circuits, protection of undisclosed information, and the control of anti-competitive practices in contractual licenses. Yet, for all its ambition, TRIPS is fundamentally flawed in its execution and impact.

Compromise That Favors the Powerful

TRIPS was conceived as a compromise between competing national interests, but in practice, it has overwhelmingly served the priorities of developed nations with entrenched IP industries. The agreement imposes minimal obligations, offering flexibility to WTO members, but this flexibility largely benefits those with the legal, financial, and technological infrastructure to exploit it.

Critically, TRIPS is woefully outdated. Since its introduction in 1995, global intellectual property landscapes have undergone seismic shifts, particularly with the rise of artificial intelligence, digital trade, and biotechnology.

The agreement remains stuck in the past, unable to regulate or address these emerging complexities. Calls for modernization through bilateral or regional Free Trade Agreements (FTAs) are now gaining traction, as TRIPS alone appears incapable of evolving at the pace of innovation.

Structural Disparities: The Case Against TRIPS

The most persistent and glaring flaw of TRIPS is its structural bias towards wealthy nations. This bias is evident in several key areas:

- **A System Rigged for the Rich**: Developed countries, home to pharmaceutical giants, media conglomerates, and tech monopolies, extract disproportionate benefits while leaving developing nations struggling with compliance.

- **Implementation as an Economic Burden**: Many developing nations lack the legal expertise, resources, and institutional capacity to implement TRIPS effectively. Instead of fostering economic progress, TRIPS often acts as a regulatory burden that exacerbates economic inequalities.

- **The Public Health Crisis**: Nowhere is the failure of TRIPS more pronounced than in its handling of essential medicines. The rigid patent protections on life-saving drugs place profits over human lives, restricting access in poorer nations and fueling global health inequalities.

Challenges and Systemic Failures

- **Global IP Apartheid:** TRIPS enforces a system where intellectual property rights serve as a tool of economic dominance rather than innovation-sharing.

- **Weak Dispute Resolution:** The WTO's consensus-based dispute system is slow, highly politicized, and often ineffective in delivering meaningful enforcement.

- **Excessive Ambiguity:** While the agreement's flexibility could have been an advantage, it has instead created loopholes for powerful nations to exploit, rendering many of its supposed protections meaningless.

The Case for Overhaul, Not Just Reform

The WTO claims TRIPS is a comprehensive and effective framework, yet the reality is that it is a relic in dire need of reconstruction. The following reforms should be prioritized:

1. **Modernization of IP Laws**: TRIPS must be expanded to regulate AI-generated content, digital intellectual property, and cross-border data protection.

2. **Public Health Over Patents**: The agreement must introduce binding exceptions that prioritize public health over corporate monopolies, allowing for broader access to essential medicines.

3. **Equitable Enforcement Mechanisms**: TRIPS dispute resolution must be restructured to prevent developed nations from wielding disproportionate influence.

4. **Decentralization Through FTAs**: Encouraging regional and bilateral agreements that set higher, more equitable IP standards beyond TRIPS' limited scope.

5. **Developing Country Protections**: Meaningful assistance, including financial and technological aid, to help developing nations implement and benefit from IP protections rather than suffer under them.

Conclusion: A System at a Crossroads

TRIPS was a significant achievement in 1995, but in 2025 and beyond, it risks becoming an outdated obstacle rather than a trade facilitator.

Its failure to address modern technological advancements, entrenched global inequalities, and humanitarian concerns is glaring. Without drastic and immediate reform, TRIPS will continue to entrench a world where intellectual property serves as a tool of corporate imperialism rather than a mechanism for global progress.

The world cannot afford to let TRIPS stagnate. Its next iteration must be bold, just, and tailored to the needs of a rapidly evolving digital and economic landscape. The time for piecemeal reform is over—the time for radical reinvention has arrived.

Chapter 39

Special Requirements Related to Border Measures Under the TRIPS Agreement

1. Introduction

The Agreement on Trade-Related Aspects of Intellectual Property Rights (TRIPS) was discussed in the previous chapter. This chapter focuses on Section 4 of the TRIPS Agreement, which deals with "Special Requirements Related to Border Measures."

This aspect of TRIPS is enshrined in many WTO members' domestic legislation and was crafted to enable intellectual property rights holders to prevent the importation of counterfeit and pirated goods.

While this provision is well-intentioned and remains relevant in principle, practical enforcement—especially in developing economies—has proven challenging due to limited resources and evolving customs procedures. This chapter examines the merits of these provisions, their implementation difficulties, and their applicability in the modern trade environment.

2. Key Provisions and Objectives

The border measures outlined in Articles 51 to 60 of the TRIPS Agreement focus on granting customs authorities the ability to suspend or delay the release of suspected infringing goods, provide due process for importers, and offer remedies for IP right holders. The primary objectives of these provisions are:

- Enabling right holders to apply for the suspension or delay of counterfeit and pirated goods at the border (Article 51);

- Requiring right holders to provide adequate evidence of IP infringement (Article 52);
- Establishing safeguards such as security deposits to prevent abuse of the system (Article 53);
- Ensuring prompt notification and due process for both the right holder and the importer (Articles 54 and 55);
- Providing indemnification for importers in cases of wrongful detention (Article 56);
- Allowing both right holders and importers to inspect detained goods (Article 57);
- Empowering customs authorities to act ex officio in appropriate cases (Article 58);
- Prescribing remedies, including the destruction of infringing goods (Article 59);
- Exempting de minimis imports (Article 60).

To fully comprehend the application of these measures, it is crucial to define the key terms as outlined in the Agreement:

- **Counterfeit Trademark Goods**: Goods, including packaging, that bear without authorization a trademark identical to a validly registered trademark or one that is indistinguishable in its essential aspects. These goods infringe the trademark owner's rights under the laws of the country of importation. For example, fake designer handbags bearing the logo of a luxury brand without authorization fall under this category.

- **Pirated Copyright Goods**: Copies made without the consent of the right holder or authorized entity in the country of production. These copies are made directly or indirectly from an original work where reproduction would have constituted a copyright infringement under the laws of the country of importation. A common example is unauthorized movie DVDs or software replicating protected content without the creator's approval.

SPECIAL REQUIREMENTS RELATED TO BORDER MEASURES UNDER TRIPS

3. Strengths of the Provisions

The TRIPS border measures regime was a significant step forward in international IP protection when first introduced in 1994. It established a standardized framework for customs enforcement, reinforcing the importance of preventing counterfeit and pirated goods from entering markets. Several aspects of this framework remain praiseworthy:

- **Uniform Enforcement Mechanism**: The TRIPS provisions harmonized border enforcement across WTO members, creating a structured system to prevent the circulation of infringing goods.

- **Customs Authority Empowerment**: Granting customs officials the ability to suspend infringing goods ex officio (Article 58) reduces the burden on right holders to detect and report violations.

- **Legal Safeguards**: Provisions such as Article 53 (security requirements) and Article 56 (indemnification for importers) introduce checks and balances that prevent abuse of the system and protect legitimate businesses from undue harm.

- **Focus on Deterrence**: The possibility of destruction of counterfeit goods under Article 59 discourages large-scale counterfeiting operations.

4. Challenges and Limitations

Despite these strengths, the implementation of TRIPS border measures has faced significant obstacles, particularly in developing economies where customs resources are strained:

- **Resource Constraints**: Customs authorities in many countries, particularly developing nations, lack the financial and personnel resources to effectively monitor and intercept infringing goods. The process of identifying counterfeit or pirated goods requires specialized training, which is not always available.

- **Evolving Trade Practices**: The digital economy and changes in trade practices, including increased e-commerce and small-package shipments, have made it more difficult for customs agencies to apply traditional TRIPS border enforcement measures effectively.

- **Aging Legal Framework**: The provisions were drafted in a pre-digital era when physical goods were the primary medium of intellectual property infringement. Today, digital piracy, 3D printing, and decentralized manufacturing present new challenges that the existing framework does not adequately address.

- **Reduction of Investigation Offices**: Many jurisdictions have experienced a decline in specialized customs investigation units due to budgetary constraints, making it even more difficult to enforce these provisions.

5. The Need for Modernization

Given the changing landscape of IP infringement, the TRIPS border measures framework requires updates to align with contemporary realities. Potential improvements include:

- **Increased Funding and Training**: Developing nations need targeted assistance from international organizations to build the capacity of customs authorities in detecting and handling IP violations.

- **Adaptation to E-Commerce**: The growth of online marketplaces necessitates new measures tailored to small parcel shipments and digital IP enforcement.

- **Enhanced Public-Private Collaboration**: Strengthening partnerships between right holders and customs agencies could facilitate more effective enforcement through shared intelligence and technological advancements.

- **Utilization of AI and Digital Tracking**: Artificial intelligence and blockchain technology could be leveraged to improve the detection and tracking of counterfeit goods across borders.

Author's Commentary: Reimagining TRIPS Border Measures for the 21st Century

The TRIPS border measures provisions were groundbreaking at their inception, providing an internationally harmonized approach to intellectual property (IP) enforcement at customs. However, the economic, technological, and trade landscapes have evolved dramatically since 1994, necessitating a rethinking of

SPECIAL REQUIREMENTS RELATED TO BORDER MEASURES UNDER TRIPS

how border measures operate in a way that both preserves their effectiveness and modernizes their enforcement mechanisms.

The current framework faces structural inefficiencies that weaken its ability to curb counterfeiting and piracy, particularly in the context of digital commerce and decentralized manufacturing. Moreover, the one-size-fits-all approach under TRIPS does not account for the diverse economic realities of WTO members, many of whom lack the necessary infrastructure to implement these provisions effectively. Reform must be holistic—addressing enforcement gaps, leveraging emerging technologies, and ensuring that the system remains fair for all stakeholders, including businesses, right holders, consumers, and governments.

1. Beyond Traditional Borders: The Need for Digital Enforcement Mechanisms

The primary weakness of TRIPS border measures today is their failure to address non-traditional trade flows such as digital piracy, small parcel shipments through e-commerce, and illicit trade in 3D-printed counterfeit goods. The rise of decentralized manufacturing, on-demand production, and global supply chain fragmentation means that counterfeit goods may never pass through traditional customs inspections in bulk form.

Proposed Innovation:

- **International E-Commerce IP Enforcement Protocol**: TRIPS should be expanded to include obligations for digital marketplaces, requiring them to implement AI-driven content recognition, seller verification, and automated takedown systems for counterfeit goods.

- **Cross-Border Digital Tracking Systems**: Customs authorities should collaborate with tech firms to develop a blockchain-based tracking system for IP-protected goods, allowing real-time verification of authenticity and origin.

- **3D Printing Safeguards**: The TRIPS framework should explore the feasibility of digital watermarking or licensing frameworks for 3D design files, preventing the illicit production of counterfeit goods outside of traditional supply chains.

2. Rethinking Enforcement: The Role of AI and Smart Customs Technology

Customs agencies are often overburdened with high trade volumes, limited staff, and insufficient resources. Traditional physical inspections are impractical given the scale of global trade today. Instead of solely relying on manual detection, AI-driven customs screening should be the future.

Proposed Innovation:

- **AI-Powered Customs Inspections**: Governments should invest in AI models trained to recognize counterfeit goods using automated image recognition and machine learning algorithms, reducing reliance on manual detection.

- **AI-Supported Risk Profiling**: Customs databases should integrate big data analytics to assess shipment risk based on patterns of fraudulent activity, allowing high-risk shipments to be flagged for further inspection.

- **Remote Verification Systems for Customs Officials**: Mobile apps and smart databases could be deployed to allow field agents to instantly verify the authenticity of goods by cross-referencing with manufacturer records.

3. Trade Fairness: Addressing the Needs of Developing Nations Without Weakening IP Enforcement

Developing countries often struggle to implement TRIPS border measures due to inadequate customs infrastructure, limited funding, and competing economic priorities. However, reform should not simply relax enforcement obligations—doing so would risk making these nations hubs for illicit trade, undermining both their own legitimate industries and global IP protections. Instead, a tiered compliance model should be considered.

Proposed Innovation:

- **Tiered TRIPS Compliance Model**: A three-tier system could be established, distinguishing between:
    - High-capacity enforcement countries (with full AI-integrated customs systems).

SPECIAL REQUIREMENTS RELATED TO BORDER MEASURES UNDER TRIPS

- o Medium-capacity countries (receiving AI-assisted training and digital verification tools).
- o Low-capacity countries (offered alternative means such as digital tracking and cooperative agreements).

- **IP Enforcement Subsidies & Public-Private Partnerships**: International organizations such as the WTO, WIPO, and private sector IP holders should jointly fund customs modernization projects in low-resource nations.

- **Shared Regional Customs Networks**: Neighboring developing countries could form regional customs alliances, pooling resources to strengthen enforcement without overburdening individual economies.

4. Revisiting De Minimis Exemptions and Small Parcel Trade

Article 60 of TRIPS exempts de minimis imports (small personal shipments) from enforcement, a provision that made sense when trade was dominated by bulk shipments. However, the modern reality is that counterfeiters exploit this loophole through e-commerce, sending thousands of small parcels instead of single large shipments to evade detection. Reform is urgently needed.

Proposed Innovation:

- **De Minimis Threshold Recalibration**: Countries should be given flexibility to lower their de minimis thresholds for IP-infringing goods, preventing large-scale abuse of small parcel shipments.

- **Automated E-Commerce Vendor Identification**: Online marketplaces should be required to submit vendor data to customs authorities, allowing authorities to track suspicious sellers engaging in systematic counterfeit sales.

- **Pre-Screening for High-Risk Packages**: Logistics companies should partner with governments to use AI-driven risk analysis on small parcels before they reach customs, reducing workload and improving efficiency.

5. Strengthening International Coordination and Cross-Border Intelligence Sharing

Illicit trade networks are highly adaptive, shifting their operations to jurisdictions with weak enforcement. A fragmented enforcement system across borders makes TRIPS less effective. To counteract this, customs agencies should establish real-time cross-border intelligence-sharing agreements beyond the current sporadic cooperation models.

Proposed Innovation:

- **Global Customs Data Exchange on Counterfeits**: Establish an AI-powered international IP enforcement database where countries share real-time data on counterfeit shipment trends, repeat offenders, and high-risk transit points.

- **Trade & IP Enforcement Diplomacy Units**: Countries should designate special IP enforcement attaches who work within regional trade blocs (e.g. ASEAN, MERCOSUR, AfCFTA) to coordinate regional crackdowns on counterfeit networks.

- **Global IP Crime Task Force**: Expanding beyond customs, TRIPS reform should explore the creation of an Interpol-led special enforcement unit targeting global counterfeit operations.

Conclusion: Future-Proofing TRIPS Border Measures

The TRIPS Agreement's border measures remain vital to preserving the integrity of global trade and protecting intellectual property, but they must evolve beyond their 1994 framework.

A modernized TRIPS enforcement model should emphasize:

- AI and automation for customs enforcement to improve efficiency.

- Better integration with digital and e-commerce trade realities to prevent loopholes.

- Support for developing countries through smart, scalable compliance models that don't compromise enforcement integrity.

- Stronger international intelligence-sharing mechanisms to prevent counterfeiters from exploiting weak jurisdictions.

SPECIAL REQUIREMENTS RELATED TO BORDER MEASURES UNDER TRIPS

The future of IP enforcement is no longer just about what happens at physical borders—it is about digital tracking, AI-assisted screening, and transnational cooperation. TRIPS must be reimagined not as a static framework but as a living, adaptable system that can respond dynamically to emerging trade threats. Only then can it continue to serve as the cornerstone of global IP protection in a rapidly evolving marketplace.

Chapter 40

The Agreement on Trade-Related Investment Measures (TRIMs)

The TRIMs Agreement is an integral part of the World Trade Organization (WTO) framework, addressing the relationship between trade and investment policies. It ensures that investment measures do not distort trade or contravene the principles of the General Agreement on Tariffs and Trade (GATT). This chapter explores the scope, obligations, and implications of the TRIMs Agreement, supported by WTO commentary, case law, and insights.

Objectives of the TRIMs Agreement

The TRIMs Agreement aims to:

1. **Eliminate Trade Distortions**

   - The agreement ensures that trade-related investment measures do not create barriers to international trade or distort competitive conditions between imported and domestically produced goods.
   - By prohibiting measures such as local content requirements, it fosters a level playing field for international businesses.

2. **Promote Transparency**

   - It requires member states to notify the WTO of any measures inconsistent with the agreement, providing clarity and predictability for traders and investors.
   - Transparency ensures accountability and reduces the risk of disputes arising from unclear or opaque investment policies.

3. **Support Non-Discrimination**

- The TRIMs Agreement reinforces the principles of most-favored-nation (MFN) and national treatment under GATT, ensuring that foreign investors and their products are not treated less favorably than their domestic counterparts.

Illustrative Case: *Indonesia – Certain Measures Affecting the Automobile Industry (DS59)*

To better illustrate the application of TRIMs, it is useful to refer to a pertinent example. This case highlights the complexities of implementing investment measures that may conflict with WTO obligations.

Background

In 1996, the United States requested consultations with Indonesia concerning its National Car Program, which provided tax and tariff benefits to encourage the development of a domestic automobile industry. The program offered incentives to companies that met specific local content requirements, favoring the use of Indonesian-made components.

The United States contended that these measures violated Indonesia's obligations under GATT 1994, the TRIMs Agreement, and the Agreement on Subsidies and Countervailing Measures (SCM Agreement).

Key Issues

1. **Local Content Requirements:** Indonesia's program mandated that a certain percentage of components in domestically produced automobiles be sourced locally to qualify for tax and tariff incentives. The United States argued that this requirement was inconsistent with Article 2 of the TRIMs Agreement, which prohibits investment measures that violate Article III (National Treatment) of GATT 1994.

2. **Trade-Related Investment Measures:** The dispute centered on whether Indonesia's measures constituted trade-related investment measures inconsistent with the TRIMs Agreement, particularly those requiring the purchase or use of domestic products by an enterprise.

3. **Subsidies and Countervailing Measures:** The United States also contended that the incentives provided under Indonesia's program constituted prohibited subsidies under the SCM Agreement, as they were contingent upon the use of domestic over imported goods.

THE AGREEMENT ON TRADE-RELATED INVESTMENT MEASURES (TRIMS)

Panel Findings

The WTO Panel found that Indonesia's local content requirements were inconsistent with Article 2.1 of the TRIMs Agreement, as they violated Article III:4 of GATT 1994 by affording less favorable treatment to imported products. The Panel also concluded that the measures constituted import substitution subsidies prohibited under Article 3.1(b) of the SCM Agreement.

Outcome

Following the Panel's report adoption in 1998, Indonesia agreed to bring its measures into conformity with its WTO obligations. This case highlights the importance of adhering to the TRIMs Agreement's provisions, particularly regarding local content requirements and their impact on trade and investment.

Scope of the TRIMs Agreement

The TRIMs Agreement applies to trade-related investment measures that affect trade in goods. It does not address investment policies broadly or measures affecting trade in services, which are covered under the General Agreement on Trade in Services (GATS).

Key Provisions:

1. **Prohibition of Trade-Restrictive Measures**

    - The agreement prohibits investment measures that are inconsistent with GATT Articles III (National Treatment) and XI (Elimination of Quantitative Restrictions).
    - Examples include measures that favor domestic over imported goods or impose restrictions on the volume of imports.

2. **Illustrative List of Prohibited Measures**

    An annex to the TRIMs Agreement provides specific examples of measures that violate WTO rules:
    - **Local Content Requirements:** Mandating the use of domestically produced goods over imports as a condition for investment.
    - **Trade Balancing Requirements:** Requiring firms to limit their imports to a certain proportion of their exports.

- **Foreign Exchange Restrictions**: Imposing constraints on foreign exchange availability tied to trade performance.

Author's Commentary: The Need for Reform

The TRIMs Agreement, while instrumental in curbing trade distortions, has increasingly shown its limitations. Global economic transformations necessitate a re-evaluation of its scope and applicability. Several key areas require urgent reform:

1. **Broadening the Scope**: The exclusion of investment measures affecting services limits the Agreement's effectiveness. Given the increasing importance of digital trade, cross-border data flows, and intellectual property protections, expanding the Agreement's provisions is crucial.

2. **Enhancing Flexibility for Governments:** Governments must have the ability to pursue industrial policies that foster strategic growth without violating WTO principles. The current rigidity of TRIMs impedes the ability to respond to economic exigencies such as the promotion of emerging industries or sustainability initiatives.

3. **Addressing Compliance Gaps:** Developing countries struggle with compliance due to economic constraints. The Agreement should offer more tailored transitional arrangements, including capacity-building initiatives to assist nations in implementing fair trade policies while achieving developmental objectives.

4. **Periodic Review and Update Mechanism:** Global trade evolves rapidly, and static agreements become obsolete. The TRIMs Agreement (now 30 years since commencement) should include provisions for periodic review and amendment to reflect emerging trade challenges and investment trends.

The WTO TRIMs Agreement has played a crucial role in maintaining fair competition and preventing trade distortions. However, its limitations hinder its effectiveness in addressing the complexities of contemporary global economies.

Reforming the Agreement is not an abandonment of its foundational principles but an acknowledgment of the need for adaptability. Expanding its scope, introducing greater flexibility, and improving compliance mechanisms would ensure that it remains relevant in the evolving landscape of international trade and investment.

Part 9
Sector-Specific WTO Agreements

Chapter 41

The Agreement on Agriculture (AoA)

The Agreement on Agriculture (AoA) is a foundational component of the World Trade Organization (WTO) framework, governing the international trade of agricultural products.

It was conceived to introduce greater market discipline, promote fair competition, and establish a level playing field for agricultural trade.

Concluded during the Uruguay Round (1986-1994), the AoA marked a significant step in integrating agriculture into the multilateral trading system, an area that had previously been largely insulated from trade liberalization efforts under the General Agreement on Tariffs and Trade (GATT) 1947.

While the AoA has been instrumental in reducing protectionist barriers, it remains one of the most contentious trade agreements due to ongoing debates about equity, development concerns, and the strategic importance of agricultural self-sufficiency.

This chapter examines the content, objectives, and scope of the AoA, highlights key dispute cases, and offers a critical commentary on its effectiveness and future trajectory.

Overview and Objectives of the AoA

Historically (and up to 1995), agriculture was largely excluded from global trade liberalization efforts due to its political sensitivity and the strategic need for food security.

Many nations, particularly developed countries, maintained high tariffs, quotas, and extensive subsidy programs to protect their domestic agricultural sectors. The AoA was designed to rectify these distortions by introducing rules governing agricultural policies, with core objectives to:

- **Promote Market Access:** Reduce trade barriers, increase transparency, and facilitate access to agricultural markets.

- **Curtail Domestic Support:** Impose limitations on subsidies that distort trade.

- **Eliminate Export Subsidies:** Prohibit or reduce subsidies that give unfair advantages in global markets.

- **Encourage Development:** Provide special provisions for developing and least-developed countries to support food security and rural development.

The AoA's preamble underscores the long-term goal of establishing a fair and market-oriented agricultural trading system, balancing trade liberalization with concerns for food security and rural livelihoods.

Structure of the AoA

The AoA is built upon three key pillars, each addressing different aspects of agricultural trade policy:

1. Market Access (Article 4)

One of the primary goals of the AoA was to replace non-tariff barriers, such as import quotas and restrictive licensing schemes, with tariffs (a process known as "tariffication") and subsequently reduce those tariffs over time. This was aimed at ensuring greater transparency and predictability in agricultural trade.

- **Case Example:** *United States—Restrictions on Imports of Sugar (WT/DS77)*: Argentina challenged U.S. restrictions on sugar imports, arguing that they violated the AoA's market access commitments. The WTO panel ruled against the U.S., reinforcing the principle that protectionist policies in agricultural trade must comply with agreed tariff reduction schedules.

While tariffication improved transparency, many developed nations employed complex tariff rate quotas (TRQs) and sanitary and phytosanitary (SPS) measures to continue restricting imports, leading to concerns over the true effectiveness of these reforms.

THE AGREEMENT ON AGRICULTURE (AOA)

2. Domestic Support (Article 6)

The AoA classifies agricultural subsidies into three categories or "boxes," based on their potential trade-distorting effects:

- **Amber Box:** Trade-distorting subsidies subject to reduction commitments.

- **Blue Box:** Subsidies tied to production-limiting programs, exempt from reduction commitments.

- **Green Box:** Non-trade-distorting subsidies, such as environmental and rural development programs, permitted without limits.

- **Case Example:** *Canada—Dairy (WT/DS103):* The United States successfully challenged Canada's domestic support for its dairy industry, arguing that the subsidies exceeded amber box commitments. The ruling highlighted the challenge of distinguishing between permissible and impermissible domestic support.

A major criticism of the domestic support framework is that developed countries continue to exploit legal loopholes to maintain high levels of subsidies, often shifting them into the green box to avoid reduction commitments.

For example, the United States and the European Union have provided substantial subsidies under environmental and conservation programs, which indirectly benefit domestic producers while technically complying with WTO rules.

3. Export Subsidies (Article 9)

Export subsidies, which artificially lower the price of agricultural goods in international markets, have long been a contentious issue. The AoA sought to reduce and eventually eliminate these subsidies to ensure fairer competition.

- **Case Example:** *European Communities—Export Subsidies on Sugar (WT/DS265):* Brazil, Thailand, and Australia successfully challenged the EU's sugar export subsidies, leading to a landmark ruling that required the EU to modify its policies. The case exemplified the systemic problem of developed nations subsidizing their agricultural exports at the expense of global market competition.

Despite reductions, certain forms of indirect export assistance, such as export credit guarantees and state trading enterprises, remain significant challenges. Many developing nations argue that export competition remains skewed in favor of wealthier economies, where governments provide extensive support to agribusiness exporters.

4. **Special and Differential Treatment (Articles 6 and 12)**

Recognizing the unique vulnerabilities of developing countries, the AoA includes provisions for special and differential treatment (SDT), allowing:

- Longer implementation periods for trade liberalization commitments.
- Greater flexibility in reducing tariffs and subsidies.
- Special provisions for food security and rural development.
- **Illustrative Example**: India's public stockholding programs for food security have been a subject of WTO scrutiny but remain permissible under special provisions for developing nations, as reaffirmed in the Bali Ministerial Declaration (2013). However, developed countries have criticized such programs for distorting global grain markets.

Challenges and Criticisms

While the AoA has facilitated significant reforms, it remains highly controversial, particularly in the following areas:

- **Persistent Loopholes:** Developed nations continue to provide substantial agricultural support by shifting subsidies into WTO-compliant categories.
- **Imbalances in Trade Benefits**: Developing nations contend that the agreement disproportionately favors wealthier economies, particularly regarding market access and export competition.
- **Enforcement and Compliance Issues**: Dispute cases, such as those involving U.S. cotton subsidies and EU sugar export policies, illustrate the difficulties in ensuring compliance and effective enforcement.
- **Food Security Concerns**: Critics argue that liberalization may compromise national food security by making developing nations overly reliant on volatile global markets.

The Future of Agricultural Trade

As global trade dynamics evolve, the AoA's framework requires adjustments to address emerging concerns:

- **Reforming Domestic Support Rules:** Stricter disciplines are needed to prevent developed countries from exploiting green box subsidies.

- **Enhancing SDT for Developing Nations**: Improved mechanisms are required to ensure that trade liberalization does not undermine food security and rural livelihoods.

- **Aligning Trade Rules with Environmental and Sustainability Goals**: The growing impact of climate change and environmental sustainability necessitates integrating new considerations into agricultural trade policy.

Author's Commentary: Rethinking Agricultural Trade in a New Global Era

When the AoA was introduced, it was heralded as a transformative step toward a fair and market-oriented agricultural trading system. However, more than three decades later, its core principles remain riddled with contradictions and inefficiencies.

The AoA was designed to reduce trade distortions, yet its framework has been repeatedly manipulated by powerful economies to maintain structural advantages. The fundamental question is no longer whether the agreement should be reformed, but rather whether it is capable of delivering true agricultural trade fairness in its current form.

One of the AoA's most glaring weaknesses is its failure to anticipate the long-term consequences of subsidy reclassification. The system of amber, blue, and green box subsidies has created an illusion of discipline while allowing developed nations to legally repackage their protectionist policies.

The United States, for instance, has transitioned billions of dollars in agricultural support into "environmental" programs that disproportionately benefit its own producers while technically remaining WTO-compliant.

A bold reform would involve redefining green box subsidies to ensure they do not create indirect market advantages—perhaps introducing a "climate impact index" that measures whether subsidies genuinely serve environmental purposes or are merely disguised protectionist tools.

Another major oversight of the AoA is its inability to reconcile trade liberalization with food security. While developing nations were granted Special and Differential Treatment (SDT) provisions, these have largely been inadequate in safeguarding their agricultural sovereignty. The increasing volatility of global food markets—exacerbated by climate change, geopolitical instability, and supply chain disruptions—suggests that agricultural trade rules must incorporate a food security safeguard mechanism.

This could take the form of an emergency trade adjustment clause that allows nations to temporarily adjust tariff commitments or provide direct market intervention when global supply shocks threaten national food stability. Without such protections, developing economies risk becoming overly dependent on an unpredictable global market that operates in the interests of the most powerful agricultural exporters.

A particularly underexplored avenue for reform lies in incorporating sustainability and climate-resilient agriculture into the AoA framework. Current trade rules were drafted in an era when climate considerations were secondary to economic liberalization. In the 21st century, however, the environmental footprint of agricultural trade cannot be ignored.

A modernized AoA should introduce carbon-adjusted tariffs on agricultural exports, ensuring that nations benefiting from large-scale subsidized agribusiness must also account for the environmental costs of their production. This would create a more balanced playing field by incentivizing sustainable agricultural practices rather than rewarding volume-driven production backed by government subsidies.

Ultimately, the AoA's survival depends on its ability to evolve beyond its original limitations. Instead of merely tweaking existing provisions, a radical reconsideration of how agricultural trade is governed is needed—one that places food security, environmental responsibility, and true market equity at the heart of global trade rules.

Without such reforms, the AoA risks becoming a relic of an outdated trade system, protecting the interests of agricultural superpowers while failing the developing nations it was intended to support.

Chapter 42

The Agreement on Sanitary and Phytosanitary Measures (SPS)

The Agreement on Sanitary and Phytosanitary Measures (SPS Agreement) is a critical component of the World Trade Organization (WTO) framework, designed to balance the facilitation of international trade with the protection of human, animal, and plant health.

Adopted during the Uruguay Round (1986-1994), the SPS Agreement seeks to establish clear rules for the application of food safety and animal and plant health regulations, ensuring that such measures are scientifically justified and not disguised trade barriers.

What Does "Sanitary and Phytosanitary" Mean?

- **Sanitary Measures**: Measures related to the protection of human and animal health from risks arising from diseases, pests, or contaminants.

- **Phytosanitary Measures**: Measures to protect plant health from pests, diseases, or other harmful organisms.

These measures encompass quarantine restrictions, inspection protocols, and food safety standards, ensuring the safe import and export of agricultural and food products.

Case Study: The New Zealand Apples Case: A landmark WTO dispute illustrating the SPS Agreement's enforcement is the *New Zealand Apples Case*. This case demonstrated the tension between legitimate biosecurity concerns and the misuse of SPS measures as protectionist tools.

The Dispute: Background and Context

For over 80 years, Australia imposed restrictions on the importation of New Zealand apples, citing concerns about the bacterial disease fire blight and other plant health risks.

These restrictions effectively constituted a trade ban, which New Zealand challenged at the WTO in 2007, arguing that Australia's measures lacked scientific justification and violated the SPS Agreement.

New Zealand contended that modern scientific evidence and robust phytosanitary controls mitigated the risk of fire blight introduction. Australia maintained that its stringent biosecurity measures were necessary to protect its domestic apple and pear industries.

Trade Barriers Created by Australia's Measures

Australia imposed 16 specific conditions on New Zealand apple imports, including:

1. **Complete Restriction on Fire Blight-Exposed Fruit**: Only apples from orchards free of fire-blight bacteria were eligible for export.

2. **Extensive Orchard Inspections**: Mandatory inspections were required to certify orchards as fire-blight-free.

3. **Surface Sterilization of Apples**: Chemical treatments were mandated to eliminate contamination.

4. **Packing and Quarantine Protocols**: Strict packaging and post-entry quarantine requirements were imposed.

5. **Prohibitive Treatment Costs**: High compliance costs rendered exports economically unviable.

6. **Seasonal Restrictions**: Certain periods prohibited imports altogether.

WTO Findings and the SPS Agreement

New Zealand's case was based on five key provisions of the SPS Agreement:

1. **Scientific Basis (Article 2.2)**: SPS measures must be based on scientific principles and evidence. The WTO Panel found that Australia's fire blight concerns lacked scientific justification.

2. **Risk Assessment (Article 5.1)**: Members must assess risk based on objective evidence. Australia's risk assessment was found to be overly conservative and speculative.
3. **Least Trade-Restrictive Measures (Article 5.6)**: Measures must not be more trade-restrictive than necessary. Australia could achieve its biosecurity goals through less restrictive alternatives.
4. **Consistency (Article 5.5)**: SPS measures should not create arbitrary distinctions. Australia's leniency toward other trading partners with similar risks demonstrated inconsistency.
5. **Transparency (Annex B)**: Members must notify SPS measures and provide justification. Australia's lack of transparency further weakened its case.

Outcome of the Case

In 2010, the WTO's Dispute Settlement Body ruled in favor of New Zealand. Australia's restrictions were found to violate the SPS Agreement due to a lack of scientific evidence and excessively restrictive measures. Australia was required to revise its import conditions to comply with WTO obligations, ultimately allowing New Zealand apples to enter under reasonable phytosanitary standards.

Significance of the Case

The New Zealand Apples Case reinforced several key principles of the SPS Agreement:

1. **Science-Based Justification**: SPS measures must be firmly rooted in scientific evidence to avoid misuse for protectionist purposes.
2. **Balancing Trade and Biosecurity**: Governments must balance national biosecurity concerns with fair trade principles.
3. **Transparency and Risk Assessment**: Objective risk assessments and clear justifications are required for SPS measures.
4. **Precedent for Future Disputes**: The case provides guidance for resolving future SPS-related trade conflicts.

Other Notable WTO SPS Disputes

1. ***EC—Measures Concerning Meat and Meat Products (Hormones) (WT/DS26):*** The WTO ruled against the EU's ban on hormone-treated beef due to insufficient scientific justification.

2. ***India—Agricultural Products (WT/DS430):*** India's blanket ban on U.S. poultry due to avian influenza concerns was found to be more trade-restrictive than necessary.

3. ***Japan—Apples (WT/DS245):*** The WTO found Japan's restrictions on U.S. apple imports to be excessive and lacking a scientific basis.

Commentary on the SPS Agreement and the Role of Artificial Intelligence

The SPS Agreement aims to balance trade liberalization with the need for stringent health and safety protections. However, challenges remain in ensuring that these measures are applied fairly and scientifically.

1. **The Potential for AI in SPS Risk Assessments**

   - AI can revolutionize risk assessments by analyzing vast amounts of data more efficiently than traditional methods.
   - Machine learning models can predict potential risks based on historical patterns, improving decision-making for SPS measures.

2. **Challenges of AI Implementation**

   - Algorithmic Bias – AI-driven risk assessments could reflect biases in data, disproportionately impacting certain exporters.
   - Transparency Issues – Governments may struggle to explain AI-driven decisions, raising concerns about due process in trade disputes.
   - Regulatory Disparities – AI models must align with WTO-sanctioned methodologies to ensure consistency and fairness.

3. **Ensuring Equitable AI Integration**

   - WTO members should collaborate on AI governance frameworks for SPS compliance.

- Developing countries need access to AI-based tools to prevent an imbalance in trade negotiations.

Challenges and Future Considerations

Despite its strengths, the SPS Agreement faces ongoing challenges:

- **Scientific Disputes:** Determining "sufficient scientific evidence" remains contentious, as seen in EC—Hormones.
- **Developing Country Constraints**: Many lack the resources to comply with complex SPS measures.
- **Risk of Protectionism**: While designed to prevent disguised trade barriers, SPS measures can still be misused.

Author's Commentary

The SPS Agreement is a cornerstone of the WTO framework, designed to balance fair trade practices with essential protections for public health and the environment. Given its role in regulating trade while safeguarding health standards, it should be recognized as a foundational agreement within the WTO.

Landmark cases such as *New Zealand Apples* and *EC—Hormones* demonstrate the SPS Agreement's effectiveness in preventing protectionist policies disguised as health measures.

The Evolving Role of AI in SPS Measures

Advancements in artificial intelligence (AI) and digital technologies present both opportunities and challenges for the SPS framework. One of the most pressing issues is the determination of "sufficient scientific evidence", a matter that has historically been contentious, as seen in EC—Hormones.

AI-driven risk assessment models have the potential to enhance objectivity in evaluating scientific claims, reducing ambiguity in dispute resolution and ensuring equitable, science-based trade regulations.

Bridging the Gap for Developing Nations

A persistent challenge in the implementation of the SPS Agreement is the inequality faced by developing countries in meeting stringent SPS standards.

Many lack the technical and financial resources to comply with complex regulations, placing them at a disadvantage in global trade.

International organizations such as the IMF and the World Bank should play a more active role in providing technological assistance and capacity-building initiatives to help these nations integrate into the global trading system more effectively.

The Importance of Harmonization in SPS Standards

There is strong merit in fostering the harmonization of SPS standards within international regulatory bodies. Consistency in regulations not only benefits developing nations but also streamlines trade for all stakeholders.

The success of harmonized tariff structures serves as a compelling precedent for similar efforts in SPS standardization, ensuring that producers and exporters face fewer regulatory hurdles when entering international markets.

Addressing the Misuse of SPS Measures

While the SPS Agreement was designed to prevent disguised trade barriers, certain countries continue to manipulate health and safety standards for protectionist purposes. The expanded use of AI and blockchain technologies in transparency and risk assessment could significantly curb these practices, ensuring that SPS measures serve their intended purpose rather than being exploited for economic gain.

Conclusion: The Future of the SPS Agreement

The SPS Agreement remains a vital component of the global trade system, ensuring that health and safety regulations do not become trade barriers. However, technological advancements and evolving trade dynamics necessitate ongoing adaptation.

By leveraging AI for scientific assessments, strengthening support for developing nations, promoting harmonization of standards, and enhancing transparency in SPS enforcement, the WTO can ensure that the SPS Agreement continues to fulfill its dual mandate of facilitating fair trade and protecting public health.

With the right reforms, the SPS Agreement can transition from being a defensive trade mechanism to a proactive tool that fosters global trust in the safety of international commerce.

Chapter 43

The Agreement on Technical Barriers to Trade (TBT)

The Agreement on Technical Barriers to Trade (TBT Agreement) is another crucial component of the World Trade Organization (WTO) framework. It ensures that technical regulations, standards, and conformity assessment procedures do not create unnecessary obstacles to international trade while allowing members to achieve legitimate policy objectives, such as protecting health, safety, and the environment.

This chapter explores the scope, application, and implications of the TBT Agreement, with reference to key cases and commentary.

Overview and Objectives of the TBT Agreement

The TBT Agreement applies to all technical regulations, standards, and conformity assessment procedures that may directly or indirectly affect international trade. It acknowledges the need for members to implement measures for legitimate objectives while ensuring they are non-discriminatory and not overly trade-restrictive. Key objectives include:

- **Promoting Transparency:** Ensuring technical measures are published and accessible to trading partners.

- **Preventing Discrimination**: Avoiding unjustifiable discrimination against imported products.

- **Encouraging Harmonization**: Aligning national measures with international standards where possible.

- **Fostering Trade Facilitation**: Ensuring technical measures do not create unnecessary barriers to trade.

Case Study: US-Tuna II (Mexico)

A landmark WTO dispute illustrating the TBT Agreement's operation is US-Tuna II (Mexico). This case highlights the challenge of balancing legitimate environmental concerns with fair trade practices.

The Dispute: Background and Context

The case revolved around U.S. dolphin-safe labeling requirements for tuna products, aimed at protecting dolphins from harmful fishing practices. Mexico, a major tuna exporter, challenged the measure, arguing that it unfairly discriminated against its tuna exports and violated the TBT Agreement.

The U.S. allowed the dolphin-safe label only if tuna was harvested without using purse-seine nets to encircle dolphins. Since this method was commonly used by Mexican fishers in the Eastern Tropical Pacific (ETP) region, they were effectively excluded from the U.S. market, despite comparable environmental outcomes with other fishing methods.

Trade Barriers Created by the U.S. Measures

1. **Fishing Method Restriction**: Tuna caught using purse-seine nets in the ETP was ineligible for the dolphin-safe label, irrespective of whether dolphins were harmed.

2. **Certification Requirements**: Independent certification was required to verify no dolphins were killed or injured, imposing higher costs on Mexican fishers.

3. **Regional Discrimination**: Tuna from other regions, using methods with similar risks (e.g. longline fishing), qualified for the label, disadvantaging Mexico.

4. **Consumer Perception**: The labeling system implied that Mexican tuna was unsustainable, despite contrary evidence.

5. **Lack of Flexibility**: The U.S. failed to consider alternative, less trade-restrictive ways to achieve its environmental objectives, such as recognizing Mexico's dolphin protection programs.

THE AGREEMENT ON TECHNICAL BARRIERS TO TRADE (TBT)

WTO Findings Under the TBT Agreement

Mexico initiated a WTO dispute in 2008, claiming violations of the TBT Agreement, particularly:

- **Non-Discrimination (Article 2.1)**: The U.S. measures treated Mexican tuna less favorably than comparable products from other countries.

- **Avoiding Unnecessary Obstacles to Trade (Article 2.2)**: The regulations were more trade-restrictive than necessary to achieve environmental goals.

- **Transparency and Fair Procedures (Articles 5.1 and 5.2)**: Conformity assessment procedures imposed disproportionate burdens on Mexican fishers.

The WTO's Dispute Settlement Body (DSB) ruled in favor of Mexico, concluding that the U.S. dolphin-safe labeling regulations violated Article 2.1 by unfairly discriminating against Mexican tuna. While the U.S. could pursue environmental objectives, its measures were not applied evenly. The DSB directed the U.S. to modify its measures to comply with WTO rules.

Significance of the Case

The US-Tuna II (Mexico) case illustrates key principles of the TBT Agreement:

1. **Balancing Trade and Policy Objectives**: Regulations must not unnecessarily restrict trade or unfairly discriminate while pursuing legitimate objectives.

2. **Non-Discrimination in Practice**: Even neutral-seeming measures can be discriminatory if they disproportionately impact certain trading partners.

3. **Proportionality and Least Restrictiveness**: WTO members must use the least trade-restrictive means to achieve policy goals.

4. **Transparency and Fair Access**: Conformity assessment procedures must be fair and not impose excessive burdens.

5. **Impact on Global Trade**: The ruling reinforced the need for evidence-based, science-driven regulations that respect international trade principles.

Additional Case Study: EC—Trade Description of Sardines

Background

The EU reserved the name "sardines" exclusively for Sardina pilchardus, a species found in European waters. Peru challenged the regulation, arguing it excluded other species commonly known as sardines in international trade.

WTO Findings

- The panel found the EU regulation violated Article 2.4 of the TBT Agreement, as it did not align with the Codex Alimentarius Commission's international standard.
- The Appellate Body upheld the decision, reinforcing the need for harmonization with international standards.

Outcome

The EU was required to amend its regulation to allow other sardine species, improving market access for Peruvian products.

Author's Commentary on the TBT Agreement and the Role of Artificial Intelligence

The TBT Agreement plays a dual role in facilitating trade while preserving regulatory autonomy. Striking this balance remains one of its greatest challenges. While the agreement seeks to prevent protectionism disguised as technical regulations, it must also respect each member's right to set its own policies.

A fundamental issue is the conflict between trade and sovereignty. Many governments introduce technical regulations for consumer protection, public health, and environmental reasons, but these can inadvertently restrict trade. The difficulty lies in distinguishing between genuine regulatory measures and disguised protectionism.

Another challenge is the unequal capacity of developing countries to comply with TBT requirements. Wealthier nations often have the infrastructure and expertise to implement and adapt to new regulations, while developing countries may struggle with the costs of compliance. The lack of technical resources means some nations cannot participate effectively in dispute resolution, leaving them at a disadvantage in the global trading system.

Moreover, artificial intelligence (AI) is poised to transform the landscape of trade regulations and conformity assessment. AI-driven compliance tools can streamline conformity assessments, improving efficiency and reducing trade barriers. However, AI also raises concerns about algorithmic bias, regulatory disparities, and data sovereignty.

If AI-driven assessments favor wealthier nations with advanced technology, developing countries could face additional obstacles. Additionally, AI-based conformity systems must align with international standards to ensure fairness and avoid unintended discrimination in global markets.

Challenges and Future Considerations

Looking ahead, the TBT Agreement must evolve to:

- Enhance technical assistance for developing countries.
- Strengthen international standards to reduce trade barriers.
- Address emerging challenges, such as digital trade, AI-driven regulatory assessments, and environmental sustainability.

The TBT Agreement remains an important tool within WTO trade governance, fostering cooperation while upholding regulatory autonomy. The *US-Tuna II (Mexico)* and the *Sardines* cases confirm its impact in resolving trade disputes and promoting greater fairness in international commerce.

Part 10
Customs Valuation Rules Under WTO

Chapter 44

Customs Valuation under Article VII of GATT and the WTO Customs Valuation Agreement (CVA)

Introduction

Customs valuation is a critical aspect of international trade, directly influencing the amount of duty payable on imported goods. Accurate customs valuation ensures fair competition, compliance with trade rules, and predictability for businesses.

This chapter explores the framework provided by Article VII of the General Agreement on Tariffs and Trade (GATT) and the more detailed Customs Valuation Agreement (CVA) adopted under the WTO, highlighting their scope, obligations, and practical applications.

Importance of Customs Valuation

Customs valuation is central to determining the dutiable value of imported goods, which has a significant impact on various aspects of international trade. The calculation of import duties often relies on the customs value of goods, influencing overall pricing and market competition.

When valuation practices are inconsistent or opaque, businesses may struggle to assess the true costs of imported products, leading to distortions in market pricing and unfair trade advantages for certain players.

Beyond tariff calculations, customs valuation ensures that importers can accurately determine the total landed cost of goods. This includes duties, taxes, and additional charges that affect profitability and pricing strategies.

Standardized valuation practices promote fairness by preventing manipulation of customs values, whether through undervaluation to reduce tax liabilities or overvaluation for illicit financial purposes.

Article VII of GATT: The Foundation of Customs Valuation

Article VII of GATT establishes fundamental principles for customs valuation, aiming to create a transparent and fair system for assessing the value of imported goods. The core principles include:

- **Fairness and Neutrality**: Customs valuation must be applied consistently, without arbitrary or punitive elements.
- **Transaction Value**: The primary method of valuation should be based on the actual price paid or payable for the goods in the course of international trade.
- **Consistency**: The customs valuation process should accurately reflect the economic reality of transactions, avoiding speculative or fictitious pricing practices.

Despite these fundamental guidelines, the application of Article VII remained inconsistent among WTO members. Varying interpretations led to disputes, prompting the need for a more comprehensive framework under the WTO Customs Valuation Agreement.

The WTO Customs Valuation Agreement

The CVA, formally known as the Agreement on Implementation of Article VII of GATT, provides a structured approach to customs valuation, ensuring transparency and uniformity across WTO members. It sets out detailed rules for determining the customs value of goods and reinforces the transaction value principle as the primary method of assessment.

Transaction Value (Article 1)

Under Article 1, transaction value is defined as the price actually paid or payable for goods sold for export to the importing country. This approach is preferred because it aligns customs valuation with real-world trade practices, fostering consistency and predictability.

Key Elements of Transaction Value

- **Price Actually Paid or Payable:** Includes all forms of payment, whether direct or indirect, such as monetary compensation, bartered goods, or other considerations.

- **Adjustments to Transaction Value:**
    - **Inclusions:** Commissions, brokerage fees (except buying commissions), packing costs, assists (such as free or reduced-cost materials provided by the buyer), royalties, license fees, and transportation costs up to the point of importation.
    - **Exclusions:** Post-importation costs such as assembly and maintenance, as well as distinguishable interest charges for deferred payment.

- **Conditions and Restrictions:** The transaction value method is applicable only if the sale is free from conditions that could distort pricing, and if the buyer and seller's relationship does not influence the price.

- **Related Party Transactions:** When the buyer and seller are related, customs authorities **"must"** ensure the price reflects genuine market conditions. There are serious questions around the use of the word "must" in this text. It doesn't appear to be ambiguous to the author but few Customs administrations accept this mandatory obligation. Where the relationship affects pricing, alternative valuation methods should generally be applied.

Practical Challenges in Applying Transaction Value

Transfer Pricing and Multinational Transactions

Multinational corporations frequently engage in inter-company transactions that raise concerns over whether the declared customs value aligns with market-based pricing. Transfer pricing—the pricing of transactions between related entities—can result in manipulation of customs values, either to minimize duties or to shift profits across jurisdictions. The CVA requires customs authorities to periodically review such transactions, but in practice, these reviews often lack the necessary scrutiny.

Royalties and License Fees

Royalties and license fees present another complex challenge in customs valuation. These payments, if required as a "condition of the sale", must be included in the customs value. In global trade in goods, a legitimate but unanswered question (since 1995) is: what royalty payments are a "condition of the sale" of goods? This question has not been satisfactorily answered in 30 years yet it is an important issue impacting on thousands of importers and exporters. The answer is probably: None!

Disputes frequently arise over this issue. Specifically, the issue is whether such royalty payments are genuinely tied somehow to the imported goods or if they relate to broader intellectual property rights unrelated to the sale of goods. Given the evolving nature of licensing agreements, greater clarity is needed to ensure consistent application of the WTO valuation principles.

Discounts, Rebates, and Price Adjustments

Price adjustments occurring post-sale, such as volume discounts and rebates, introduce additional complications. Customs authorities must determine whether these adjustments affect the transaction value and whether they should be reflected in the final customs assessment. Ambiguities in defining applicable price adjustments can lead to disputes between importers and regulatory authorities.

Other Valuation Methods

If the transaction value cannot be used, the CVA outlines five alternative methods, applied in sequential order:

1. **Transaction Value of Identical Goods**: Uses the customs value of identical goods imported under comparable conditions.

2. **Transaction Value of Similar Goods**: Expands the identical goods principle to include goods with comparable characteristics and uses.

3. **Deductive Value**: Bases valuation on the resale price of the goods in the importing country, deducting costs and markups.

4. **Computed Value**: Calculates the customs value from production costs, including labor and material expenses.

5. **Fall-Back Method**: Allows customs authorities to determine value using reasonable means consistent with GATT principles.

Challenges and Criticisms

- **Complexity:** The multi-method hierarchy can be difficult for businesses and customs authorities to navigate.

- **Overlap with Transfer Pricing Rules:** The interaction between customs valuation and transfer pricing regulations leads to inconsistencies and potential double taxation.

- **Resource Constraints in Developing Nations:** Many countries lack the technical infrastructure to fully implement the CVA's provisions, leading to uneven enforcement.

Author's Commentary: Reimagining Customs Valuation for the 21st Century

Customs valuation is one of the most overlooked yet critical components of international trade. It directly influences tariff revenues, trade competitiveness, and compliance burdens for businesses.

The WTO CVA was meant to bring structure, transparency, and uniformity to valuation practices, yet in many respects, it has failed to live up to its promise. Instead of ensuring fairness across global markets, it has created a complex, loophole-ridden system that allows strategic manipulation by both businesses and governments.

One of the most glaring failures of the CVA is its inability to effectively regulate related-party transactions. Multinational corporations routinely engage in inter-company trade, often using transfer pricing strategies to shift profits and minimize duty liabilities. While the OECD has developed comprehensive guidelines for transfer pricing in taxation, there is no equivalent global standard for customs valuation between related entities.

The result? WTO members apply widely varying interpretations of related-party valuation, creating inconsistencies that distort trade. A bold reform would involve establishing a global "Customs Transfer Pricing Framework" that aligns customs valuation with modern corporate structures. This would prevent companies from gaming the system by exploiting jurisdictional differences in customs valuation methodologies.

Another pressing issue is the outdated approach to royalties, license fees, and intellectual property payments. The current CVA framework assumes that customs valuation should focus primarily on tangible goods. Yet, in today's economy, a significant portion of trade value is embedded in intangible assets—software, trademarks, patents, and proprietary technologies.

Multinationals increasingly use royalty agreements and service fees to shift profits and manipulate customs values. The WTO must redefine the scope of customs valuation to account for the modern, digitalized economy. This could mean implementing a hybrid customs valuation model that factors in both tangible and intangible value contributions, ensuring that valuation reflects the true economic substance of a transaction rather than an artificial breakdown of costs.

Furthermore, customs valuation rules are alarmingly outdated when it comes to supply chain flexibility and dynamic pricing models. Modern global trade operates on real-time pricing mechanisms, algorithm-driven cost adjustments, and post-sale rebates. The CVA's rigid, linear approach to transaction valuation does not account for the real-world complexities of just-in-time production, volume-based pricing agreements, or AI-driven procurement strategies.

To keep pace with contemporary trade practices, a reformulated CVA should introduce a "Dynamic Valuation Mechanism," which allows customs authorities to consider post-importation price adjustments (beyond those currently in existence) where commercially justified. This would enhance fairness while reducing unnecessary disputes between importers and regulators.

Finally, after nearly 80 years, it is clear that the CVA is ripe for a complete rewrite. It remains a technically intricate, bureaucratically cumbersome agreement that lacks the precision and adaptability required for today's trade realities. If the WTO is serious about modernizing global commerce, it must abandon the assumption that customs valuation should be a static, one-size-fits-all process.

Instead, it should move toward a principles-based, technology-driven valuation system—one that reduces manipulation, increases predictability, and ensures that customs practices reflect the complexities of 21st-century trade. If this does not happen, the CVA will continue to be a playground for regulatory arbitrage rather than a tool for trade fairness.

Chapter 45

The Harmonized Tariff System

Introduction

The Harmonized Tariff System (HTS), formally known as the Harmonized Commodity Description and Coding System (HS), is a standardized nomenclature for classifying traded goods.

Managed by the World Customs Organization (WCO), the HTS provides a common language for international trade, ensuring consistency in the classification of goods across countries.

While not a WTO agreement, the HS system complements the WTO's objectives of trade facilitation and transparency by simplifying customs procedures and reducing disputes.

Historical Background

The origins of the harmonized tariff can be traced to the Brussels Tariff Nomenclature (BTN) established in 1950.

Recognizing the need for a universal system to classify goods in an increasingly globalized economy, the WCO developed the Harmonized System in the 1980s. Officially adopted in 1988, the HS replaced disparate national classification systems, creating a uniform structure for tariff schedules and trade statistics.

The system's adoption was driven by the desire to streamline international trade, reduce administrative costs, and provide a common framework for negotiating trade agreements. Today, the HS is updated every five years to reflect technological advancements and changes in global trade patterns.

Structure and Current Format

The Harmonized System is structured as a six-digit code, which provides a hierarchical framework for classifying goods:

1. **Chapters (2 digits):** The first two digits identify the broad category of goods (e.g. Chapter 62 for apparel).

2. **Headings (4 digits):** The next two digits specify a more detailed category within the chapter (e.g. 6203 for men's or boys' suits).

3. **Subheadings (6 digits):** The final two digits offer further granularity (e.g. 6203.22 for suits made of cotton).

Many countries expand on this six-digit structure with additional digits to accommodate national tariff schedules or statistical needs. For example:

- The European Union uses an eight-digit system.
- The United States employs a ten-digit system known as the Harmonized Tariff Schedule of the United States (HTSUS).

As of 2023, over 200 countries and territories use the HS system, accounting for more than 98% of global trade. Its widespread adoption underscores its critical role in facilitating international commerce.

Key Features and Benefits

- **Standardization:** The HS provides a universally accepted language for classifying goods, reducing misunderstandings and disputes.

- **Trade Facilitation:** By harmonizing classification criteria, the system simplifies customs procedures, reducing delays and administrative burdens.

- **Statistical Analysis:** Governments and international organizations use HS data to monitor trade flows, inform policy decisions, and negotiate trade agreements.

- **Revenue Collection:** Accurate classification ensures the correct application of tariffs and taxes, safeguarding government revenue.

THE HARMONIZED TARIFF SYSTEM

Role of Tariffs and National Autonomy

While the HS system provides a uniform classification framework, individual countries retain full autonomy to set their own tariff rates based on national priorities, including industrial policy, revenue generation, or protection of domestic industries.

These tariff rates are published in national schedules that often extend the HS's six-digit structure with additional digits for specificity.

However, countries must adhere to their commitments under the General Agreement on Tariffs and Trade (GATT) 1994, particularly the "bound rates."

Bound rates represent the maximum tariff levels a country has agreed not to exceed as part of its WTO commitments.

Countries are free to set applied tariff rates—the rates actually charged—below these bound rates, but they cannot exceed them without renegotiating their commitments with affected trading partners.

For example:

- A country may apply a 5% tariff on imported machinery to promote technological development but is obligated not to exceed its bound rate of 10%.

- In contrast, sensitive products such as agricultural goods might have applied tariffs close to or at the bound rate to protect domestic farmers.

This dual system allows countries to balance domestic economic needs with their international obligations, ensuring flexibility while maintaining a predictable trading environment.

Dispute-Prone Areas in Tariff Classification

Tariff classification is one of the most contentious areas in international trade, second only to customs valuation. Disputes often arise over the interpretation of HS codes, as minor differences in classification can result in significant variations in tariff rates. For instance:

- **Pharmaceuticals vs. Chemicals:** Disagreements may arise over whether a product qualifies as a pharmaceutical (often tariff-free under WTO agreements) or as a chemical (subject to higher tariffs).

- **Consumer Electronics:** The classification of multi-functional devices, such as smartphones, can lead to disputes over whether they fall under headings for telecommunications devices or computers, each carrying different tariff rates.

These disputes are typically resolved through national customs authorities, in some cases, the WTO's Dispute Settlement Body (DSB) or the WCO.

Relationship with WTO Agreements

Although the HS is not a WTO agreement, it plays a vital role in the functioning of the multilateral trading system. WTO members use the HS for scheduling tariff commitments under the General Agreement on Tariffs and Trade (GATT) 1994. The HS also facilitates the implementation of other WTO agreements, such as those on customs valuation and trade facilitation.

For example:

- **Customs Valuation Agreement:** The HS ensures consistency in classifying goods, enabling accurate valuation for tariff purposes.
- **Trade Facilitation Agreement (TFA):** The HS supports TFA objectives by standardizing procedures, reducing transaction costs, and enhancing predictability.

Challenges and Disputes

While the HS has significantly improved trade efficiency, it is not without challenges:

1. **Interpretation Disputes:** Differences in interpreting HS classifications can lead to disputes between trading partners. For instance, disagreements over whether a product qualifies as a machine or a part of a machine can result in tariff misapplication.
2. **Complexity**: The HS's detailed structure can be difficult for small businesses to navigate, necessitating capacity-building initiatives to ensure compliance.

Case Law Examples

1. ***India – Classification of Electrical Products:*** In this dispute, India's classification of certain electrical products under a higher tariff heading was challenged by trading partners. The WTO Panel emphasized

the importance of adhering to the HS's interpretative rules to ensure consistency.

2. ***European Communities – Classification of Computer Equipment:*** The European Union faced a challenge over its classification of certain computer components. The WTO Appellate Body highlighted the need for members to base their classifications on HS principles, underscoring the system's role in facilitating transparent trade practices.

Future Developments

The WCO continues to update the HS to reflect technological advancements and evolving trade patterns. For example, the 2022 edition introduced new provisions for classifying electronic waste and novel medical devices. Future updates are expected to address emerging sectors such as renewable energy and artificial intelligence.

Author's Commentary: Rethinking the Harmonized Tariff System for a Digital and Automated Trade Era

However, despite its long-standing role in trade facilitation, the HS is increasingly showing its age—struggling to keep pace with the rapid evolution of digital trade, automation, and the complexities of modern supply chains. If the HS is to remain relevant in the 21st century, it must undergo fundamental reforms that go beyond periodic technical updates.

One of the greatest shortcomings of the HS is its inability to adapt quickly to technological advancements. The classification of goods within the HS follows a rigid structure that often lags behind real-world innovations.

Consider, for example, multi-functional electronic devices, AI-integrated machinery, and digital goods—these do not fit neatly into the traditional categories envisioned when the HS was developed. The result? Prolonged classification disputes, inconsistencies across jurisdictions, and tariff misapplications that disrupt global supply chains.

A more dynamic classification system—perhaps one that incorporates AI-driven classification tools—could automate the tariff determination process, reducing disputes and ensuring greater consistency between national customs authorities.

Another major challenge is the excessive reliance on subjective human interpretation in tariff classification disputes. Minor classification differences can result in significant variations in tariff rates, trade costs, and legal obligations.

The current system places the burden on businesses to interpret and comply with complex classification rules, often leading to disputes between importers and customs authorities.

A forward-thinking solution would be to develop a blockchain-based global customs database, where historical classifications, WTO dispute rulings, and real-time updates from customs authorities worldwide could be referenced instantly. This would reduce the ambiguity surrounding product classifications and create a single source of truth for trade compliance.

Perhaps the most underexplored issue is the potential for strategic manipulation of tariff classifications by major economies. The HS was intended to be a neutral system, yet it is often used as a trade weapon—whether through selective reclassification of goods to impose higher duties or through "tariff engineering" strategies where businesses deliberately design products to fit into lower-duty categories.

To counteract this, a global oversight mechanism could be established under the WCO to monitor and audit tariff classifications, ensuring that no country or business exploits classification loopholes for economic advantage.

Finally, digital trade remains largely unaccounted for in the HS framework. The classification system remains heavily focused on physical goods, yet global trade is increasingly dominated by data flows, intellectual property transactions, and digital services. Should a downloadable 3D printing template for manufacturing machinery be classified under the same heading as the physical machinery itself?

How should cloud computing services bundled with hardware sales be treated? The current HS system has no coherent methodology for incorporating the trade value of digital goods and services, leaving a growing gap in tariff policy. The future of the HS should include a digital trade classification annex, ensuring that trade rules remain relevant as commerce continues its shift toward digital and intangible products.

While many argue that the HS is too complex and should be simplified, its multiplicity of uses—from tariff determination to statistical data collection—makes this complexity justifiable.

However, complexity should not mean rigidity. A more flexible, technology-driven, and globally coordinated approach to customs classification could eliminate ambiguities, reduce disputes, and ensure that the HS remains a vital tool for international trade rather than an outdated bureaucratic hurdle.

Chapter 46

The Agreements on Rules of Origin (ARO)

Background and Objectives

The rules of origin are important elements in international trade, determining the "economic nationality" of goods.

Within the World Trade Organization (WTO) framework, two key agreements address rules of origin: the Agreement on Rules of Origin (ARO) and Article IX of the General Agreement on Tariffs and Trade (GATT) 1994, which deals with marks of origin.

Together, these agreements seek to ensure a harmonized approach to the application of origin criteria, fostering trade transparency and minimizing trade distortions.

The ARO, concluded during the Uruguay Round, establishes disciplines for the application of non-preferential rules of origin.

It complements Article IX of GATT 1994, which focuses on labeling requirements for origin marks.

While both agreements deal with rules of origin, their scopes differ: the ARO primarily governs the determination of origin for tariff and trade policy purposes, whereas Article IX addresses the proper marking of goods to indicate their origin to consumers.

Scope of Coverage

1. **The Agreement on Rules of Origin (ARO):** The ARO applies to non-preferential rules of origin, used in the application of:
    o **Most-Favored-Nation (MFN) Treatment:** Ensuring goods receive the appropriate tariff rate under MFN obligations.

- **Trade Remedies:** Determining the country of origin for the imposition of anti-dumping and countervailing duties.
- **Other Trade Policy Instruments:** Including safeguards, labeling, and statistical data collection.

2. **Article IX of GATT 1994:** Article IX governs the marking of imported goods with their country of origin. This ensures that consumers are informed about the origin of products and that labeling requirements do not create unnecessary trade barriers. For example:
   - Goods imported into the United States must be marked with their country of origin unless exempted under specific provisions.
   - Labels such as "Made in Japan" or "Product of Canada" ensure transparency for consumers but must comply with WTO rules to avoid being overly restrictive or discriminatory.

Key Provisions

1. **Harmonization Work Program (ARO):** Article 9 of the ARO outlines the commitment of WTO members to develop a single set of harmonized non-preferential rules of origin. This initiative aims to eliminate discrepancies among members' national systems.

2. **Transparency and Notification (ARO and GATT):** Members must publish their rules of origin and notify the WTO of any changes. Similarly, under Article IX, members must ensure that marking requirements are clearly communicated and consistent with WTO principles.

3. **Non-Discrimination (ARO):** The ARO mandates that rules of origin must not be used as disguised restrictions on trade. They should apply equally to all WTO members in accordance with MFN principles.

4. **Consumer Protection (GATT):** Article IX focuses on ensuring that marks of origin do not mislead consumers while avoiding unnecessary obstacles to international trade.

THE AGREEMENTS ON RULES OF ORIGIN (ARO)

Application and Implementation

- **Customs Valuation and Documentation:** Non-preferential rules of origin are applied during customs clearance to verify the origin of goods for tariff and statistical purposes. For instance, a product assembled in Vietnam using components from China may require a determination of "substantial transformation" to establish its origin.

- **Labeling Requirements**: Article IX obligations are frequently applied in consumer goods sectors. For example, electronic devices exported to the European Union must display their country of origin in compliance with EU labeling laws.

Case Law Analysis

1. *India – Measures Relating to Rules of Origin for Textile and Apparel Products:* This case centered on India's rules of origin for textiles, which complainants argued were overly stringent and burdensome for exporters. The WTO Panel emphasized that such rules should be clear and predictable, avoiding disguised trade restrictions. The Panel's findings underscored the importance of aligning rules with transparency obligations under the ARO.

2. *United States – Origin Marking Requirements:* The United States faced challenges over its labeling requirements, which mandated specific origin markings on imported goods. The complainants argued that these measures created unnecessary obstacles to trade. The WTO Panel found that while origin marking is permissible under Article IX, it must not discriminate against foreign products or impose undue compliance burdens.

Examples of Distinctions Between ARO and Article IX

1. **Substantial Transformation (ARO):** Under the ARO, a good's origin is determined based on substantial transformation criteria—for instance, a car assembled in Mexico using Japanese parts may be deemed Mexican origin under specific rules.

2. **Marking of Origin (GATT):** A product such as "Made in Italy" wine must comply with labeling requirements under Article IX, ensuring consumers are aware of its origin, even if some production steps occur elsewhere.

Author's Commentary: Rethinking Rules of Origin for a Fragmented Global Economy

Rules of origin have long served as the gatekeepers of international trade, defining which goods qualify for preferential tariffs and ensuring transparency in product labeling. However, in an era where supply chains are no longer linear but multi-jurisdictional, the current framework for determining and certifying origin is becoming increasingly obsolete.

Trade agreements are multiplying, manufacturing is becoming decentralized, and digital technology is transforming how goods are produced and tracked. The WTO's Agreement on Rules of Origin (ARO) and Article IX of GATT are foundational, but they are woefully outpaced by the realities of modern trade. The time has come for a radical rethinking of how rules of origin operate, not just in terms of efficiency, but in their very conception.

One of the most pressing issues is the lack of a universal definition of origin that applies across all trade agreements. While the WTO aims to harmonize non-preferential rules, preferential trade agreements continue to layer complexity upon complexity, with each agreement maintaining its own original criteria. A product assembled in Vietnam using Chinese components may qualify as "Vietnamese" under one agreement but not another, creating regulatory uncertainty and increasing compliance costs for businesses.

Should the definition of origin continue to be tied to rigid tariff-based classifications, or should it evolve to reflect economic realities, such as value-added metrics, labor content, or sustainability factors? While some agreements incorporate these issues a new approach could involve a "Hybrid Origin Model," where origin determination integrates both material inputs and the economic contribution made within a given country. Uniformity is the key.

Another major inefficiency in the current system is the outdated, paper-based nature of origin certification. Trade remains bogged down by physical documentation, manual approvals, and fragmented verification procedures that increase the risk of fraud and administrative bottlenecks.

Blockchain technology and digital trade networks could revolutionize this process. A universal, blockchain-based origin certification system would allow customs authorities, businesses, and trade regulators to verify origin claims in real time, reducing fraudulent misclassification and dramatically improving trade facilitation. Instead of relying on static country-of-origin certificates that can be easily falsified, goods could be assigned a digitally authenticated "origin identity" that traces the entire supply chain from raw materials to finished products.

THE AGREEMENTS ON RULES OF ORIGIN (ARO)

Perhaps the most underexplored aspect of rules of origin is their role in shaping global trade power dynamics. While origin rules are often viewed as technical mechanisms, they are also political tools that can be manipulated to favor certain economies. Countries frequently adjust their rules of origin requirements to restrict access for specific trading partners, using them as disguised protectionist measures.

This raises the question: Should the WTO introduce a dispute resolution mechanism specifically for rules of origin disputes? While the current system relies on national authorities for enforcement, a WTO-supervised "Rules of Origin Tribunal" could help prevent misuse and ensure that origin classifications are based on economic principles rather than political agendas.

In conclusion, the current patchwork of rules of origin is unsustainable. Without reform, it will continue to undermine the efficiency of trade agreements and impose unnecessary burdens on businesses. The future lies in a digital, harmonized, and economically rational system—one that aligns with modern production processes rather than outdated bureaucratic structures. By integrating blockchain verification, universal origin standards, and independent dispute resolution mechanisms, the global trading system can transform rules of origin from a regulatory hurdle into a true facilitator of international commerce.

Chapter 47

The Agreement on Pre-shipment Inspection

Background and Objectives

The Agreement on Pre-shipment Inspection (PSI), part of the World Trade Organization (WTO) framework, involves the verification of the quality, quantity, and price of goods before they are exported to the importing country.

Instituted under the Uruguay Round negotiations, the PSI Agreement entered into force in 1995 with the establishment of the WTO.

Its primary objectives are to ensure transparency, fairness, and efficiency in international trade while safeguarding the interests of both exporters and importers.

Background

Pre-shipment inspections were initially adopted by many developing countries as a mechanism to prevent customs fraud, mis-invoicing, and other irregularities in international trade transactions.

By outsourcing the verification process to independent inspection agencies, these countries aimed to enhance customs revenue collection and mitigate the risk of undervaluation or overvaluation of imported goods. However, the system has also faced criticism for creating additional costs and delays, leading to debates on its overall efficacy.

Scope of the Agreement

The PSI Agreement governs the conduct of pre-shipment inspection activities to ensure they align with WTO principles, particularly those of non-discrimination, transparency, and impartiality. The agreement applies to:

1. **Exporters and Importers:** Ensuring that exporters are not subjected to unnecessary or discriminatory inspections, and importers are provided with accurate data to facilitate customs clearance.

2. **Inspection Agencies:** Mandating that agencies conducting inspections operate in a transparent, independent, and non-discriminatory manner.

3. **National Authorities:** Requiring WTO members utilizing PSI to adhere to specific obligations, including the publication of relevant laws and regulations, and the provision of adequate legal recourse mechanisms.

Illustrative WTO dispute case on the PSI

The PSI establishes guidelines to ensure that pre-shipment inspections are conducted fairly and transparently, preventing unnecessary delays and discrimination in international trade.

While disputes specifically citing the PSI Agreement are relatively rare, one notable case provides insight into its application: *Indonesia – Certain Measures Affecting Imports*

Background

In 2013, the European Union (EU) requested consultations with Indonesia concerning certain measures affecting the importation of horticultural products, animals, and animal products. The EU alleged that Indonesia's import licensing regimes and pre-shipment inspection requirements were inconsistent with various WTO agreements, including the Agreement on Pre-shipment Inspection.

Key Issues

- **Pre-shipment Inspection Requirements:** The EU contended that Indonesia's mandatory pre-shipment inspection requirements imposed unjustifiable delays and administrative burdens on exporters, potentially violating the PSI Agreement's provisions. These provisions stipulate that inspections should not cause unnecessary delays or be applied in a discriminatory manner.

Outcome

The dispute was settled through consultations, and Indonesia agreed to modify its import licensing procedures and pre-shipment inspection requirements to align with WTO rules. This case underscores the importance of adhering to the PSI Agreement's principles to facilitate smooth international trade operations.

Key Takeaways

1. **Non-Discrimination**: Pre-shipment inspections must be applied uniformly to all trading partners without favoritism.

2. **Avoidance of Unnecessary Delays**: Inspections should be conducted promptly to prevent undue hindrance to trade.

3. **Transparency**: Clear information regarding inspection procedures and criteria should be provided to exporters to ensure compliance and predictability.

Conclusion about Case

This case illustrates the WTO's role in resolving disputes related to pre-shipment inspections and highlights the necessity for member countries to implement inspection procedures that comply with international trade agreements.

By ensuring transparency, non-discrimination, and the avoidance of unnecessary delays, the PSI Agreement continues to play a critical role in promoting fair and efficient trade practices.

Key Provisions of Agreement

1. **Non-Discrimination:** Article 2 of the PSI Agreement requires member countries to ensure that the procedures for pre-shipment inspections are applied uniformly to all exporters, regardless of their nationality or country of origin. This provision is aimed at preventing protectionist practices and fostering equal treatment.

2. **Transparency**: The agreement mandates the publication of all laws, regulations, and guidelines related to pre-shipment inspection. It also requires inspection agencies to provide exporters with a clear explanation of inspection procedures and reasons for any non-compliance findings. Transparency ensures accountability and mitigates disputes arising from unclear processes.

3. **Confidentiality**: Inspection agencies must maintain the confidentiality of business information obtained during the inspection process, as

outlined in Article 3. This provision safeguards commercial interests and prevents the misuse of sensitive data.

4. **Legal Recourse:** Exporters have the right to appeal inspection decisions. Article 4 establishes an independent review procedure to address disputes arising from inspection activities. This mechanism provides exporters with a fair platform to contest adverse findings and ensures due process.

5. **Avoidance of Delays**: Article 2.6 emphasizes minimizing delays in the inspection process to prevent disruptions to international trade. Excessive delays can lead to increased costs and logistical challenges, particularly for time-sensitive shipments.

Application and Implementation

The implementation of the PSI Agreement varies significantly among WTO members. Developing countries, which are the primary users of pre-shipment inspections, often rely on external agencies to supplement their limited institutional capacity. While this can enhance customs revenue and reduce fraud, it may also introduce additional costs and procedural complexities for exporters.

To balance these challenges, some countries have integrated PSI into broader customs modernization initiatives, leveraging digital technologies to streamline the process. For instance, automation of documentation and real-time tracking systems has improved efficiency and reduced inspection-related delays in several jurisdictions.

Another Illustrative Case

Several notable cases provide substantive insights into the application and interpretation of the PSI Agreement:

Philippines – Customs Valuation: This dispute centered on allegations that the Philippines' pre-shipment inspection practices were discriminatory and inconsistent with WTO obligations.

The complainants argued that certain exporters faced undue scrutiny compared to others. The WTO Panel emphasized the importance of the non-discrimination principle enshrined in Article 2 of the PSI Agreement.

The case underscored the need for member states to ensure that PSI measures do not disproportionately impact specific trading partners or exporters.

THE AGREEMENT ON PRE-SHIPMENT INSPECTION

This additional case illustrates the role of the WTO's Dispute Settlement Body in clarifying the scope and application of the PSI Agreement, ensuring adherence to its principles while addressing emerging challenges.

Historical Significance

The PSI Agreement was designed to ensure fair and transparent pre-shipment inspections, addressing concerns such as fraud, mis-invoicing, and discriminatory practices. Its focus on accountability and uniform application played a crucial role in facilitating trade during a time when technological tools for verifying shipments were limited.

While the Agreement has undeniably been beneficial over the decades, its mechanisms now appear outdated in light of technological advancements and the evolving nature of global commerce. Many member states, particularly developing countries, still rely on pre-shipment inspections, raising the question of whether these processes could be modernized or replaced by more efficient alternatives.

Challenges and Outdated Features

1. **Reliance on Physical Inspections**: In the current age of containerized shipping, the need for manual pre-shipment inspections seems antiquated. Modern technology, such as electronic verification and blockchain, offers faster, more reliable alternatives for ensuring the authenticity of shipments.

2. **Cost Implications**: While PSI mechanisms reduce fraud and mis-invoicing, they often impose disproportionate costs on small and medium-sized enterprises (SMEs). The administrative and procedural burdens can hinder their ability to compete globally.

3. **Capacity Constraints in Developing Countries**: It is a relevant issue to recognize the importance of institutional capacity in overseeing inspection agencies and ensuring compliance. Many developing nations lack the resources to effectively implement the Agreement's provisions, resulting in inefficiencies and trade barriers.

4. **Transparency and Efficiency**: Although the PSI Agreement aims to enhance transparency, the lack of integration with modern digital tools undermines its effectiveness. Delays caused by manual inspections can disrupt global supply chains and increase costs.

Recommendations for Reform

1. **Integration of Digital Technologies**: Embrace digital tools such as blockchain and electronic verification systems to modernize the inspection process. These technologies can reduce delays, lower costs, and enhance transparency while ensuring the integrity of shipments.

2. **Targeted Capacity Building**: The WTO should recognize the importance of targeted capacity-building initiatives to support developing countries. Providing resources and technical assistance would enable these nations to transition to more efficient systems and optimize the benefits of the PSI framework.

3. **Periodic Review of the Agreement**: Conduct regular reviews of the PSI Agreement to assess its relevance and address emerging challenges in global trade. These reviews should include consultations with stakeholders, including governments, businesses, and international organizations.

4. **Phasing Out Physical Inspections**: As soon as possible replace physical inspections with electronic verification methods, ensuring a smooth transition for member states that currently rely on traditional systems.

5. **Streamlined Processes for SMEs**: Simplify procedural requirements to reduce the burden on small and medium-sized enterprises. This would promote inclusivity and enhance the participation of SMEs in international trade.

Author's Commentary: Modernizing Pre-Shipment Inspection for a Digital Trade Era

The PSI was introduced at a time when customs fraud, mis-invoicing, and revenue evasion posed major threats to global trade. Developing nations, in particular, relied on PSI as a safeguard against undervaluation and misclassification of imports.

However, while the PSI Agreement was designed to ensure fairness and transparency in trade transactions, it has increasingly become an anachronistic burden—one that now risks slowing rather than facilitating trade. In an era of big data, digital customs systems, and blockchain verification, the PSI framework must be fundamentally reimagined, not just reformed.

One of the greatest inefficiencies of the current PSI system is its heavy reliance on physical inspections—a process that is slow, labor-intensive, and prone to human error. With the globalization of supply chains and containerized shipping, the traditional model of manual pre-shipment checks is no longer fit for purpose.

The future of PSI should not be at the port of departure but within digital trade ecosystems. Automated verification systems, AI-driven risk assessments, and blockchain-based tracking of shipments could replace much of the outdated PSI model, making customs clearance faster, more reliable, and less susceptible to manipulation. A new "Smart PSI" framework could leverage these technologies to provide real-time fraud detection and eliminate unnecessary delays.

Another major issue is the high cost of PSI compliance, particularly for small and medium-sized enterprises (SMEs). While large multinational corporations can absorb the added administrative burdens of pre-shipment inspections, SMEs often struggle with excessive fees, opaque procedures, and inconsistent requirements across jurisdictions.

Rather than ensuring fair competition, PSI inadvertently benefits large-scale players while discouraging market entry by smaller businesses. The WTO should introduce a tiered compliance model, where trusted traders and low-risk shipments are exempted from costly pre-shipment checks, while high-risk transactions undergo enhanced scrutiny. This would ensure better allocation of resources while reducing trade barriers for SMEs.

Perhaps the most overlooked flaw of the PSI framework is its lack of synergy with modern trade facilitation initiatives. While the WTO's Trade Facilitation Agreement (TFA) aims to reduce red tape, digitalize customs processes, and streamline border controls, the PSI system still operates within an outdated, paper-based paradigm.

A radical but necessary step would be to merge PSI mechanisms with the TFA's digital infrastructure, ensuring that inspections align with modern e-commerce supply chains, electronic invoicing, and AI-based risk profiling. PSI should no longer be treated as a separate regulatory hurdle but as an integrated part of the digital trade ecosystem.

In conclusion, the PSI Agreement in its current form is no longer fit for the realities of global commerce. The WTO must move beyond marginal improvements and fundamentally rethink the purpose of pre-shipment inspections.

Rather than relying on outdated manual processes, PSI should evolve into a data-driven, technology-enabled verification system. If pre-shipment inspections are to continue playing a role in trade governance, they must be smarter, faster, and seamlessly integrated into the digital trade revolution. Without such reforms, PSI risks becoming a relic of a bygone era—an obstacle rather than a facilitator of international trade.

Chapter 48

Publication and Administration of Trade Regulations under Article X of GATT and WTO Agreements

Introduction

Article X of the General Agreement on Tariffs and Trade (GATT) 1994 addresses the publication and administration of trade regulations, emphasizing transparency and predictability in international trade.

It mandates that trade-related laws, regulations, judicial decisions, and administrative rulings of general application must be published promptly to enable traders and governments to become acquainted with them. The provisions of Article X aim to reduce uncertainty in trade and ensure fairness in the administration of trade regulations.

The World Trade Organization (WTO) has expanded on these principles through several agreements, most notably the Trade Facilitation Agreement (TFA), which builds on Article X by addressing modern trade challenges.

Other WTO agreements, such as the Agreement on Customs Valuation, the Agreement on Import Licensing Procedures, and the Agreement on Technical Barriers to Trade (TBT), also incorporate transparency and administrative fairness.

These agreements collectively provide mechanisms for importers to obtain clarity and ensure compliance before goods enter a market.

Historical Background

Article X originated in the original GATT 1947 framework and was carried over into the GATT 1994 under the WTO umbrella.

Its inclusion reflected a recognition that trade liberalization alone is insufficient without transparent and predictable administration of trade rules. Over time, the need for more specific and actionable provisions led to the negotiation of the TFA, which came into force in 2017.

The TFA provides detailed disciplines on publication, consultation, and appeal mechanisms, complementing the broad principles of Article X.

Key Provisions of Article X of GATT

1. **Publication:**

   - Article X:1 requires that all trade-related laws, regulations, judicial decisions, and administrative rulings of general application be published promptly.
   - This ensures traders have access to relevant information to comply with import and export requirements.

2. **Uniform Administration:**

   - Article X:3 mandates that trade regulations be administered in a uniform, impartial, and reasonable manner.
   - This provision aims to prevent arbitrary or discriminatory application of trade rules.

3. **Right of Appeal:**

   - Article X:3(b) provides that traders have the right to seek prompt review and correction of administrative actions relating to customs matters.

WTO Agreements Expanding on Article X

1. **Trade Facilitation Agreement (TFA):**

   - **Transparency Measures:** The TFA requires members to publish trade-related information online, including procedures for importation, exportation, and transit.
   - **Advance Rulings:** Members must issue binding advance rulings on tariff classification, origin, and other trade-related matters to provide certainty to traders before importation. This provision

is critical for ensuring that importers can address compliance requirements proactively.
- **Appeals Mechanisms:** The TFA strengthens provisions for appeals, requiring members to provide accessible and transparent review mechanisms.

2. **Agreement on Customs Valuation:**
   - This agreement requires customs authorities to provide clear explanations of valuation decisions and ensure traders have the right to appeal.

3. **Agreement on Import Licensing Procedures:**
   - Transparency and publication requirements under this agreement ensure that traders are aware of licensing criteria and procedures, reducing uncertainty in trade transactions.

4. **Agreement on Technical Barriers to Trade (TBT):**
   - The TBT Agreement includes provisions on publishing technical regulations and standards to ensure they do not create unnecessary obstacles to trade.

Importance of Advance Rulings

One of the most critical aspects of these agreements is the obligation to provide advance rulings.

Advance rulings allow importers to seek binding decisions from customs authorities regarding the classification, valuation, or origin of goods before importation. This reduces the risk of disputes arising after goods enter the market, saving time and costs for traders. For example:

- An importer of electronic components may request an advance ruling to confirm whether a product qualifies for preferential treatment under a free trade agreement.
- Advance rulings ensure that importers can calculate duties and taxes accurately, avoiding unexpected liabilities.

The importance of advance rulings lies in their ability to prevent post-importation disputes, which are often costly and disruptive to business operations. By providing clarity upfront, advance rulings enable importers to incorporate compliance costs into their pricing models and avoid penalties.

Application and Scope

The principles of transparency and uniform administration apply across all WTO members. Key aspects include:

1. **Publication of Regulations:** Members must ensure timely publication of trade-related laws and regulations in accessible formats, such as official gazettes or online portals.

2. **Simplification of Procedures**: Agreements like the TFA encourage members to streamline customs processes, reducing delays and administrative burdens for traders.

3. **Dispute Prevention**: Advance rulings and transparent appeals mechanisms help prevent costly disputes by clarifying requirements before goods are imported.

4. **Regulatory Predictability**: By mandating uniform administration of trade rules, Article X and related agreements ensure that importers face consistent regulatory environments, reducing the risk of arbitrary or discriminatory practices.

Case Law Analysis

1. *European Communities – Customs Classification of Frozen Boneless Chicken Cuts:*
   - This dispute involved differences in the classification of chicken cuts, leading to tariff discrepancies. The WTO Appellate Body emphasized the importance of consistent and transparent application of customs rules under Article X.

2. *United States – Section 301 Trade Act:*
   - The Panel addressed concerns about the lack of transparency and procedural fairness in U.S. trade measures, highlighting the need for clear publication and administration of trade regulations.

3. *India – Import Restrictions on Agricultural Products:*

- India's failure to notify and publish trade restrictions on agricultural imports was found to violate transparency obligations under Article X. The case underscored the importance of timely publication to prevent trade barriers.

Challenges and Opportunities

1. **Implementation Gaps:**

   - Many developing countries face challenges in implementing transparency and publication requirements due to limited administrative capacity.

2. **Technological Solutions:**

   - Digital tools, such as online customs portals and automated systems, can enhance compliance with publication and transparency obligations. For instance, electronic submission of advance ruling requests can streamline the process.

3. **Capacity Building:**

   - Technical assistance and capacity-building programs can support members in meeting their obligations under Article X and related WTO agreements.

Author's Commentary: Transforming Transparency into a Competitive Advantage

The principles enshrined in Article X of GATT and its expansion through WTO agreements are fundamental to the stability of international trade. Without transparency, uniformity, and procedural fairness, the global trading system would collapse into a web of arbitrary regulations, administrative inconsistencies, and protectionist maneuvering. While Article X has served as a bulwark against regulatory opacity, the real challenge lies not in the existence of these rules, but in their effective implementation and modernization to meet the demands of an increasingly digital, data-driven trade environment.

One of the most underutilized aspects of Article X is the potential for transparency itself to become a competitive advantage. Traditionally, discussions around trade regulations and their publication have focused on compliance obligations and reducing uncertainty for traders.

However, nations that prioritize radical transparency, streamlined procedures, and real-time regulatory updates could attract higher volumes of trade and foreign investment. Imagine a scenario where customs authorities not only publish trade regulations but also provide AI-powered predictive insights on upcoming regulatory changes, enabling businesses to adapt well in advance.

This would shift transparency from being a mere compliance function to a strategic trade enabler, allowing governments to differentiate themselves as "high-certainty" trade hubs in an otherwise unpredictable global market.

Furthermore, the principle of uniform administration—while essential—remains largely aspirational in many WTO member states, particularly in developing economies with fragmented bureaucratic structures.

A practical solution would be the development of an independent WTO-supervised "Transparency and Compliance Index" that ranks member states on their adherence to Article X obligations. Countries with high rankings would benefit from enhanced credibility in trade negotiations, while low rankings would serve as a red flag for businesses seeking predictable regulatory environments.

Such an index could act as a market-driven enforcement tool, encouraging governments to maintain high standards of transparency not just to comply with WTO obligations, but to remain attractive trading partners.

Advance rulings, one of the most practical tools arising from Article X, must also evolve. While advance rulings provide certainty in areas like tariff classification, valuation, and rules of origin, their current limitations—bureaucratic delays, inconsistent interpretations, and the lack of global mutual recognition—diminish their potential benefits.

A next-generation approach could involve automated, blockchain-verified advance rulings, ensuring that once an importer receives a ruling in one jurisdiction, it is automatically recognized across other WTO member states—at least for comparable transactions. This would eliminate the need for redundant approvals, reduce administrative burdens, and accelerate trade flows.

Ultimately, Article X and its related agreements should not just be about transparency for its own sake—but about transforming clarity into a tool that enhances global trade efficiency.

By integrating real-time regulatory intelligence, leveraging digital governance tools, and introducing competitive transparency benchmarks, trade facilitation can move beyond passive rule publication to an active driver of economic growth. Nations that recognize transparency as a source of trade competitiveness rather than just an administrative obligation will be the ones that shape the future of global commerce.

Part 11:
Future of International Trade and WTO Reforms

Chapter 49

The WTO Trade Facilitation Agreement – A Framework for Easier Trade

Introduction: A New Chapter in Global Commerce

The World Trade Organization (WTO) Trade Facilitation Agreement (TFA) represents a pivotal effort to streamline international trade and reduce barriers to cross-border commerce.

Entering into force on February 22, 2017, the TFA was the first multilateral agreement concluded by the WTO since its establishment in 1995.

It is important to emphasize that this is the first new multinational WTO agreement in 22 years. This agreement nevertheless, reflects a shared understanding among WTO members of the need to simplify and harmonize customs procedures, thereby fostering greater integration and efficiency in global trade.

This chapter explores the background, objectives, and key provisions of the TFA.

By examining the agreement's substantive elements and real-world examples, we can understand how the WTO aims to enhance free trade, reduce trade costs, and unlock economic potential across member countries.

Background: The Need for Trade Facilitation

The genesis of the TFA lies in the recognition of the complexities and inefficiencies inherent in international trade. Despite significant progress in liberalizing trade through tariff reductions and market access commitments, non-tariff barriers—such as cumbersome customs procedures, inconsistent documentation requirements, and inadequate infrastructure—remained a major obstacle to global commerce.

These inefficiencies disproportionately affected developing and least-developed countries (LDCs), where capacity constraints often led to higher trade costs and delays.

For instance, before implementing trade facilitation reforms under the TFA, Kenya experienced significant delays at the Port of Mombasa. Inefficient customs procedures and a lack of coordination among border agencies led to extended clearance times for shipments.

By adopting streamlined processes and risk management techniques outlined in the TFA, Kenya reduced cargo clearance times from 11 days to under four days, significantly boosting trade efficiency.

Negotiations on trade facilitation began as part of the Doha Development Round in 2001. The objective was to address procedural and administrative hurdles at borders, which were estimated to account for significant trade costs.

After years of discussion and compromise, the TFA was adopted at the WTO Ministerial Conference in Bali in 2013 and entered into force in 2017 following its ratification by two-thirds of WTO members.

Objectives of the TFA

The TFA's overarching goal is to expedite the movement, release, and clearance of goods across borders. By creating a more transparent and predictable trading environment, the agreement seeks to:

1. **Reduce Trade Costs**: Simplified customs procedures and improved cooperation among border agencies aim to lower the time and expense associated with international trade. *Example*: In Rwanda, the implementation of a single electronic window for customs processing, inspired by the TFA's principles, reduced the average time for cross-border trade by 40%, providing a significant boost to its export competitiveness.

2. **Enhance Global Supply Chains**: Efficient trade facilitation strengthens supply chain reliability, enabling businesses to operate with greater certainty. *Example*: In Southeast Asia, the ASEAN Single Window, aligned with TFA principles, facilitates electronic data exchange among member countries, reducing documentation duplication and speeding up cargo movement.

3. **Promote Inclusive Growth**: By addressing systemic inefficiencies, the TFA benefits smaller economies and businesses, particularly in developing and least-developed countries. *Example*: In Bangladesh, small-scale exporters of textiles have benefited from simplified export procedures, enabling them to compete more effectively in international markets.

4. **Encourage Investment and Competitiveness**: Predictable and streamlined processes often better attract foreign investment and help countries integrate into the global trading system.

Substantive Elements of the TFA

The TFA is structured into three sections, each addressing critical aspects of trade facilitation. These provisions collectively aim to modernize and harmonize customs and border practices among WTO members.

1. **Section I: General Substantive Provisions**

This section outlines the substantive commitments of members to facilitate trade. Key provisions include:

- **Publication and Availability of Information**: Members are required to make trade-related information, such as customs procedures, fees, and penalties, publicly available. This ensures transparency and empowers traders with the knowledge needed to comply with regulations. *Example*: In Colombia, the creation of a publicly accessible customs information portal has reduced disputes and improved compliance rates among traders.

- **Advance Rulings**: Customs authorities must provide binding advance rulings on tariff classification and origin matters, offering predictability to traders. *Example*: Exporters in Morocco now benefit from advance rulings on tariff classifications, allowing them to plan shipments with greater confidence.

- **Simplification of Formalities**: Members must adopt measures to streamline documentary requirements and reduce the complexity of customs formalities. This includes transitioning to electronic systems where feasible. *Example*: India's introduction of paperless customs clearance reduced clearance times at ports and cut documentation costs for exporters.

- **Risk Management and Post-Clearance Audit**: The agreement encourages risk-based customs inspections, focusing resources on high-risk consignments while expediting the clearance of low-risk goods. *Example*: Brazil's implementation of risk management systems halved the inspection time for compliant traders.

- **Release and Clearance of Goods**: Provisions aim to minimize delays by mandating expedited clearance procedures, particularly for perishable goods. *Example*: In Peru, the prioritization of fresh produce for expedited clearance has bolstered the competitiveness of agricultural exports.

- **Border Agency Cooperation**: Enhanced coordination among border agencies, both domestically and across borders, is emphasized to reduce duplication and improve efficiency. *Example*: Collaborative border management between Tanzania and Uganda has reduced waiting times at their shared border crossings.

2. **Section II: Special and Differential Treatment for Developing and Least-Developed Countries**

Acknowledging the varying capacities of WTO members, the TFA includes provisions for special and differential treatment (SDT). Developing and least-developed countries (LDCs) are given flexibility in implementing their commitments, allowing them to determine their own timelines and priorities.

Key features include:

- **Categorization of Commitments**: Members can self-designate provisions into three categories:
    - Category A: Provisions implemented upon the agreement's entry into force.
    - Category B: Provisions requiring additional time for implementation.
    - Category C: Provisions necessitating capacity-building assistance. *Example*: Ethiopia categorized several provisions under Category C, leveraging international technical assistance to modernize its customs systems.

- **Technical Assistance and Capacity Building**: Developed countries and international organizations, such as the WTO and the World Bank, provide financial and technical support to help developing countries meet their commitments.

3. **Section III: Institutional Arrangements and Final Provisions**

This section establishes the institutional framework for the TFA's implementation and monitoring. Key elements include:

- **Committee on Trade Facilitation**: The WTO Trade Facilitation Committee oversees the agreement's implementation, providing a platform for members to share best practices and resolve disputes.

- **National Trade Facilitation Committees**: Each member is required to establish a domestic committee to coordinate the implementation of the TFA at the national level. *Example*: Kenya's National Trade Facilitation Committee has played a key role in monitoring progress and ensuring accountability in implementing TFA commitments.

- **Dispute Settlement**: Disputes arising under the TFA are subject to the WTO's dispute settlement mechanism.

Conclusion: A Pathway to Greater Integration

The WTO Trade Facilitation Agreement is an illustration of the power of cooperation in addressing shared challenges. By harmonizing customs procedures and simplifying cross-border formalities, the TFA is a genuine attempt to lay the groundwork for a more predictable, efficient, and inclusive global trading system.

Illustrative examples from across the globe highlight how the TFA's provisions are being implemented to achieve real-world impact. From streamlined customs in Kenya to collaborative border management in Southeast Asia, the TFA demonstrates how targeted reforms can unlock economic potential and foster greater integration.

As this chapter has outlined, the TFA's success lies in the international trading community's ability to balance ambitious goals with practical flexibility, recognizing the diverse capacities of WTO members. For countries willing to invest in its implementation, the agreement appears to offer a pathway to greater integration, competitiveness, and economic prosperity— which of course is the cornerstone of the WTO's stated vision for free and fair trade.

As of January 2025, the WTO TFA which came into force in 2017, has not yet been the subject of any formal disputes under the WTO's Dispute Settlement Understanding (DSU).

While there have been no disputes directly citing the TFA, its principles have influenced various aspects of international trade practices. For instance, the TFA emphasizes the importance of transparency, streamlining customs procedures, and reducing bureaucratic barriers, which are common themes in trade facilitation discussions.

Author's Commentary: Future-Proofing the Trade Facilitation Agreement for the Digital Age

The WTO Trade Facilitation Agreement (TFA) was a groundbreaking achievement when it came into force in 2017, marking the first major multilateral trade agreement since the WTO's creation. It addressed a long-overdue need to simplify, standardize, and digitalize customs procedures, reducing non-tariff barriers that disproportionately affected developing economies.

However, despite its progress, the TFA is already showing signs of age in a rapidly evolving trade environment. The very nature of international commerce has shifted dramatically in the past decade, with technological advancements outpacing many of the agreement's provisions.

While the TFA introduced paperless trade as a goal, it did so in a pre-blockchain, pre-AI, pre-IoT (Internet of Things) era.

Digital trade corridors, smart logistics, and real-time customs processing were not fully integrated concepts at the time of its negotiation. If the TFA is to maintain its relevance, it must evolve beyond static digitalization measures and embrace cutting-edge trade technologies.

A natural progression would be the establishment of a WTO-backed Global Trade Digitalization Framework (GTDF)—a next-generation system that seamlessly integrates blockchain-verified trade documents, AI-powered customs risk assessments, and IoT-enabled shipment tracking. This would ensure not just faster trade clearance but real-time, fraud-resistant, fully automated customs processing.

Another pressing issue is that the TFA remains heavily geared toward traditional trade logistics—focusing on port efficiency, border delays, and customs paperwork—while failing to adequately address the rise of digital trade.

The global economy has rapidly shifted toward e-commerce, digital services, and intangible trade, yet the TFA remains predominantly designed for containerized shipments and physical goods. A fundamental expansion of the TFA's scope could introduce E-Commerce Facilitation Provisions, ensuring that trade rules support digital transactions, cross-border data flows, and digital customs clearance mechanisms.

The question is no longer just how to move physical goods faster, but how to regulate and facilitate the trillions of dollars in global trade that never physically crosses a border.

Another area of innovation could involve an AI-driven, dynamic trade facilitation index, where WTO members are continuously ranked on the efficiency, transparency, and automation of their trade processes. This would introduce competitive pressure for governments to actively implement TFA provisions, rather than simply signing on and letting bureaucratic inertia delay progress.

The index could incorporate real-time trade data, providing businesses with predictive analysis of customs efficiency worldwide, enabling companies to choose supply chain routes based on up-to-date trade facilitation performance, rather than outdated bureaucratic assurances.

Ultimately, the success of the TFA will not be measured by its original commitments but by its ability to remain adaptable in a trade landscape defined by rapid technological shifts.

The next evolution of the agreement should not just reduce bureaucratic delays but actively drive the adoption of modern trade technology. By embedding blockchain, AI, IoT, and e-commerce-specific provisions into its framework, the TFA could transition from a mere regulatory document into a forward-thinking enabler of global trade efficiency.

The WTO must recognize that trade facilitation is no longer just about borders—it is about data, automation, and the seamless movement of goods and services in a hyper-connected world.

Chapter 50

Reforming the Anti-Dumping Regime – Addressing the Misuse of Country Market Power

Introduction

The global trade system is increasingly challenged by the misuse of country and corporate market power, a phenomenon that distorts competition and undermines the principles of free trade. Traditional anti-dumping measures under Article VI of GATT and the WTO Anti-Dumping Agreement (ADA) were originally designed to counteract predatory pricing.

However, these measures have proven ineffective, prone to manipulation, and, in many cases, used as disguised protectionist tools. Rather than fostering fair trade, anti-dumping laws often entrench power imbalances and create inefficiencies in global markets.

This chapter critiques the inadequacies of the current anti-dumping regime and proposes a novel alternative: the Misuse of Country Market Power Framework, which shifts the focus away from subjective cost analyses and instead evaluates the actual distortive impact of a nation's trade practices.

This approach, rooted in competition law principles, provides a more transparent, objective, and effective means of addressing unfair trade practices.

Understanding Article VI of GATT and the Anti-Dumping Agreement

Article VI of GATT provides the legal foundation for anti-dumping measures, allowing member states to impose duties on imported goods that are sold at prices lower than their "normal value" if such pricing causes material injury to domestic industries. The WTO Anti-Dumping Agreement (ADA) further refines these provisions, establishing procedures for investigations, injury assessments, and dispute resolution.

Key Provisions of the Anti-Dumping Agreement

1. **Definition of Dumping**: Goods are considered dumped if their export price is lower than the comparable price in the exporting country under normal trade conditions.

2. **Material Injury Requirement**: Anti-dumping duties can only be imposed if dumping causes or threatens material injury to the domestic industry.

3. **Investigation Procedures**: Investigations must be transparent, evidence-based, and conform to due process.

While these anti-dumping measures aim to safeguard domestic industries, their real-world implementation has led to unintended consequences, including economic distortions and retaliatory trade actions. The process for determining "normal value" is often subjective, enabling governments to construct artificial cost structures that unfairly justify anti-dumping duties.

The Failings of the Current Anti-Dumping Regime

Despite its intended purpose, the anti-dumping framework suffers from multiple structural and procedural flaws:

1. Manipulation Through Notional Normal Values

Many national governments construct artificial cost structures and profit margins to justify anti-dumping measures. Since WTO rules allow importing countries to estimate the "normal value" of goods in the exporting country, there is vast room for subjective interpretation.

2. Protectionism in Disguise

Anti-dumping measures frequently serve as a front for protecting domestic industries rather than addressing genuine predatory pricing. Governments use these laws as a means of economic nationalism, undermining the principles of competitive global trade.

3. Market Distortions and Trade Retaliation

The overuse of anti-dumping duties has led to trade wars and retaliatory measures that disrupt global supply chains. The ongoing U.S.-China trade dispute and European Union's restrictions on Chinese steel imports illustrate how anti-dumping laws have become instruments of economic aggression rather than tools of fairness.

4. Imbalance of Power in Dispute Resolution

Larger economies with legal expertise and financial resources disproportionately influence WTO dispute resolutions, leaving developing nations vulnerable to unfounded anti-dumping accusations.

A New Approach: The Misuse of Country Market Power Framework

The WTO's current anti-dumping regime is outdated, opaque, and vulnerable to political manipulation. Instead of addressing true predatory pricing, it often serves as an economic weapon, allowing major economies to impose unjustified tariffs on foreign competitors.

A more transparent, objective, and economically sound approach would be the Misuse of Country Market Power Framework—a model inspired by domestic competition laws. This framework shifts the focus away from speculative cost calculations and instead evaluates actual distortions in global trade.

Comparative Legal Basis for the Framework

The proposed framework draws inspiration from existing competition law principles used in several jurisdictions to regulate market power abuses.

Below is a comparative overview of how different legal systems address market dominance and distortive trade practices.

The proposed new approach explained below has been uplifted from the best features of the 4 jurisdictions' competition law provisions.

Comparative Overview of Market Power Regulations

Jurisdiction	Relevant Law	Market Power Definition	Key Prohibited Conduct	Intent Requirement	Penalties for Breach
Australia	Competition and Consumer Act 2010 (Cth), Sec. 46	Substantial market power in any market	Conduct that has the purpose, effect, or likely effect of substantially lessening competition	Not required; effect-based test applies	Fines up to $50M or three times the benefit gained
New Zealand	Commerce Act 1986, Sec. 36	Substantial degree of market power	Taking advantage of market power for an anti-competitive purpose	Intent required	Monetary fines, cease orders, director bans
United States	Sherman Antitrust Act, Sec. 2	Monopoly power in a relevant market	Monopolization, attempt to monopolize, or conspiracy to monopolize	Intent is crucial	Fines, treble damages, criminal penalties
European Union	TFEU, Article 102	Dominant position in the internal market	Abuse of dominant position (e.g. unfair pricing, limiting production, discrimination)	No need to prove intent	Fines up to 10% of global turnover, structural remedies

Based on the key elements of the above 4 jurisdictions the proposed replacement for anti-dumping law would be a model called for example **Misuse of Country Market Power.**

This table illustrates that modern competition law principles focus on market power and trade distortions rather than subjective pricing calculations. The Misuse of Country Market Power Framework applies these principles to international trade, creating a rules-based system to prevent trade distortions.

Key Features of the Proposed Framework

To ensure fair and transparent enforcement, the WTO should establish a three-step investigation process, modeled after global antitrust frameworks.

Step 1: Preliminary Market Distortion Review

- A specialized WTO Market Power Oversight Panel would assess trade distortions in specific sectors.
- If distortions are linked to excessive market concentration or unfair state support, an investigation is launched.

Step 2: Full Market Power Assessment

- A dedicated expert panel evaluates the country's market power using key metrics:
    - Global export share in a specific industry (e.g. China in rare earth minerals).
    - Restrictions on imports or monopolistic control of critical industries.
    - State-sponsored industrial policies that distort competition.

Step 3: Targeted Remedies & Sanctions

- Instead of blanket anti-dumping duties, penalties would be sector-specific and time-limited.
- Remedies could include:
    - Market access adjustments (ensuring fair entry for foreign competitors).
    - State-subsidy restrictions (curbing unfair government support).
    - Sectoral trade balance measures (ensuring no country dominates an entire supply chain).

Author's Commentary

The Misuse of Country Market Power Framework presents a compelling alternative to the flawed anti-dumping regime, yet its adoption would require a significant shift in global trade governance. The underlying principles—borrowed from competition law—are well-established in domestic legal systems, but applying them at the international level introduces complexities that merit further discussion.

If international trade is to remain fair, predictable, and dynamic, a modernized regulatory approach is not optional—it is inevitable. The question is not whether reform is needed, but how quickly it can be realized.

This framework is not just about replacing anti-dumping laws but about creating a more equitable, transparent, and competition-driven international trade order. It offers a model that benefits all stakeholders—developed and developing nations alike—by ensuring that trade policies serve economic efficiency rather than political maneuvering.

The transition will not be immediate, nor will it be free from opposition. However, incremental adoption, starting with pilot industries such as high-tech manufacturing, steel, and agriculture, could prove its effectiveness and pave the way for a broader global acceptance of competition-based trade regulation.

If the WTO and its members are serious about ensuring free and fair trade, they must acknowledge that anti-dumping laws are relics of a bygone era—the future belongs to a market power-driven regulatory framework that fosters genuine economic growth and stability.

Part 12:
Final Reflections – The Future

Chapter 51

Author's Commentary: Final Reflections on WTO Reform

The World Trade Organization (WTO) stands at a crossroads. Across the 50 chapters of this book, there has been an examination of the profound challenges facing the WTO and the global trading system—challenges that, if left unaddressed, will render the organization increasingly obsolete.

Economic nationalism, regional trade blocs, and the growing misuse of national security exceptions have all contributed to the erosion of a rules-based multilateral trade framework.

The WTO, once the cornerstone of global economic stability, now struggles to enforce its own agreements, resolve disputes, and adapt to the rapidly evolving nature of international trade.

This book has argued for transformative reforms rather than piecemeal adjustments. The issues plaguing the WTO—particularly its failure to prevent the misuse of trade measures, the stagnation of dispute resolution mechanisms, and the failure to modernize trade rules for the digital era—demand bold, innovative solutions.

The WTO must embrace modernization, technological integration, and a renewed commitment to enforceable trade principles if it is to remain relevant in the 21st century.

The Future of the WTO: A Call for Urgent Reform

The collapse of the WTO's Appellate Body is one of the starkest examples of the organization's declining authority. Without a functioning dispute resolution system, WTO agreements risk becoming unenforceable diplomatic aspirations rather than binding international obligations.

The establishment of ad hoc alternatives, such as the Multi-Party Interim Appeal Arbitration Arrangement (MPIA), fails to resolve the fundamental issue: without a universally recognized mechanism for resolving trade disputes, the rules-based system disintegrates. Restoring the Appellate Body is not optional—it is essential to the credibility of the WTO.

Similarly, Article XXI of GATT, which allows trade restrictions under the pretense of national security, has been weaponized by governments to justify arbitrary economic policies. This undermines predictability in trade relations and creates an environment where any trade restriction can be excused under vague security concerns.

Unless clear, legally binding limitations are imposed on the misuse of this provision, the WTO will continue to see its authority eroded by politically motivated economic measures.

Beyond structural reforms, this book has advocated for the digital transformation of the WTO's administration. The future of global trade governance lies in harnessing blockchain for secure trade documentation, artificial intelligence for trade surveillance, big data for policy analysis, and automated dispute resolution mechanisms.

These technological advancements offer the best chance at reducing bureaucratic inefficiencies, increasing transparency, and ensuring fairer trade outcomes. The WTO cannot afford to lag behind while private industries and individual economies move toward digitalization. Potential technological applications include:

1. **Blockchain for Trade Documentation**: A decentralized and secure system for managing trade documents can reduce fraud, streamline customs procedures, and increase regulatory compliance.

2. **Artificial Intelligence in Trade Monitoring**: AI-driven analytics can help identify patterns of unfair trade practices, optimize tariff structures, and improve real-time trade surveillance.

3. **Big Data for Trade Policy Analysis**: The use of predictive analytics can aid policymakers in assessing the impact of trade policies before implementation, ensuring that regulations are data-driven rather than politically motivated.

4. **Automated Dispute Resolution Systems**: AI-enhanced mediation and arbitration mechanisms can provide a more efficient alternative to prolonged trade disputes, reducing backlogs and enhancing compliance.

AUTHOR'S COMMENTARY: FINAL REFLECTIONS ON WTO REFORM

Reclaiming the WTO's Relevance

The past few decades have seen the rise of regional trade agreements, often at the expense of WTO-led multilateralism. While these agreements serve an important role in facilitating economic cooperation, they also risk fragmenting global trade into competing regulatory regimes.

The WTO must take proactive steps to integrate these regional frameworks into a coherent, enforceable multilateral order, ensuring that the fundamental principles of non-discrimination and fair competition remain intact.

Moreover, the WTO must address the growing misuse of anti-dumping measures. As demonstrated in earlier chapters, many nations employ anti-dumping duties not as protective measures against predatory pricing, but as tools of economic warfare.

The book has proposed the Misuse of Country Market Power Framework as a viable alternative—one that targets actual economic distortions rather than relying on subjective and often politically influenced cost analyses.

A Call to Action

This book does not merely diagnose problems; it presents solutions. The WTO's future depends on decisive action from policymakers, trade negotiators, and international stakeholders. The following six key reforms are essential to revitalizing global trade governance:

1. **Restore the WTO Appellate Body** to ensure that dispute resolution remains binding and enforceable.

1. **Reform Articles VI and XXI of GATT** to eliminate anti-dumping and prevent the abuse of national security exceptions as a tool of economic coercion.

2. **Promote technological integration** to modernize WTO administration and trade monitoring mechanisms.

3. **Align trade policies** with the realities of the 21st century by updating WTO agreements on digital commerce, sustainability, and evolving supply chain challenges.

4. **Strengthen protections for developing economies** by ensuring that WTO processes are fair, inclusive, and reflective of the diverse needs of all members.

5. **Enhance WTO accountability and transparency** by implementing regular audits, independent oversight, and real-time public reporting on trade rule compliance.

The WTO is at a defining moment. It can either embrace the necessary reforms outlined in this book and reclaim its role as the primary arbiter of global trade, or it can continue its slow decline into irrelevance. The time for half-measures is over. The world cannot afford to let multilateral trade governance collapse.

A Final Thought

This book is a call to action, not a historical account of WTO failures. The trade system is too vital to be left to stagnate. The coming years will determine whether global commerce is governed by fair, transparent, and enforceable rules or by the whims of economic nationalism and unchecked geopolitical maneuvering.

The WTO must rise to meet the demands of modern trade, or it will fade into obscurity. The choice is clear. The time for reform is now.

www.ingramcontent.com/pod-product-compliance
Lightning Source LLC
Chambersburg PA
CBHW052237220526
45471CB00001B/85